Christ and the Council

Christ and the Council

Conflict, Politics, Theology, and the Outrageous,
Extraordinary Story of the Church's First Creed

Ben Wyatt

CASCADE *Books* · Eugene, Oregon

CHRIST AND THE COUNCIL
Conflict, Politics, Theology, and the Outrageous, Extraordinary Story of the Church's First Creed

Copyright © 2025 Ben Wyatt. All rights reserved. Except for brief quotations in critical publications or reviews, no part of this book may be reproduced in any manner without prior written permission from the publisher. Write: Permissions, Wipf and Stock Publishers, 199 W. 8th Ave., Suite 3, Eugene, OR 97401.

Cascade Books
An Imprint of Wipf and Stock Publishers
199 W. 8th Ave., Suite 3
Eugene, OR 97401

www.wipfandstock.com

PAPERBACK ISBN: 979-8-3852-3720-3
HARDCOVER ISBN: 979-8-3852-3721-0
EBOOK ISBN: 979-8-3852-3722-7

Cataloguing-in-Publication data:

Names: Wyatt, Ben, author.

Title: Christ and the Council : conflict, politics, theology, and the outrageous, extraordinary story of the church's first creed / Ben Wyatt.

Description: Eugene, OR: Cascade Books, 2025 | Includes bibliographical references and index.

Identifiers: ISBN 979-8-3852-3720-3 (paperback) | ISBN 979-8-3852-3721-0 (hardcover) | ISBN 979-8-3852-3722-7 (ebook)

Subjects: LCSH: Council of Nicaea (1st : 325 : Nicaea, Turkey). | Council of Constantinople (1st : 381 : Constantinople). | Trinity—History of doctrines—Early church, ca. 30–600.

Classification: BT109 W93 2025 (paperback) | BT109 (ebook)

VERSION NUMBER 071425

For all who find truth amidst controversy; meaning amidst chaos; and God in the confusing, outrageous, and unpredictable lives of mortals.

For all who seek to understand, inasmuch as we can, the mystery of the incarnation.

The past is never dead. It's not even past.

—William Faulkner, *Requiem for a Nun*

Contents

Acknowledgments | IX
Introduction: The Long Reach of Antiquity | XI
List of Abbreviations | XVII

PART 1

Chapter 1
The Church of 300 AD | 3

Chapter 2
Early Trinitarian Thought | 18

Chapter 3
The Cross of Christ and the Sword of Empire | 30

Chapter 4
The Beginnings of a Controversy | 43

Chapter 5
The Council to Settle It All (Or Not) | 57

PART 2

Chapter 6
The Eusebii Strike Back | 69

Chapter 7
Who Needs the Homoousios? Anti-Nicene Theologies | 82

Chapter 8
We Need the Homoousios! Pro-Nicene Theologies | 97

Chapter 9
Homoousian Struggle and the Blasphemy of Sirmium | 121

Chapter 10
Religion After Julian | 134

PART 3

Chapter 11
The Council to (Mostly) Settle It All | 147

Chapter 12
Creeds and Outlaws, Orthodoxy and Heresy | 157

Chapter 13
Religious Violence After Nicaea | 168

Chapter 14
Nicaea and the Suffering, Relational God | 180

Chapter 15
One Body, Many Councils | 191

Appendix A
A (Mostly) Jargon-Free Glossary of Key Terms | 203

Appendix B
A (Mostly) Jargon-Free Glossary of Key Players and Their Relationships | 206

Bibliography | 211
Scripture Index | 217
Authors Index | 219
Topic Index | 221

Acknowledgments

EVEN A BOOK WITH one author is a team sport. This book would not have been possible without the unwavering help and support of many people. The Rev. Dr. Chris Corbin, Ellie Singer, and the whole team at Forward Movement were crucial in launching the podcast on which this book was based. I am eternally grateful to Rachel Wyatt, Dr. Meg Harper, Dr. Jonathan Sanchez, the Rev. Benjamin Crosby, Sarah Killam Crosby, Anna Rosas, Brother Ronan Patrick, and the Rev. Frank Impicciche for their feedback on drafts of this manuscript. I also thank Acacia Chan, longtime friend and indexer extraordinaire, for her work on the project. I also wish to thank Church of the Nativity, Indianapolis for their understanding and support of this aspect of my priestly vocation. I am forever indebted to my clergy group for their wisdom, good humor, and unwavering support. All glory, laud, and honor go to my editor, Rodney Clapp, and the whole team at Cascade.

Introduction

The Long Reach of Antiquity

THE CHURCH IS CONFLICTED. It is probably never more conflicted than when it is trying to understand its conflicts.

A quick glance at religious news on any given day will offer a window into a smorgasbord of Christian fights: over gender and sexuality, over structure and organization, over racial tensions and nationalism, over worship and music, even over the nature of salvation itself. The sheer magnitude of disagreement among those who call themselves Christians is staggering. Even more staggering is the fact that so many people involved in these conflicts *are absolutely certain they are right!* If you take up the melancholy burden of reading the hundreds of articles, blog posts, video essays, and books devoted to any one of these controversial topics, you are likely to find authors who are so convinced they are right that they are confident anyone who thinks otherwise is not really a Christian. In 2011, author and pastor Rob Bell published his book *Love Wins*. In the book, Bell questioned the doctrine of an eternal hell and suggested God would save every person who has ever lived. In response, theologian John Piper infamously tweeted, "Farewell, Rob Bell." Piper's implication appears to have been that Bell's questions were beyond the pale of what a Christian could ask in good faith—and perhaps that Bell had condemned himself to the hell he was skeptical of.

Even that exchange was relatively mild by historical standards. Church conflicts have often led to bloodshed, as the Protestant Reformation repeatedly proved. When churches do not resort to violence, their conflicts often produce heartbreak and acrimony. Jesus prayed that his church would be one;[1] today, there are over forty-five thousand different Christian denominations, many of which have condemned and disfellowshipped each other. As churches split among themselves over questions of gender and sexuality,

---

1. John 17:21.

that number is likely to increase. Nor is the local parish free of conflict. I know of one church that was embroiled in a long-running feud between two prominent families. Each family had donated part of their land to form the church grounds, and each family insisted they had given more land than the other. Eventually, one family convinced most of the church that they were the bigger givers. The losing family was so incensed that they left the church—and exhumed their dead ancestors from the church graveyard to boot!

Why does the church fight this way? Is there any hope of resolving our profound disagreements?

Looking to the Past

One way to answer those questions is to look at the church's history. We are not the first Christians to live in a time of conflict and controversy. In fact, one of the largest and most consequential of all Christian conflicts happened seventeen centuries ago. In the midst of church-rending disagreement, theologians produced one of the most sweeping and universally accepted statements of church doctrine that history has ever seen. We are still living in its wake.

Three hundred and twenty-five years after the birth of Jesus of Nazareth, faith leaders from all across the Roman Empire gathered in the town of Nicaea, only about forty-three miles from the newly minted imperial capital city. That meeting was something new in the history of Christianity: for the first time, Christians leaders responded to controversy by gathering to argue, reason, compromise, and then eventually promulgate a set of doctrines regarding the identity of Jesus Christ—all with the blessing and protection of the Emperor Constantine, who had just made Christianity the official religion of the Roman Empire.

You may know the document that emerged from that council, usually referred to as the Nicene Creed. The version most Westerners are familiar with reads something like this:

> *We believe in one God,*
>   *the Father, the Almighty,*
>   *maker of heaven and earth,*
>   *of all that is, seen and unseen.*
> *We believe in one Lord, Jesus Christ,*
>   *the only Son of God,*
>   *eternally begotten of the Father,*
>   *God from God, Light from Light,*

true God from true God,
begotten, not made,
of one Being with the Father.
Through him all things were made.
For us and for our salvation
    he came down from heaven:
by the power of the Holy Spirit
    he became incarnate from the Virgin Mary,
    and was made man.
For our sake he was crucified under Pontius Pilate;
    he suffered death and was buried.
    On the third day he rose again
        in accordance with the Scriptures;
    he ascended into heaven
        and is seated at the right hand of the Father.
He will come again in glory to judge the living and the dead,
    and his kingdom will have no end.
We believe in the Holy Spirit, the Lord, the giver of life,
    who proceeds from the Father and the Son.
With the Father and the Son he is worshiped and glorified.
He has spoken through the Prophets.
We believe in one holy catholic and apostolic Church.
We acknowledge one baptism for the forgiveness of sins.
We look for the resurrection of the dead,
    and the life of the world to come. Amen.

    It is hard to overstate how central the Nicene Creed is to the worship and belief of millions of Christians the world over today. Many denominations recite the Nicene Creed as part of their weekly Sunday worship, including Roman Catholicism, Eastern Orthodoxy, Anglicanism, and some branches of Lutheranism. Even Christians who do not recite the Nicene Creed often agree with its basic doctrines: the full divinity of Jesus Christ and the equality of the members of the Trinity. Churches often use the creed as a litmus test for what churches count as Christian. Many denominations refuse to acknowledge the Church of Jesus Christ of Latter-day Saints (Mormonism) as Christian because it does not affirm the Nicene Creed.

    Many are certain the Nicene Creed is not just true, but obviously true. For these folks, opposing the creed can seem tantamount to damnation. While in college, I attended a Greek Orthodox liturgy as part of a class assignment. After the service, one of my classmates asked the priest if his church believed that only members of Eastern Orthodox churches would go to heaven. The priest told us that the Eastern Orthodox church did not proclaim *anyone* to definitively be damned no matter what their faith. Then he paused, and after a moment of thought added, "Well, except for Arius. They're pretty sure he's in hell."

As you will learn in this book, Arius was the priest whose denial of Jesus Christ's true divinity prompted the Council of Nicaea. This Orthodox priest's claim struck me as extraordinary. Here was a man unwilling to say that Judas was damned for selling Jesus out to be crucified, but quite sure that Arius was damned for saying the wrong thing about his divinity!

Antiquity has a long reach. The Nicene Creed's impact on Christian history is hard to overstate—even if you are not so sure that its detractors are doomed. The thinkers who had the largest say in its creation and defense have gone down in history as some of the most venerated theologians of all time. In Eastern Orthodoxy, figures from this time period are lauded with titles like "the Great," "Holy Hierarch," and even "the Theologian." In the Christian West, the Nicene Creed was one of precious few documents that held together Roman Catholic and Protestant believers. Martin Luther, John Calvin, and many other Protestants were ready to rethink almost all of Christian doctrine, and were extremely skeptical of the authority of church councils. Yet Protestants by and large refused to reject the Nicene Creed. This artifact of church tradition was so precious to all that it commanded acceptance from both Protestants and Catholics even as they painted the fields of Europe red with each other's blood.

The story of the Nicene Creed has much to teach us today. It can show us how Christians have handled and mishandled power, how they have navigated ethnic and theological differences, and why two people who attend the same church can have profoundly different beliefs. A full understanding of the Nicene Creed can also make sense of that strange doctrine that Jesus Christ is both fully human and fully divine. Most of all, it can reveal the deep, underlying factors behind church conflicts that make those conflicts feel so impossible to resolve.

In this book, we are going to investigate these questions by hearing the story of this ancient controversy. We will meet its key players and walk with them, argument by argument, as they journey through the Nicene conflict. In the midst of all the enormous questions and controversies raised, we will also get to see all of the human oddities and mistakes that make the story such a good one. We will meet a bishop who accidentally insulted the emperor's mother and lost his post, an emperor who yearned for the life of a cabbage farmer, a lone controversialist who managed to get exiled five times in the course of his life, a heretic who had a reputation for doing miracles but chose to give dry and lengthy lectures instead, and even Santa Claus! My hope is that the story of Nicaea will help you confront twenty-first century conflict with more understanding, more courage, and more good humor.

Only when we can see and accept the human elements in our disagreements can we discern the divine opportunities they present.

Technical Notes

As we delve into the story of Nicaea, we are going to encounter some Greek and Latin words that may be unfamiliar to you. When I introduce a new word, I will give its pronunciation in parentheses, if needed, and explain what it means. You will also encounter the names of a number of ancient cities and regions that no longer exist (or are called by different names): Bithynia, Constantinople, and more. When I introduce these cities, I will tell you the modern-day names they correspond to. As you will soon learn, many of the figures in this controversy had the poor manners to share the same name. I will do my best to help us keep our Constantiuses, Gregories, and Eusebii straight as we walk through the bewildering array of ancient names.

Readers with scholarly backgrounds will notice that the story I tell closely follows standard scholarly text on this subject: R. P. C. Hanson's *The Search for the Christian Doctrine of God*. While I occasionally disagree with Hanson's analysis (especially his assessment of Athanasius of Alexandria), I am deeply indebted to his scholarship for making this book possible. My reason for writing this book was to condense the discoveries of modern patristic scholarship (both Hanson's and others) into a form digestible for busy seminarians, busier clergy, and extremely busy laypeople.

The story of Nicaea unfolds in three parts. Part 1 covers the background of the fourth-century church and the initial council. Part 2 discusses the long controversy regarding the Nicene Creed after the council. Part 3 covers the controversy's eventual resolution and its continuing legacy for the church today.

Attempting to tell the story of a fourth-century controversy for a twenty-first-century audience is a daunting endeavor. Any time we translate a story from one context to another, we risk watering down its questions and history so much that we make it unrecognizable. At the same time, if we simply reproduce events as they happened, using the words that the people of the time did, then we have failed to translate the story at all. We have simply kept it in its fourth-century context, no more comprehensible to us than when we started. In this book, I have erred on the side of making things comprehensible. I have taken a conversational, "chatty" tone of writing. I have simplified (though not, I believe, distorted) arguments, summarized lengthy processes of argumentation and political back-and-forth, and introduced modern analogies where I believe them to be helpful. My goal is to provide enough understanding of the period that those who desire a more scholarly treatment will be equipped to read one.

In other words, I have not attempted to follow every minor twist and turn of the Nicene controversy. Instead, I have tried to tell its story: a wild roller coaster of clashing personalities, theological depth, historical drama, and human oddities. It is a story both timely and timeless, and we will understand much about the church of today by looking at the church of the fourth century. To that church we shall now turn.

List of Abbreviations

ANF *Ante-Nicene Fathers*
NPNF *Nicene and Post-Nicene Fathers of the Church*
PG *Patrologia Graeca*

PART 1

Chapter 1

The Church of 300 AD

The Nicene controversy would have been unthinkable to Christians living just a few generations earlier Unbeknownst to them, there were hidden fault lines in the church that were just waiting to be activated by the right combination of personalities and events. To understand the Nicene conflict, we must understand the church that preceded it. Only then will we grasp how the culture, beliefs, practices, and historical context of the conflict's participants all combined to make such a massive conflict possible.

Fortunately, there are five simple words that sum up our knowledge of the early church. Unfortunately, those five words happen to be: we are not quite certain.

There is much about the early church we simply do not know. Our usual way of learning about history is to read texts from that period. In the ancient world, writings were expensive to produce and were written on papyrus, which had an annoying habit of degrading very quickly. The only books that survived were books that people cared about so passionately that they were willing to pay the high costs to copy and recopy over centuries. Most books did not inspire that level of devotion, and hence have been lost to us. We simply do not have the level of detailed knowledge that we would need to describe the ancient church in full detail. So if you started this chapter hoping to read punishingly intricate meeting minutes of some ancient church committee, you are tragically out of luck.

The Growth of the Church

However, even with the relative paucity of materials, we know quite a bit about the Christians of 300 AD. For starters, we know that there were a lot more of them than there had been before. The church had remained relatively small during its first two centuries of existence. It was a movement that demanded much from its followers, and many were unwilling to make the necessary sacrifices. It also suffered from the fact that it was illegal. The Roman Empire's religious laws were pretty simple: you could worship whatever gods you wanted, so long as you also worshiped the Roman pantheon. The required worship included making a yearly sacrifice for the health of the Roman emperor, who was believed to become a god upon his death. Christians were unwilling to make this sacrifice, as they believed in one God and considered sacrifices to the emperor to be idolatrous.

Their strict monotheism left Christians in an awkward place within the empire. Most of the time, Roman officials were simply too busy to care about a small band of religious renegades who refused to make their government-mandated sacrifices. There were taxes to collect, renegades to crush, political rivals to fend off, revolting peasants to crush, new emperors to acknowledge, rebellions against the aforementioned new emperor to crush, and more. However, Roman officials were all too happy to use the Christians as punching bags when they needed a scapegoat to blame their problems on. Unfortunately for beleaguered Roman officials, persecutions occasionally backfired by creating sympathy for suffering Christians.[1] While persecutions were sporadic, they still had a chilling effect on the growth of the church. Many were unwilling to join a group that might become the target of imperial ire, and gathering for public worship on Sunday was an

---

1. Perhaps the most famous example of this phenomenon is the third-century text known as the *Passion of Perpetua and Felicity*. (See Heffernan, ed., *Passion*.) The work is supposedly the diary of Perpetua, who describes her imprisonment for her faith. She is kept in prison while pregnant. Her father begs her to renounce her faith; she calmly states that she is a Christian and cannot call herself by another name. Her father is so angry that he almost physically attacks her, but she calmly persists in her decision. After giving birth, Perpetua is hauled before a governor and sentenced to death for her faith. She waves off several more attempts by her desperate father before coming to the gladiatorial pits where she is to be executed. She is to be decapitated by a gladiator, who turns out to be a young man terrified of combat. Eventually Perpetua puts the soldier's sword on her neck so that he can get the job over with. Perpetua's calm demeanor in the face of violence and death was a profound contrast with the cowardice and injustice of the pagan men around her. While the Christian editors of this text may have exaggerated the story, Roman citizens became quite uncomfortable with the idea of putting young mothers to the sword.

inherently risky proposition when troops could arrive to arrest you at any moment.

However, Christianity enjoyed substantial growth during the third century. The Roman emperors of this century mostly embraced a policy of toleration for Christians. In fact, Christians enjoyed complete respite from persecution from 260 to 303 AD. This time of toleration allowed Christians to make their case to the outside world without fear of reprisal. They were quite successful in doing so. Our best estimates suggest that Christians made up about 10 percent of the population of the Roman Empire by 300 AD.[2] Their numbers were comparable to modern-day atheists and agnostics in the United States, who currently make up 11 percent of the population. While Christians were nowhere close to a majority, they were common enough that most people would have met at least a few Christians and formed opinions about them. Many pagan Romans would have had a Christian friend or two.

Christianity was especially popular in those parts of the Roman Empire where class boundaries were most fluid. Land-owning aristocrats were very much tied to the history of ancient Rome, including its traditional gods. Rural peasants were generally off the beaten track of Christian evangelists, and more likely to continue worshiping the same gods their ancestors had as they farmed the land their ancestors had. But in the cities, and especially among the civil servants and a rising middle class, Christianity found an audience. The church of the Roman Empire was a place where a powerful imperial official might sit in the pews while listening to a sermon preached by his former slave, all while nobility and commoners who would never otherwise rub shoulders shared a communal meal.[3]

The inclusive, class-defying church of the fourth century was popular, paradoxically enough, because of its theological exclusivity. Unlike most other religions in antiquity, Christianity claimed that there was only one God, who created the entire world and all that is in it. Depending on which Christian you asked, all the "gods" of other religions were either figments of pagan imagination or demons who had tricked the people of the world into worshiping them. Despite the trouble their monotheism caused them with local politicians, the Christian belief that they alone worshiped the true God created an extraordinary sense of belonging that most other religions simply could not emulate. Many Roman citizens felt deeply unmoored at the dawn of the fourth century. Cherished traditions had changed or died off, massive political instability in the third century had rocked Romans' faith

---

2. Hopkins, "Christian Number and Its Implications," 185.
3. Brown, *World of Late Antiquity*, 66.

in governance, and the empire was shrinking rather than growing. Being a part of a group dedicated to a purpose greater than oneself is a powerful antidote to anxiety, and traditional Roman religion could not provide that for an increasing number of folks. Christians, by contrast, had a very strong sense of group solidarity. Not only did they see themselves as the harbingers of God's salvation, but they also had a strong ethic of care for one another. Pagan critics of Christianity noted with alternating scorn and begrudging admiration the way that Christians cared for their poor, widowed, and sick members. While not all churches were equally charitable, for many Romans being a Christian meant having a kind of social insurance: no matter what happened to you in life, you would not have to go through it alone.

Life in the Church

Those seeking to join this unique community began with a period of instruction and guidance in the faith. People in this phase of faith were called catechumens (kat-eh-CYOO-mens), and the period of time was called the catechumenate. The length of the catechumenate varied depending on how each particular church practiced, but it almost certainly lasted at least a year, and ended with baptism. Catechumens were welcome to come to church, but were sent home halfway through the service after the Bible had been read and the sermon preached. Most churches celebrated the Eucharist[4] every week, but catechumens were not able to partake of the mystical bread and wine. That was available only to those who were baptized. So before the Eucharist began, the catechumens were dismissed from the service and only the baptized remained.

You might think that most catechumens were eager to get baptized so they could participate in the full service, including the Eucharist. Shockingly, the opposite was true. It was not uncommon for people to spend most of their lives in the catechumenate. Some people, of course, moved quickly to baptism and happily spent their Sundays on the extended version of church, sacraments and all. Most were more hesitant—and not because they enjoyed skipping out of church early to enjoy the rest of their day. The main reason for their hesitation had to do with Hebrews 6:1–6.

> Therefore let us go on toward perfection, leaving behind the basic teaching about Christ and not laying again the foundation: repentance from dead works and faith toward God, instruction

---

4. There are many names for the Eucharist: the Lord's Supper, Holy Communion, Mass, etc. I will stick to calling it the Eucharist throughout this book, but other terms are equally applicable.

about baptisms and laying on of hands, resurrection of the dead and eternal judgment. And we will do this, if God permits. For it is impossible to restore again to repentance those who have once been enlightened and have tasted the heavenly gift and have shared in the Holy Spirit and have tasted the good word of God and the powers of the age to come and then have fallen away, since they are crucifying again the Son of God to their own harm and are holding him up to contempt.[5]

Many early Christians thought the letter's reference to the "basic teaching about Christ" described the catechumenate. They thought that once you had left the catechumenate by being baptized and taking the Eucharist, you could not be forgiven if you sinned! Anyone who committed a sin after baptism (especially a big sin, like adultery or murder) was doomed to hell with no hope of redemption. Faith leaders repeatedly told their flocks that this was a bad interpretation of the passage. They railed against the practice of delaying baptism. Still, many pious, faithful Christians were unwilling to take the chance of being wrong on such a critical matter. Thus the majority of the church's members spent their lives on the doorstep of the church, accepting baptism only on their deathbeds.

Whether catechumen or baptized, the centerpiece of the ancient Christian life was Sunday worship. What was a church service like? We are not quite certain. (I told you to expect those words!) Churches in different regions of the world worshiped in different ways: different hymns, different prayers, different dress, and different sacramental customs. Moreover, we have very few documents that describe complete worship services. Modern churches make all kinds of conjectures about how the first Christians worshiped. Funnily enough, these conjectures often imply that early Christians worshiped in basically the same way as the person making the guess!

While the first few centuries of worship are quite mysterious, we have more information about how churches worshiped by 300 AD. While the earliest Christians met in believers' homes to worship, the Christians of the fourth century usually worshiped in dedicated church buildings. Most services began with prayers and readings from the Bible. After this, a community leader (usually, but not always, an ordained person) would preach a sermon. The length of sermon could vary depending on the expectations of the church and the skill of the preacher. Most of the evidence we have for sermons comes from larger churches, in which the sermon could easily last thirty to forty-five minutes. In one particularly infamous case, a preacher

---

5. All biblical citations are from the NRSV unless otherwise noted.

went on for seven days!⁶ In any event, the sermon was followed by a celebration of the Eucharist, which appears to have been a weekly occurrence for most churches. While some of the earliest Christians celebrated the Eucharist as a full, sit-down meal,⁷ the churches of 300 AD usually consumed only a cup of wine and a bit of bread.

There were several kinds of church leaders who went by different names. Some of the epistles attributed to St. Paul describe three distinct types of leadership. At one level we find deacons, or *diakonoi* (dee-AH-koh-noi) in Greek, who distributed alms to the poor and participated in the church's worship. Then we find a level of leadership referred to as the *presbyteros* (pres-BOO-ter-os) in Greek—the same root word from which Presbyterian comes. The translation of *presbyteros* is one of the most contentious questions in the church. Some denominations translate this word as "priest," others as "pastor" or "minister," still others as "elder," and still others as "that person who preaches too long and makes my family late to our brunch reservation." (Okay, that last one is not an *official* title for ordained people, but there are few among us who haven't *thought* something like that at least once.) For the purposes of this book, I will usually refer to this group of people as either priests or presbyters, but any of the other translations can apply equally well. A *presbyteros* was charged with administering worship, presiding over the sacraments, and caring for the people of the church. The third and highest level of leadership was the *episkopos* (eh-PIS-ko-pos)—the Episcopal Church takes its name from this word. *Episkopos* is often translated as "bishop" but more literally means "overseer." As an overseer, the *episkopos* was the one ultimately in charge of the ministries of the priests and deacons. After all, you cannot oversee others very well if you are not in charge of them.

Of course, the duties of a church overseer change as the church changes—and the church was about to change a lot. In fact, one way to understand the story of the Nicene controversy is as the saga of the changing role of the bishop. In the early days of Christianity, when a church might have been six people gathering at someone's house, the bishop may have simply been the one setting up tables and chairs and making sure everybody showed up on time. By the fourth century, though, churches had grown, and with them the responsibilities of leadership. Their core responsibilities grew in size and complexity: keeping unity and addressing conflict in their churches. As the centuries passed, many bishops found themselves engaged in a ceaseless

---

6. This preacher was not completely without mercy. The congregation was allowed to go home each night.

7. For example, 1 Corinthians 11:17–34 describes such a practice.

struggle against the two forces constantly threatening the church: heresy and schism.

The Bishop's Foes: Heresy and Schism

Heresy and schism are going to be our constant companions throughout the Nicene controversy, so let's take a minute to make sure we know what they mean. A schism is when someone in the church decides they dislike the job someone else is doing and declares that they are now in charge instead. While schisms are painful and destructive, they are not necessarily related to issues of belief and doctrine. A schism is not about what the church teaches, but about who is in charge and how good of a job they are doing—or not doing, depending on which side of the schism you fall on.

We have good evidence of schisms going back almost to the beginning of Christianity. A bishop named Ignatius of Antioch, who may have been a direct disciple of St. Peter, wrote a series of letters to churches in his care in the early first century. Among the many topics of his letters was a schism that roiled his congregations. It seems that a group of young men had decided that the older generation of priests and deacons were doing a poor job of leading the church, so they simply ordained themselves to those roles and gave their senior colleagues the boot. Ignatius was adamant that this kind of behavior is unacceptable. He went so far as to say that anyone who behaves in such a manner will not inherit the kingdom of God. Part of the reason he was so verklempt about all of this is that he could not actually do all that much to stop it. Christian bishops ultimately operated on persuasion rather than force; there was no mechanism to force these young schismatics to knock it off. Especially in these early centuries, when each church was fending for itself, the possibility of a schism succeeding was substantial.

In addition to schisms, the early church also faced a set of movements that would be known as heresies. Heresy is a highly contested word. Some people will call any belief that they disagree with a heresy. Others will speak as though a heresy is any odd or unconventional belief, like using tarot cards to help one make decisions or treating Jesus as a Hindu guru on one's quest to attain enlightenment. Both ways of speaking are inaccurate. The early church had plenty of diverse beliefs, and many Christians combined their faith with other spiritual practices without being called heretics. "Heresy" comes to us from a Greek word that means choice. The early church used the word to describe those who had decided to use the church's authority to proclaim a message that came from themselves rather than the teaching of Jesus. In other words, heretics were teachers or authorities who had heard the message of Jesus and, having been insufficiently impressed by it, chose to make some modifications to bring it into line with what they thought was right.

The most notorious heretic in the early church was a man named Marcion of Sinope. Marcion taught that there were actually two Gods, not one. The God of the Old Testament was a cruel, vengeful, and bloodthirsty being who demanded sacrifice and had created the world as a result of his own pride. The reason the material world is full of suffering is because it was created by an evil God. The God of the New Testament was a completely separate being, all-good and loving, who had sent Jesus Christ into the world to break the false God's sway and rescue people from the evil world they were trapped in. Marcion's teachings ran into a few problems when reading the Bible, because Jesus says there's only one God, who revealed himself to Abraham, Isaac, and Jacob, gave the Jewish law to Moses in the Old Testament, and has now sent Jesus to be incarnate. Marcion solved this contradiction by just saying that those bits of the Bible were fake. Marcion thought the only books that were truly biblical were the Gospel of Luke and most of St. Paul's letters. The entire Old Testament and the rest of the New were thrown out.

You can probably see why Marcion was not good for the early church's collective blood pressure. They were aghast at his habit of revising or outright rejecting essential components of Christian teaching and Scripture while claiming to be a faithful Christian. His heresy was not a rejection of faith. It was an attempt to warp and distort faith—which many Christians found far more dangerous than mere rejection.

Bishops had several tools for responding to heretical teachings. Most obviously, they could ban heretics from teaching where they had authority. They had no power to prevent heretics from teaching in other churches, though. Moreover, those labeled heretics were occasionally bishops themselves. In these cases, communities engaged in a long, drawn-out battle of persuasion, with each side trying to convince the other that their approach to God was the more faithful one.

In so doing, teachers would often appeal to a nifty little idea called the rule of faith. A rule of faith was not a set of rules like the Ten Commandments. It was more like a modern ruler or straightedge: a standard by which you could measure your own teaching. Rules of faith would list out the basic matters of Christian teaching that defined the church's witness. A really good example of a rule of faith that has come down to us today is the Apostles' Creed, which reads as follows:

I believe in God, the Father almighty,
> creator of heaven and earth.

I believe in Jesus Christ, his only Son, our Lord,
>> who was conceived by the Holy Spirit
>> and born of the Virgin Mary.
>> He suffered under Pontius Pilate,
>> was crucified, died, and was buried;
>> he descended to hell.
>> The third day he rose again from the dead.
>> He ascended to heaven
>> and is seated at the right hand of God the Father almighty.
>> From there he will come to judge the living and the dead.

I believe in the Holy Spirit,
>> the holy catholic church,
>> the communion of saints,
>> the forgiveness of sins,
>> the resurrection of the body,
>> and the life everlasting. Amen.

There was no singular rule of faith that all communities accepted as authoritative. However, most rules of faith shared a number of common themes that we see in the Apostles' Creed: the Father; the Son who became incarnate as Jesus Christ; the Holy Spirit; and the events of Jesus' life, including his birth, death, resurrection, and ascension. Such a rule of faith would then become the basis on which to accuse a leader of heresy. For example, Marcion taught that Jesus was *not* the Son of the God who made heaven and earth, which contradicted the rule of faith and hence made him a heretic.

Their use of rules of faith tells us that early Christians knew something many modern Christians struggle to grasp: just reading the Bible was not going to resolve an argument. Early Christians knew full well that the Bible could be confusing, and parts of it apparently contradicted each other. A nonexclusive list of all the odd things in the Bible would include ghosts of saints being controlled by evil witches,[8] rules against mixing linens,[9] some extremely prejudicial opinions about people from Crete,[10] confusing

---

8. 1 Samuel 28:3–25.
9. Leviticus 19:19.
10. Titus 1:12.

instructions on food offered to idols,[11] and God attempting to kill Moses immediately after sending him to free the Israelites from Egypt![12]

Ancient Christians did not believe that these strange passages were inexplicable. The Bible was not a book you could pick up, read once, and understand all there was to know about life. Instead, it was like a set of mosaic tiles. Depending on how you arranged the pieces you could make almost any image you wanted. A rule of faith simply described the picture you were supposed to make. It is a set of instructions about how to read the Bible created by highlighting particular bits of Scripture that they perceived as especially important—a sort of SparkNotes version of the gospel.

The bishops were the custodians of their rules of faith. Their public preaching expounded the rule of faith they had inherited and proclaimed it to the next generation. They did so from positions of institutional power and held all the advantages of institutional leadership: their teachings were frequent, public, and relatively clear. They were educated clergy who had spent a lifetime in prayer and service. But bishops also had all the disadvantages of institutional leadership. They were a bit ossified and inflexible in the face of change. They had a lot of obligations and so were pressed for time and attention. Sometimes the wrong person became bishop and simply did a bad job. Christians were often hungry for a different sort of authority than bishops provided, one grounded more in individual charisma and godly living than in lines of succession and church politics.

The Teacher over the Bishops: Origen of Alexandria

Individual teachers of the faith who were renowned for their intellectual achievement and holiness could achieve a level of influence to rival any bishop. By the dawn of the fourth century, no one was as renowned for both as Origen of Alexandria (185–253 AD). Origen was easily one of the most brilliant thinkers Christianity produced in the first millennium. He wrote more books than almost any other early Christian thinker—and if we had all of his manuscripts that have been lost to history, he might take the top slot. At the height of his power he kept a whole team of scribes busy copying out his manuscripts, day and night, which tells you something about how full of ideas he was.

---

11. 1 Corinthians 8 seems to leave open the possibility of participating in meals with food offered to idols, while 1 Corinthians 10:14–22 suggests that to do so is to associate with demons.

12. Exodus 4:24–26.

Origen's works ranged from defenses of Christian teaching against pagan criticism to biblical commentary to inventing whole new fields of study. His work *On First Principles* is the first attempt to systematically discuss all major topics of Christian theological teaching, and is still required reading in many seminaries today. Above all else, Origen cared about the Bible. He was the first Christian scholar to attempt a massive analysis of existing biblical manuscripts. This manuscript is called the *Hexapla,* and it sets out six different texts of the Bible in parallel columns so that the scholar could compare the biblical text across different Hebrew and Greek manuscripts. Since all biblical texts were copied out by hand, "typos" and clerical errors were a fact of life. The *Hexapla* allowed scholars to set out different texts against each other to correct errors and gain insight into how a passage's meaning might change across translations. Because some people get all the talent, Origen also happened to be a brilliant teacher who was beloved by his students. His fame would grow so great that in his later years the emperor's mother would seek him out as her personal tutor in philosophy.

In addition to being sickeningly brilliant, Origen was a man of irreproachable character. Origen was sixteen years old when an empire-wide persecution of Christians broke out. The emperor of the time ordered all Christians to be executed. As was usual with these persecutory impulses, the order was never completed; busy Roman provincial officers had better things to do than track down every member of what seemed to them like an odd but harmless cult. Some officials did obey the order, however, and among those executed was Origen's father. As a wealthy and prominent member of the community, Origen's father was an easy person to make an example of—and proved to the bloodthirsty emperor that *some* Christians were being killed. The persecution left a young Origen, as the oldest son, to care for his family of nine.

Care for them Origen did. A year later he got a job teaching at the prestigious academy in Alexandria. When he was not teaching, writing, or caring for his family at barely twenty years old, Origen meditated on his life and apparently decided he was simply not being challenged enough. He adopted the self-denying lifestyle of many Greek philosophers in order to better concentrate on the pursuit of wisdom. He ate a simple diet and abstained from alcohol, regularly walking barefoot and wearing only a single cloak, and probably reduced his sleep in order to spend more time praying.

Origen's brilliance and reputation for holiness opened the whole Christian world to him. Once he had established himself in the intellectual ferment of Alexandria, Origen visited Rome and Arabia, and spent an extended amount of time in Palestine after local unrest caused him to flee Alexandria. There, the local bishops admired him so much that they asked him to preach sermons even though he was not ordained. The process appears to have been this: Origen would stand up, ask the bishop which of three to four Scripture passages that had been read that day he would preach on, the bishop would choose one, and Origen would start preaching on the spot.[13] He spoke extemporaneously for up to an hour while scribes quickly recorded his brilliant insights for posterity.

Not only did bishops love Origen so much that they allowed him to assume their prerogative to preach, they occasionally brought him in as a one-man anti-heretical task force to oversee the doctrines of other bishops. This practice was unheard of. Bishops were the overseers of the church; their job was to correct others, and most bishops would only accept discipline from a more senior bishop.[14] The idea that a non-bishop would have authority to correct a bishop's teaching speaks to how powerful Origen's reputation was. When the bishop Heracleides taught an erroneous doctrine of the Trinity, a regional group of bishops called upon Origen to examine him. Heracleides apparently would say that Christians worshiped "two Gods," the Father and Son, who have "one power." The bishops wanted Origen to determine if this was an adequate formulation of the faith. We have a transcript of the dialogue, and it's a fascinating master class in how Origen worked. After questioning Heracleides, Origen gently told him that his doctrine was incorrect, and then gave a discourse to all the bishops in attendance about the proper way to account for divine unity and duality. Origen was rather embarrassed for poor Heracleides, but felt the need to speak strongly so that others were not misled. He treated a powerful bishop like he was a misbehaving child in Origen's classroom—and he got away with it.

There was one bishop that Origen defied more than any other. That bishop was his own. The bishop of Alexandria was a fellow named Demetrius who was hard at work building his institutional power. In the course of his ministry, he learned a timeless lesson: it is very hard to get people to listen to you when a once-in-a-millennium genius is busy preaching about the same Bible as you, working with the same people as you, and generally

---

13. Examples of Origen's spontaneous preaching can be found in his *Homilies on Jeremiah and 1 Kings 28*.

14. Are you wondering how bishops determined seniority? So do many scholars! Some churches appear to have determined seniority based on length of service. In such churches, the "bishop" might simply have been the title of the longest-serving priest. Other churches determined seniority on the basis of how important one's territory was. We know that bishops who worked near major cities like Rome, Alexandria, or Antioch would look to the bishop of that city to resolve disputes. Since Christianity usually started in a city and then spread to the surrounding countryside, those bishops may have looked to their urban bishop (sometimes called the metropolitan) as the head of their "mother church."

being a better person than you. Demetrius's jealousy hounded Origen, but to little effect. He wrote angry letters to the bishops who allowed Origen to preach without being ordained. The bishops denied his demands that Origen desist. When Origen decided he was called to be a priest, Demetrius refused to ordain him. The next time Origen went on a speaking tour, a sympathetic bishop ordained him on the spot. One imagines the bishop starstruck at the chance to ordain such a great man; perhaps he asked Origen for a commemorative sermon or autographed papyrus to mark the occasion. Demetrius was livid, but his protests again fell on deaf ears. After Origen's death, Demetrius spread nasty rumors about Origen's character to damage his reputation. They, too, failed—at least in the short term. Origen showed just how far a teacher could go in defying a petty and mediocre bishop, provided one had enough brilliance and chutzpah.

Origen's life ended in a fashion he probably would have wanted. In the year 250 AD, the emperor Decius began a persecution of Christians, whom he blamed for causing a bad plague that had swept the empire in the previous year. This time, Origen did not escape Rome's notice. He was imprisoned and tortured for two long years before being released after Decius's death and the end of the persecution. Release came too late to save him, though, and he died within the year at the age of sixty-nine. Origen had been a wunderkind: a teacher of unparalleled reputation, a thinker of extraordinary brilliance, a priest with more power than his bishop. But he ended his adult life the way he almost began it: as a martyr for his faith.

The Call of the Desert: The Authority of the Monks

Origen's stature would loom large over the Nicene controversy. However, not everyone can be a once-in-a-millennium genius and martyr to boot. Most people had to take a different path to spiritual power, and several decades after Origen's death, a powerful new movement began to take shape in the Christian world: one that we today call monasticism. At the dawn of the fourth century, Christians were fleeing the cities and towns their families had lived in for centuries to live lives of poverty and hardship in the desert. These Christians came from all walks of life: rich and poor, urban and rural, men and women. The movement happened all over the empire, at about the same time: in Egypt, in Syria, in Palestine, in Turkey. Anywhere there was a desert, there were Christians living in it. While the first generation of ascetics did not set out calling themselves monks, nuns, or anything else (they probably thought coming up with a name for themselves was a pointless distraction from prayer and self-denial), the movement they spawned led directly to the forms of monasticism that continue in many Christian denominations today.

Nobody is quite sure why this happened, and historians love few things more than arguing about the origins of monasticism. Some think that the monks were mostly peasants who had to flee their farms due to the increasingly unbearable tax burdens of the fourth-century empire. Others think that the earliest monks were reacting against the increasing respectability of their religion by following Jesus into the dangerous wilderness of the desert. Still others suggest that the monastic movement was started by wandering Buddhist monks who made it over to Egypt! Nobody really knows for sure. What we do know is that the monks quickly established distinctive forms of life that would make them famous—and a reputation for holiness so powerful that there are many today who choose to live a monastic lifestyle.

Monks spent their time in prayer and manual labor. Monks usually chose to occupy their time with simple, repetitive activities like braiding rope or basket-weaving. Such work left their minds free to continue praying while their hands were busy. The earliest monks lived in solitude and simplicity. Most of them just found a nice hole in a cave somewhere to call home. They would gather together with other monks in their vicinity for worship on a regular basis—perhaps once or more per day for more social monks, and as rarely as once per week for less social monks. They ate little more than bread and water and fasted several times per week, regularly stayed up all night in prayer vigils, and owned as few possessions as they possibly could. Some of the monks engaged in more extreme lifestyles than others. In the fifth century, a group of Syrian monks became known as the "pillar fathers" because, annoyed that too many people were finding them and asking them for advice and counsel, they decided to beat the crowds by moving to the top of little stone pillars left over from old ruins in the desert. This did not discourage the crowds; if anything there were more people now, and the pillar fathers couldn't get away on account of having only a couple square feet of living space. But the Syrian example is an extreme case. Most monks lived humble lives on the ground, giving their bodies the minimum needed for sustenance and focusing on cultivating prayer and virtue.

Communities of monks usually gathered around a charismatic ascetic, referred to as *abba* or *amma*—father or mother in Aramaic, respectively. These abbas and ammas were extraordinary teachers who were thought to have such keen spiritual insight that they could see into a person's soul and give them advice uniquely tailored to their plight. Many monastics treated the words of their leaders with the same absolute reverence as the words of Scripture. Desert fathers and mothers were considered to be authoritative sources of wisdom because their unique style of life brought them close to

God. The most famous monastics carry the distinct whiff of legend around their lives. Anthony the Great, widely regarded with some inaccuracy as the founder of monasticism, is said to have battled demons, engaged in superhuman feats of self-denial, resolved the burdens of troubled souls with a single brilliant sentence of advice, and even to have prophesied the entire Nicene controversy before it happened.

Anthony is not the only monk to have such stories told about him. Almost every desert father and mother is credited with some kind of supernatural power. So when many people had questions about their lives, or whether a loved one was in heaven, or whether their soul was clean, they did not turn to their bishop for guidance. They made a journey out into the desert to consult these holy people, who had given up more for God than most fourth-century Romans could imagine.

Bishops, of course, did not care for this. Nor did they like the fact that the monks were out there, having church in the desert, without even *asking* the bishop whether they were allowed to do so or not. After all, as the overseers of the community, bishops were responsible for approving all new churches! Moreover, monastic communities were not small. Some of them grew to be as large as seven thousand people by the end of the fourth century.

These different sources of power—ascetic, episcopal, and intellectual—would come into conflict in the Nicene controversy. In addition to the doctrinal arguments that each side waged, there was significant disagreement as to who would have the final word on the matter. Would it be the bishops, appointed overseers of the church? If so, which bishops held the most authority? Would it be teachers with charisma and brilliance? If so, how would the church agree which teachers to follow? Or would it be wonder-working monks in the desert? If so, could they even be persuaded to take part in such worldly debates? Christians would explore each of these possibilities over the course of the long controversy. Before we can understand why the church's power struggles played out as they did, we must understand the other side of the coin: the deeply held and deeply disputed beliefs about the Trinity that would come to be challenged in the fourth century.

Chapter 2

Early Trinitarian Thought

Now that we know who the Christians of the fourth century church were, we can start getting a handle on what they believed about God. As they sought to understand the God they worshiped, they continually looked to three different sources of authority: the Bible, the rule of faith, and their worship practices.

You might find that collection of sources odd. Referring to the Bible might be pretty standard; Christians have been appealing to the Bible to resolve disagreements since the Bible was written. The rule of faith is a bit more problematic since (as we saw in chapter 1) there was no one set rule of faith that everyone had access to. And how can human-made prayers and worship practices be a source of divine truth?

To understand why the early Christians thought this way, I need to ramble for a minute about something that will sound completely unrelated to ancient history.[1] It actually *is* related to ancient history, and I promise it will be worth the wait, but it might not seem that way at first. If you need to take a break and recharge your attention, then do whatever you need to do—drink your water, go for a walk, take another round of Adderall—and join me at the top of the next paragraph.

---

1. A different writer could probably make the point more concisely, but I am a minister by training, and long rambling stories are my natural form of information sharing. The longer I minister, the worse this problem gets.

Proper Praise, Right Belief

My great uncle died several years ago. There was no minister on hand who knew him well, so my family called in a chaplain to officiate his funeral. During the sermon, the chaplain stood up and said of my great uncle, "Jerry has finally joined his mother, father, and sister in heaven." Several members of my family found this statement odd. Many others took offense at it. What was the reason for their offense? My grandmother, my great uncle's sister, happened to be very much alive and was sitting in the first row of pews. The family did *not* appreciate that the chaplain had said she was dead.

I have sometimes wondered what the chaplain would have said in her defense if she had talked to my grandmother. I suppose she could have said, "There is no reason to be offended! I don't know your family. I learned as much as I could before the service started, but I do not know everything. So I made an assumption that proved to be wrong. Everyone makes mistakes! Why are you so upset with me?"

That would be a valiant defense. I certainly would have been sympathetic to her if she had said that. However, my family could have said in return that her whole job was to know us. If she was not sure about the details of the family tree, she should have asked more questions or simply not made assumptions about who had already shuffled off their mortal coil. Her job was to proclaim the gospel and speak words that would comfort the family in a time of sorrow; she could not do this without knowing my great uncle and his family. To speak on what she did not know about, while understandable and forgivable, was ultimately a form of pastoral malpractice.

The early church understood that one of its core responsibilities was to praise God in their weekly worship: to tell the story of God's incredible deeds; to rejoice in the splendor of God's mercy, love, faithfulness, etc. The church wished to encourage Christians to live in a way that a being of such resplendent goodness would approve of. The church could not accomplish those aims if it was saying things about God that are not true. To say something false about God, even something that sounds good and appropriate, would be no better than telling a nice-sounding fable about a deceased person at their funeral. It does a grieving family no good to tell stories about how their loved one was a courageous firefighter who saved hundreds of lives if the person was actually an investment banker.

Interestingly enough, the Greek word for beliefs about God was the same as the word for the praise of God: *doxa*. We get our word "orthodoxy" from this root. *Ortho* means "right" or "proper" in Greek. Thus orthodoxy can mean both "right belief" and "proper praise." For early Christians, one could not praise God rightly without understanding who God is. One without the other was simply unthinkable.

Of course, the tight connection between belief and worship presented a problem. God is infinite, and we are finite. Our minds cannot possibly comprehend all of God's mysteries and wonders. How on earth can people possibly praise God with anything approaching acceptable accuracy? The answer, of course, is that we cannot do so on our own. Fortunately, God has not left us to our own devices. God has revealed divine truths to us throughout the ages. Those insights have been recorded in the books that make up the Bible. So when praising God, Christians would reference the Bible to ensure their words were consonant with the Scriptures. When Christians disagreed about how to praise God and all parties involved thought they had biblical support, they could reference a rule of faith as a guide to reading the Bible. Moreover, all the hard work that Christians put into understanding God's self-revelation crystallized into the words of worship that the church used across generations. Christians could compare their theologies to the worship of past saints and heroes—as well as the worship practices that had won acclaim from all the faithful.

The Trinitarian Dilemma

Of all the things one might wish to get right about God, perhaps none are more important than God's very being. If you set out to praise a person, it will do you no good to think they are a snail. Just so with God; if we cannot speak of God accurately, then our attempts to praise God are doomed from the start, and the church's mission is hopelessly compromised.

To make the problem even harder, the Bible is famously difficult to understand on this particular subject. The New Testament talks about three different persons, who are usually referred to as the Father, the Son, and the Holy Spirit. In many places the biblical texts seem to imply that these three persons are all divine, and are all God. John 1:1–3 talks about how "the Word"—that's another biblical name for the Son—was in the beginning with God, and how the Word also *was* God. That Word becomes incarnate as Jesus of Nazareth. Thus early Christians could speak of Jesus as God in the flesh. Yet Jesus regularly describes the Father as God and offers him worship like other human beings. In fact, after his resurrection he tells his disciples that he is ascending to "my Father and your Father, to my God and your God."[2] If Jesus describes the Father as his God, it's hard to see how he is Father's equal, or even divine himself.

2. John 20:17.

Further complicating this puzzle, the earliest Christians retained the Jewish belief that there was only one God. The oneness of God is not some casual aside within the church's teachings. It was and is a foundational tenet of all Jewish religious thought, and of all Christian thought. Christians had died for monotheism. They were outlawed and occasionally persecuted by the Roman government precisely because they refused to acknowledge that Jupiter, Juno, Mercury, the emperor, or any other being could have equal status to their God. So what were these three divine persons doing in a monotheistic religion? If these three persons were all divine, did that mean there were three Gods, not one?

Christians tried to find ways of talking about God that could square this apparent circle. Some of their strategies are still celebrated today as classic statements of truth. Others have been condemned as heretical innovations. Others were abandoned for being too vague, or just plain weird. A few solutions have managed to enjoy all three treatments, depending on whom and when you asked!

The Great Enemy: Modalism

In theology as in politics, the most important influence on your thinking is often the ideas you are most keen to avoid. One kind of Trinitarian theology made almost everyone cringe with disgust in the early church. While it goes by several names, we shall refer to this school of thought as modalism.[3]

In a nutshell, modalism states that the Father, Son, and Holy Spirit are all different modes or manifestations of the one God. Father, Son, and Spirit are names that we give to one aspect or "side" of God, but they are not distinct persons—or even real. Only God's oneness is real; God is only three inasmuch as God has three different aspects or modes. You have probably heard modalistic analogies for God without realizing it. Has anyone ever tried to explain the Trinity to you by comparing it to the way water can be a solid, liquid, or gas? That is a classic modalistic analogy; the same set of water molecules just take different configurations depending on temperature. Perhaps someone has explained the Trinity by comparing it to the way the same person can be a father, a son, and a cousin all at the same time. This is also modalism; the terms "father," "son," and "cousin" all describe different

---

3. You will also hear this theology referred to as Sabellianism, monarchianism, or oneness theology. I use the term "modalism" because out of all those names it does two things best: it most accurately describes the content of the theology, and it is the most fun to say out loud. Try it for yourself and see!

aspects or relationships of a being who is one and not really three except in terms of how we think about them.

Modalism was radioactive in the ancient world, and simply being labeled as a modalist could be enough to call down all kinds of ecclesiastical censure on a theologian. There were two reasons for this. First, early Christians believed that modalism made a mockery of the New Testament's portrayal of the Trinity. Jesus prayed to the Father; if Jesus and the Father are two aspects of the same being, then Jesus was praying to himself. Jesus asked the Father to receive his spirit when he died. Was he asking himself to receive his own spirit? Modalism implied as much. Most early Christians found modalism's conclusions absurd. The second reason for their disdain was that early Christians understood that modalism was equivalent to another, verbosely named belief called patripassianism. Patripassianism is the belief that the Father had suffered and been crucified on the cross. You can remember this by looking at the word's Latin etymology: it comes from *pater*, meaning "father," and *passio*, meaning "to suffer." Since modalism holds that "Father" and "Son" are two names for the same entity, to say that Jesus Christ suffered and died was equivalent to saying the Father suffered and died. It was the divine equivalent of saying that the son of Mary suffered and the teacher of Peter suffered. Both statements refer to Jesus, just in different ways.

Any implication that the Father had suffered was verboten to most Christians. For reasons we will cover in future chapters, almost all ancient intellectuals took it for granted that the source of all being was beyond pain, suffering, or change. Since the source of all being is the Father in Christian theology, that meant the Father had to be beyond suffering and pain. Only a very small minority of thinkers were willing to say otherwise. Being called a modalist in the ancient world was kind of like denying that matter is composed of atoms today. You will find a few people who are very insistent about their alternative physics, but they are viewed as frauds and quacks by virtually everyone else.

The Wunderkind: Origen of Alexandria

Naturally, the early church's best and brightest thinkers wanted to show everyone why modalism was such a problem. That included the best and brightest thinker of them all, Origen of Alexandria. When he was not busy inventing whole new fields of biblical study, getting other bishops to like him more than his own bishop did, or staying up all night to pray, Origen put pen to parchment telling people what the Trinity was *actually* like and why modalistic theology was foolish. He had two insights that his fourth-century successors would rely heavily on: his theology of biblical interpretation and his invention of Trinitarian terminology.

Origen had a particular understanding of how to interpret the Bible that most of his contemporaries shared. Origen was a very attentive reader of the Bible, and he noticed something that many people have noticed since: the Bible contains what appear to be some glaring contradictions. For example, the Gospels of Matthew, Mark, and Luke all describe Jesus entering the temple toward the end of his ministry. He becomes enraged at the money-changers and merchants doing business in the house of God, whereupon he flips over their tables, grabs a whip, and drives them all out. But the Gospel of John describes Jesus doing this at the beginning of his ministry, not the end. These contradictions are not only found in the New Testament, either. Ezekiel 29 prophesies that Egypt will be completely uninhabited for a period of several decades. Of course, no such thing ever happened—as Origen, a native-born resident of the Egyptian city of Alexandria, knew full well.

What is going on here? Well, to understand how Origen viewed the Bible's seeming contradictions, you need to know that in late antiquity, they thought about biblical "inspiration" differently than we do. Nowadays, when someone says the Bible is inspired, they often mean that they think God authored every single word of the Bible and that every single word is literally, factually true. But in the ancient world, to say that a god had inspired a text meant something different. It meant that a text contained multiple layers of meaning. There were hidden, spiritual meanings that lay behind the literal meaning of a text. These spiritual meanings were the most important ones; the literal meaning of the text was there to be a good, entertaining, and possibly edifying story for the masses. Those that wanted to go deeper—and understand their deity's real purpose in inspiring a text—needed to progress to the spiritual interpretations. For example, you may remember that in Greek mythology the king of all the gods, Zeus, causes many scandals in the realms of both gods and humanity with his frequent infidelities. Pagan Greek philosophers insisted that these stories should not be understood as literally true. Zeus was the high god of their religion, and hence was honorable and just. They argued that Zeus symbolized power, and thus his stories of infidelity were actually moral fables about the union of power with other attributes. When Zeus engages in illicit unions, it represents the union of power with injustice—which is why such stories rarely end happily.[4] They are not historical recollections of an actual affair. They are allegorical warnings about what happens when evil corrupts power.

4. Seznec, *Survival of the Ancient Gods*, 85–89.

Of course Origen did not believe the ancient Greek myths to be divinely inspired. He did, however, believe the Bible was divinely inspired. He interpreted the Bible in the same way as Greek philosophers. However, Origen did not do this because he wanted to copy his pagan philosophers' notes. Origen thought that the Bible itself taught the reader to interpret it allegorically. The fact that the literal text of the Bible contradicts itself is intentional—God puts stumbling blocks in the Bible to alert the careful reader to the fact that something else is going on. For example, Origen thought the four Gospels tell the story of the cleansing of the temple differently because that story is an allegory for how Jesus cleanses our hearts when he enters them. Origen taught that there are four kinds of souls that Jesus can enter into, and each one gets cleansed a bit differently. A similar strategy works for the tricky prophecy of Ezekiel 29. Origen pointed out that St. Paul distinguishes between a physical and spiritual Israel in Romans 9, and concluded that there must be a spiritual Egypt too. Ezekiel's prophecy of desolation refers to the spiritual Egypt, not the literal one.

Origen's approach may seem like a very strange way to interpret the Bible. You may even be thinking that it sounds like complete hogwash. However, Origen has another argument for his approach worth considering: the Bible sometimes interprets its own stories as allegories. Perhaps you remember the story of Sarah and Hagar from Genesis. God has promised Sarah and her husband Abraham that they will have a child. But Sarah is well past menopause, and after a few fruitless attempts to conceive, she tells Abraham to sleep with her much younger slave, Hagar. Abraham does so, and Hagar bears him a son. A bit later, God fulfills the promise, and Sarah also conceives. Sarah then becomes jealous of Hagar and her son, and eventually drives them out into the wilderness. On a first reading, you may think that this is a story about many things: a historical retelling of the life of a key family of faith, a cautionary tale about jealousy, or a warning about the dangers of losing faith. But St. Paul gives it a different spin. In Galatians 4, he says that this story is an allegory. It represents the relationship between the old and new covenants. While the old covenant enslaves (since it is born through and requires a slave's obedience), the new covenant inaugurated by Christ brings freedom. Hagar's slavery and Sarah's freedom point forward to the work of Jesus Christ. Origen and other early Christians did not think they were inventing a new interpretive technique, or copying a pagan interpretive practice. They were trying to use the same patterns of interpretation that they saw the Bible itself using.

Critically for Origen and his followers, the interpretive key to understanding the allegories of Scripture is Jesus himself. After all, Paul's allegory of Sarah and Hagar is all about the new covenant inaugurated by Christ.

And since Christ is the central revelation of the New Testament, Origen understood the whole Bible—both Old and New Testaments—to be pointing to Jesus in some way. This did not mean that every single passage was always about Jesus in a simplistic way. However, Origen did think that knowing who Jesus is will help us understand the whole Bible better, and vice versa.

Origen's conviction was crucial for Trinitarian debates. For centuries after he died, people argued about Jesus using scriptural texts that do not seem to be about Jesus at all. The most famous example is Proverbs 8. This chapter is a song proclaimed by the personified figure of Wisdom, who talks about how God created her at the beginning of God's works, how she was beside him like a master worker, creating all things with him, and more. At first glance this may not have much to do with the Second Person of the Trinity. For one thing, Proverbs is in the Old Testament, when nobody had heard of Jesus. For another, Wisdom never claims to be God. But in the New Testament, Christ is often referred to as the "Wisdom of God," and Origen (along with most other interpreters) took this as a clue that Proverbs 8 was an allegory for the relationship between the Father and the Son. The song's parallels to John 1 also bolstered Origen's case. His approach to interpreting the Bible was incredibly influential, and people on every side of the Nicene conflict used his methods to make their point.

Origen was not content to merely set the terms for the theological debate. He also gifted the church some of the key vocabulary that it would use to talk about the Trinity. Origen was particularly keen on one of the biblical names used for Jesus: the Word. Now in Greek the term used for "Word" is *logos,* which can also mean a story, narrative, or the process of rational thinking. Jesus is called the Word because he communicates God to us. As Origen said, "He is called 'Word' because he removes everything irrational from us and makes us truly rational beings who do all things for the glory of God."[5] Given the wide variety of meanings for the word *logos,* you could also think of Origen as saying that Jesus removes everything that is not part of God's story and brings us truly into God's story. In other words, Jesus reveals God to us and makes us as much like God as we can be. Our minds are enlightened by divine truth, our lives are guided by divine purpose, and our story is forever united with God's story. That is why Jesus himself is divine; only a divine being can communicate divinity to us. The Word is God, just like John 1 says.

Now Origen, like everyone else who did not want to be a modalist, was very concerned to emphasize the distinct existence of the Son. Father, Son, and Spirit are not different modes of the same being. They are three distinct

---

5. Origen, *Comm. John,* 1.267.

things, and Origen uses a Greek word to describe these that has become somewhat[6] famous: *hypostasis* (hoo-POH-stah-sis). *Hypostasis* indicates an underlying reality or substance, something that has its own stable reality that will not pass away. For example, I am a hypostasis. My reflection in a mirror is not a hypostasis, because when I move away the reflection will disappear.

A hypostasis, then, is something with its own existence that will "stick around," rather than a mirage that disappears or a mode of being that can change into something else (think of the way ice ceases to be when water becomes liquid). There is a problem with this terminology, though: it is so general that it tells us practically no details about God's being. Even a genius like Origen did not try to tell us what *kind* of thing God is, or what the nature of the divine *hypostases* are. But he did stress that these three hypostases are related to each other and are always found together. After all, you cannot be a Father without a Son, and vice versa. The three persons of the Trinity are bound together in such a way that, although they are three things, they cannot possibly exist apart from each other.

Just because Origen thought that the Trinity is three interrelated divine things does not mean Origen thought all three persons were equal. Origen maintained that the Son and Spirit were subordinate beings to the Father. After all, the Father may not be a Father without a Son, but the Father would still *exist* without a Son, whereas the Son receives existence from the Father. In fact, at one point Origen suggested that the Father exceeds Christ just as much as Christ and the Holy Spirit exceed the rest of us![7] Yet at the same time Origen still affirmed that the Son and the Spirit really are well and truly divine, just like the Father.

If you are wondering whether Origen can really have his theological cake and eat it too, you are in good company. It seems that he wanted the Son and Spirit to be equal to the Father in divinity but also lesser than the Father. That tension runs throughout his work, and that same tension would explode in the Nicene controversy. Yet before we judge him too harshly, we should remember that he talks this way because the Bible talks in a very similar way. John 1 says that the Word was with God and the Word *was* God, which sounds like a relationship of equality. However, in John 17:3 Jesus calls the Father the "one true God" and differentiates himself from the Father—which sure sounds like he is subordinate to the Father! Origen, for all his brilliance, probably couldn't quite crack that theological nut. Yet

---

6. "Somewhat" famous means that it is famous among curmudgeonly patristics scholars who spend their lives studying this material. Which really means it's not very famous at all, but don't tell the curmudgeonly patristics scholars that.

7. Origen, *Comm. John*, 13.151.

his thoughts on the matter provided the tools for the thinkers of the Nicene controversy to try their hands at the problem.

The Western Curmudgeon: Tertullian

Origen was not the only thinker to write influential treatises on the Trinity. Now we turn to another towering figure who did the same: Tertullian of Carthage, the greatest Christian rhetorician of the Latin-speaking Western Empire.[8]

If Origen was the shining genius of the third century, Tertullian was the curmudgeon with an axe to grind. He was an uncompromising debater, well-trained in the arts of rational argument and rhetorical takedown. He famously opened this book against the arch-heretic Marcion with a multi-paragraph description of Marcion's homeland. He opined about its terrible weather, brutish inhabitants, and dearth of culture before noting that the very worst thing about the land was the fact that Marcion had been born there.[9] Tertullian would have done well on social media.

While Tertullian's penchant for insults may rub us the wrong way, it proves that he was a highly trained debater and writer. Ancient audiences expected these kinds of insults; they were an ordinary part of intellectual debate and were considered highly entertaining by the standards of the day.[10] Nevertheless, Tertullian's style of argument was harsh even compared to his contemporaries.

All of his grumpiness does not change the fact that Tertullian had a point to make, and we owe several important insights about the Trinity to his profound grumblings. The first is that Tertullian coined the word "Trinity" (*trinitas* in Latin) to describe the Father, Son, and Holy Spirit. Christians had, of course, been talking about the three persons since the Bible itself, but they lacked a snappy label to speak of all three at once. Tertullian provided it.

---

8. Tertullian would eventually lose this title to St. Augustine of Hippo. However, St. Augustine would not come into his own until the Nicene controversy was already settled, so for our purposes Tertullian remains the greatest thinker of the West.

9. Tertullian, *Against Marcion*, 1.1, in *ANF* 3.

10. The modern church has a bad habit of idealizing the early church. Particularly in countries where Christians do not face persecution, churches sometimes pine for the days when the church was smaller and more persecuted, but (they assume) more morally pure. Tertullian himself wished that his church would have stricter moral standards for its members. His biting tongue is proof that early Christians were just as capable of embracing unkindness—especially when it was socially acceptable.

Tertullian's second contribution was an important analogy to explain how Christians can worship three persons while only proclaiming one God. The analogy goes like this: whenever you think, you create a sort of dialogue between two parts of yourself. You might say, "I've got to go to the grocery store tomorrow,"[11] and in doing so you create a second self who speaks to you in your head. Or maybe you are trying to decide between having cake or ice cream for dessert, and you feel as though there are two voices inside you, each arguing with the other as to which is the better treat. Of course, there is only one of you in actuality. But the human mind has a way of splitting itself up into two or three voices in the process of thinking. God essentially does the same thing. God's Word is simply God's inner process of reasoning and thinking—a sort of divine conversation partner for the Father. The difference from human thinking is that everything that comes from God has substance and existence. So whereas we create fictitious copies of ourselves to reason with, God generates an *actual* copy of the Father to reason with, and this second person is the Word, the Logos, the Second Person of the Trinity. Tertullian then makes a similar argument that each word has a spirit or meaning behind it, and in God this becomes the Holy Spirit.

The idea that the Son is the mind of the Father given expression and existence is an important undercurrent in Christian theology. Tertullian was trying to find a way between two bad alternatives: either proclaiming the existence of three gods, which is polytheism and therefore bad; or saying that "Father" and "Son" are just different names for the same thing, which is the despised modalistic theology. He is not the first person to try to thread this needle. One generation before, the theologian Theophilus of Antioch had tried to do the same thing by describing God as "having his own Logos innate in his own bowels, generating him together with his own Wisdom, vomiting him forth before everything else."[12] You can probably see why nobody talks about Theophilus of Antioch anymore. (Some theologies were just weird.) Tertullian's genius was finding a very clever way to describe the Son and Spirit as distinct from the Father without making them alien to him. The Son is just the mind of the Father, and is as united with the Father as we are to our own minds. The Spirit is as close to the Son and Father as our intentions are to our own words. Later Christians spilled a lot of ink parsing out exactly what this analogy entailed, but they continued to find it a useful starting point.

11. I am expanding on Tertullian's analogy here for clarity; Tertullian, of course, had no grocery stores to go to in second-century North Africa. Even if he had, he probably would have been banned from them for excoriating some poor cashier who made a harmless but poorly thought-out theological comment.

12. Theophilus of Antioch, *To Autolycus*, 2.10, in *PG* 6:1064.

Tertullian's third contribution to Trinitarian theology was the way he used the word "substance" (*substantia* in Latin) to talk about God. While *hypostasis* describes the three persons of the Trinity, Tertullian taught that they all shared the same substance—in other words, that God was one substance. The terminology of substance would prove to be incredibly controversial among Christians. Some found the word helpful as a way of saying that the Father, Son, and Spirit were all "of the same stuff." Others worried that the word was too materialistic. It might imply (as many ancient people believed) that the divine was a sort of primordial cosmic ooze scattered throughout all creation. Tertullian occasionally implied as much, talking as if divine ooze eventually split itself into three persons in the way a child pulls apart a ball of Play-Doh and shapes it into three figures. It would prove to be one of his less appreciated insights.

Interestingly enough, both Origen and Tertullian would eventually come to be on the books as heretics. Origen was condemned by the reputation of his followers several centuries after the fact. Tertullian fell in with a group called the Montanists, an apocalyptic sect who practiced an *extremely* strict ethics of self-denial and came to see their founder as the mouthpiece of the Holy Spirit. Grumpy old men with a point have been susceptible to manipulation at all times in history, and Tertullian was no exception.

But regardless of their eventual fates, both Tertullian and Origen made important contributions to the Nicene controversy. There is one more piece of the puzzle that needs to be in place before we can understand its history, though. That puzzle piece is the Roman Empire itself. The Council of Nicaea would not have been possible in the year 300 AD. Christianity was still illegal then, and the empire had just emerged from a long century of devastating civil wars. It is hard to have a church council when the emperor can decide to persecute you at any moment, or when you have to divert yourself on a road to avoid the clashing armies of two would-be contenders for the throne.

In a mere twenty-five years, the situation had changed dramatically. Christianity became the state religion of a unified and peaceful empire, bishops gained extraordinary new levels of power, and the simmering theological conflicts of the early church burst into prominence. These massive changes were made possible by the strangest of coincidences: a crisis, a rare solar event, and an aspiring cabbage farmer.

Chapter 3

The Cross of Christ and the Sword of Empire

THE FOURTH-CENTURY CHURCH HAD its hands full. Between internal power struggles, sporadic persecutions, schisms, heresies, and the constant struggle to faithfully proclaim the gospel, Christians had more than enough to occupy their attention. Soon they would have even more questions to work through. For in the first quarter of the fourth century, the political ground was shifting underneath the Christians' feet.

By 300 AD the Roman Empire was ripe for a political realignment after emerging from one of the most brutal and discouraging centuries it had ever faced. To understand this realignment, we have to understand the deep instabilities that made it necessary. Long before the fourth century, the Roman Empire had conquered all of its neighbors who could be easily conquered. Normally, that is a cause for celebration, as conquering your neighbors is high on most militaristic nations' to-do list. However, it comes with one important downside. When you have conquered all your easy-to-conquer neighbors, then you are left only with your difficult-to-conquer neighbors. Those neighbors are usually hard to conquer because they are conquerors themselves. Thus it was with Rome. By the time of the third and fourth centuries, the empire's borders were usually under threat from several directions at once: Germanic tribes to the north, the Persian Empire to the east, occasional North African raiders from the south, etc. To combat these multiple threats, the Roman Empire came to increasingly rely on professional soldiers rather than conscripted ones.[1] Professional soldiers gener-

1. Professional soldiers brought their own armor and weapons to the army, and

ally want to be paid for their hard work. Rome had problems scrounging up enough coin to pay its mercenaries. Over time, a compromise was reached. The Roman government allowed soldiers to take whatever spoils they got from their victories as payment. However, this arrangement made soldiers loyal to whatever charismatic commander could most convincingly offer them victory, good pay, and the hope of a prosperous retirement. Julius Caesar had used his soldiers' loyalty to defy the Roman Senate and create the Roman Empire centuries ago. Later rulers followed his example. It became common for emperors to ascend to the throne after being hailed by their troops, not the government. It soon came to be an open secret that it was the Roman military who had the real power to make an emperor.

Attentive readers may notice this political arrangement sounds like a great recipe for civil unrest and violent coups d'etat. Attentive readers are exactly right. In fact, charismatic military leaders developed something of a playbook for seizing power that went like this:

1. Wait for the current Roman emperor to die. Help him along to the grave, if you are feeling impatient.
2. Have your soldiers declare you to be the new emperor. If the previous emperor was so rude as to name a legitimate successor other than you, use propaganda, assassination, or sheer military force to remove your rival from the picture.
3. Fight off or buy off all rival claimants to the imperial title who had the same idea you did.
4. Enjoy your reign and try to prevent your most charismatic generals from getting a copy of this playbook.

Emperors usually did not spend much time in step 4, as they tended to be better at seizing power than holding onto it. During a forty-nine-year period historians ominously call "the crisis of the third century" (235–285 AD) twenty-seven different men claimed the title of emperor. Romans of all political persuasions agreed that was simply too many emperors. A good number of those claimants reigned for a month or less, fanning the flames of instability even further.

Christians suffered from the political instability of Rome just like their pagan neighbors. However, the third century was a time of almost complete toleration from the Roman government—probably because the government was too chaotic and disorganized to launch any formal persecutions

---

were generally already organized for battle when a war broke out. While Rome could conscript its citizens, it then had to train them, organize them, and deploy them for battle. That process cost precious time that emperors were ill-prepared to spend.

of Christians. All that would soon change, however, with the advent of the man who would single-handedly end both the political crisis and the persecutory reprieve: Diocletian.

Diocletian: Reformer, Persecutor, and Cabbage Farmer

Diocletian had a truly Roman rags-to-riches story. He was born to lower-middle-class parents in the Roman province of Dalmatia (modern-day Croatia). Diocletian served in the army and rose through the ranks until he became the head of an elite cavalry force that served at the emperor's side. Diocletian was with the emperor on a military expedition in Persia when the emperor was killed under suspicious circumstances. Diocletian was hailed by his troops as the new emperor, at which point he swore an oath to avenge the emperor's death. He then promptly blamed that death on the commander who had been his main rival for the imperial title and stabbed the rival on the spot, killing him. He knew the lessons of step 2 of the Seizing Imperial Power Playbook very well. Diocletian's message was clear: I am in charge, I am going to set things right, and I am going to bulldoze anyone who gets in my way.

Although he was not a merciful man, Diocletian was a passionate believer in the Roman Empire who worked tirelessly to reform its broken governmental systems. Earlier emperors had governed through a council in which decisions were made through a collaboration of the emperor, the senate, and the army. At least, that is how it worked in theory; in practice, the emperor made the decisions that the army would endorse, and the senate wisely chose to rubber-stamp the decisions that all the men with the very sharp swords had just made. Diocletian disbanded this council and instead created a system of various departments, each with authority over a different area of government: legal affairs, finances, and so on. Most modern-day nations still use Diocletian's model. If your country has a Department of Defense or a Ministry of Health, you can thank (or blame) Diocletian for this system.

To help each department carry out its work, Diocletian roughly doubled the number of provinces in the Roman Empire. Each province had its own dedicated administrative staff. Diocletian also created another administrative unit called the diocese, made up of several provinces and meant to cover a large but still manageable territory in the Roman Empire. Many denominations of Christianity still use the diocese as a basic unit of organization: Roman Catholicism, Eastern Orthodoxy, Anglicanism, some branches of Lutheranism, the Church of God in Christ, and more. While most churches have a more spiritual vision of the diocese than Diocletian did, the basic idea remains the same more than seventeen centuries later.

Diocletian's administrative genius was second to none. He either invented or shaped many of the fundamental features of modern-day governments. For one person to accomplish so much would be remarkable in our own time. To do it in the fourth century was extraordinary. Diocletian was not infallible, however. He tried and failed to solve the rampant inflation ravaging the Roman economy. He set severe price controls and threatened to execute merchants who sold goods above the maximum price. The merchants largely ignored him, and provincial officers had more important things to do than execute a baker over the price of a ciabatta loaf. Diocletian's threats of execution had stayed the hands of his political rivals, but it was no match for the invisible hand of the market. Before we laugh too much at Diocletian, though, we should remember that even modern governments have trouble controlling inflation. To confront such perennial problems in a fourth-century empire is itself a colossal achievement. Whether we love him or hate him—and there are plenty of people who did both—there is no denying that Diocletian put the empire on firmer ground and did much to transform the chaotic third century into the merely turbulent fourth.

Nowhere is Diocletian's organizational genius more evident than in the way that he remade the office of the Roman emperor. In keeping with his expansion of administration across the empire, Diocletian decided that one emperor was simply not enough anymore. He named three other men to be co-emperors with him. This system of governance is referred to as the tetrarchy,[2] and the group of emperors are referred to as the imperial college. Diocletian split the empire into eastern and western halves and assigned a pair of emperors to each half. Each pair consisted of a senior emperor, called the Augustus, and a junior emperor, called the Caesar. An Augustus had the power to make laws, set policy for their Caesar to enforce, and appoint new emperors. Caesars could command militaries, make judicial rulings, and generally enforce the existing order of the empire. When an Augustus died or retired, his Caesar would succeed him as the new Augustus. Interestingly, Diocletian chose to reign as the Augustus of the East, not the West, indicating the increasing importance of the Roman East and the relative decline in influence of Rome itself.

Diocletian also surrounded the tetrarchy with the aura of Roman mythology. The two Augusti styled themselves after the Roman gods Jupiter and Hercules and their Caesars followed suit. In some cases the members of the tetrarchy even claimed one of these gods as their ancestor! While

---

2. From *tetra*, meaning "four," and *arche*, meaning "power," "ruler," or "principle."

Diocletian did not claim literal divine descent, he certainly expected to be treated as a god. Supplicants were expected to prostrate themselves before Diocletian; he took the title of *dominus,* meaning "lord"; and he expanded the traditional Roman practice of referring to the emperor's actions as sacred or divine. He wanted to build up an aura of mystique around the emperors. He did this partially so that people might actually listen to the emperors instead of trying to overthrow them, and partially to further enhance his own authority over his bleeding, fractured empire. There would be four emperors now, not one, but they were all to be treated as gods on earth.

An emperor who reenergizes traditional Roman religion in the service of the state is unlikely to be the biggest fan of Christianity, and Diocletian was no exception. In his mind, the Roman Empire had gotten away from the traditional Roman virtues that had made it great. What the empire needed was a return to that greatness, which meant a return to the traditions of Rome—traditions that Christianity was decidedly not a part of. Diocletian dismissed the Christians as fools and degenerates.

Then, Diocletian's cold dismissal turned to rage.

The Great Persecution

On February 23, 303 AD, he ordered that the church in his capital city be destroyed, its Bibles burned, and its money confiscated and added to the imperial treasury. Historians are not entirely sure why Diocletian gave the order. A popular rumor of the day stated that Christian servants in the palace had ruined a divination ritual by making the sign of the cross. Diocletian, thoroughly peeved that his pagan priests' ritual had failed, decided to eradicate Christianity. There is little hard evidence for the truth of this rumor. Whatever his reasons, Diocletian was not to be dissuaded from the persecutions. The next day, he ordered that the same actions be taken against churches across the empire and forbade Christians from worshiping. The following years would become known to the church as the Great Persecution, one of the most frightening and painful times in its three hundred years of history.

As in previous persecutions, the severity of the Great Persecution varied considerably depending on location. The Western emperors did not share Diocletian's insistence on religious conformity, and so generally ignored the persecutory edicts. Even in the east, persecution was sporadic and inconsistent, depending mostly upon the proclivities of local administrators. However, when persecution happened, it was severe—many clergy were mutilated, tortured, and killed. Even Christians who were never arrested or tortured lived with the constant fear that they could be—a kind of psychological torture that pressed many to rethink or abandon their faith. The severity of the persecution was so great that most Roman pagans reacted to the torture of Christians with disgust, lessening support for the empire's repression. But Diocletian held firm despite the popular outcry, and the Great Persecution lasted for nine bloody, terrifying years.

The Great Persecution had a profound impact on the church. Some Christians thought that it portended the second coming, and saw Diocletian as an antichrist for his persecution of the faithful. News of persecution forced Christians everywhere to decide just how much they were willing to sacrifice for their faith in Jesus of Nazareth. Many of them paid the ultimate price. Many others decided to give in. They handed over their precious Bibles, insincerely renounced their faith, and lived in the world Diocletian had wrought. These apostate Christians came to be called the *traditores* (tra-DIH-tor-eys) in Latin—the same word used to describe Judas, and from which the English word "traitor" is derived. The tensions between those who remained faithful in persecution and the *traditores* dramatically changed the landscape of the fourth-century church.

Yet the persecution would not last forever, and neither would Diocletian. After twenty-one years as the Roman emperor, Diocletian retired and set up shop in a country palace near his birthplace, where he farmed cabbages.

You read that right. The most powerful man in the empire, passionately committed to reforming his government and passionately adored and reviled by the Roman world, gave up his power and security for the delights of cruciferous vegetables.[3]

Even in retirement, however, Diocletian was making a political point about the significance of traditional Roman values. One of the most revered figures in Roman politics was Cincinnatus, an aristocrat of the Republic who lived in approximately 500 BC. The story goes that he was named the dictator of Rome in the face of a severe military crisis. The city was about to be besieged by a powerful invading army, and Cincinnatus was given absolute, supreme authority over every aspect of the city in order to defeat the invaders. Cincinnatus proved more than adequate to the task at hand, and trounced the invading army at Rome's gates in a mere sixteen days. Riding high on the public adoration, and with the military and state under his full command, Cincinnatus gave up his power and retired back to his farm. Some years later his citizens again called on him to assume the mantle of dictatorship in the face of a second military crisis. Again, Cincinnatus

---

3. Perhaps after a lifetime of conquering challenge after challenge, the only struggle left for Diocletian was keeping a vegan diet.

solved it brilliantly, and again he retired to his farm. It's probable that Diocletian desired to cast himself in the same mold as this legendary hero: a citizen-servant who rose to meet the task at hand and then resigned power instead of clinging to it.

Administrators have a hard time avoiding the questions of their successors, though. Later emperors attempted to call Diocletian out of retirement to settle problems of state. Diocletian was reluctant to do so. He famously told one messenger, "If you could show the cabbage that I planted with my own hands to your emperor, he definitely wouldn't dare suggest that I replace the peace and happiness of this place with the storms of a never-satisfied greed."[4] Diocletian was one of the church's most ferocious persecutors. He may also have been one of its most principled. He deeply believed in the pagan Roman values that he sought to inculcate, even when they dictated that he should surrender power.

Constantine: The First Christian Emperor

Diocletian's tetrarchy outlived him, but not by much. It turns out that getting four power-hungry leaders to share power with one another is only possible when one of the four is powerful enough to keep the other three in line. Diocletian filled that role, but as soon as he stepped aside, others rushed in to fill the vacuum. None of them could command the same respect as their former overlord, and the empire was plunged into yet another saga of political infighting.

The eventual victor of the conflict would be a young man named Constantine. Today, Constantine is famous because he was the first Roman emperor to be a Christian, and as emperor he took the monumental step of making Christianity not just tolerated, but favored within the empire. However, the union of Christian faith and imperial power was a difficult one, and Constantine would walk a long path before he came to possess either. He was born to a successful military officer named Constantius who eventually became Diocletian's Augustus of the West. Constantine's family was as skilled in governance as they were inept in picking original names for their sons. Constantine would name his sons Constantius II, Constantine II, and in one bright brief shining moment of moderate originality, Crispus. (I try not to bother you with the names of minor characters, but all of these royals have the poor manners to be very important characters in the Nicene saga. We're going to have to keep them straight as best we can.) In fairness to Constantine and his family, naming sons this way was commonplace in

---

4. Pseudo-Aurelius Victor, *Epitome de Caesaribus*, 39.6.

the Roman Empire. In fairness to ancient history lovers, at least half of the trouble with Roman history is that it is so hard to tell fathers and sons apart, so we are still allowed to complain about it.

As the son of an Augustus, Constantine was groomed to be emperor from an early age. His family likely expected him to take the path envisioned by Diocletian: he would start out as a Caesar and then rise through the ranks to become an Augustus. However, the new Augustus of the East, a fellow named Galerius, upset the family plans. He named a different Caesar in the West who would be more pliable than Constantine. Galerius hoped to be the next overlord of the imperial college and wanted to fill the tetrarchy with emperors loyal to him. Constantine and his father responded to this slight in genius fashion: on his deathbed, Constantius appointed Constantine an emperor, as was his right. However, Constantius also specified that Constantine would take office as the new *Augustus* in the West, not the new Caesar. This had never been done before. Augusti were allowed to appoint new emperors, but they had only ever appointed them to the rank of Caesar. Diocletian had probably intended for an Augustus to only appoint Caesars; however, he had never thought to write that rule down. Constantine took advantage of that ambiguity to secure his place in the tetrarchy. Constantine began to rally his troops in the Western Empire, who quickly and duly hailed him as the new Augustus. His quick maneuvering brought Galerius to the bargaining table. Hoping to avoid a civil war, Galerius offered to recognize Constantine as an emperor so long as Constantine would accept appointment as Caesar and not Augustus. Constantine agreed. In less than a year, Constantine was hailed as Caesar by the very man who had originally blocked him from that role. Constantine had played his cards like a master, and he was only getting started.

The next few years would be ones of constant struggle for Constantine as the politics of the tetrarchy became increasingly bloody. The short version of his very confusing and reversal-ridden story is as follows. Constantine was not the only son of an emperor to be denied a place in the tetrarchy. A fellow named Maxentius had been similarly scorned. Not being as gifted a politician as Constantine, Maxentius was unable to win recognition no matter what he tried. So he started a rebellion in the West. The Western Augustus Severus (whom Galerius had appointed in place of Constantine) attempted to put it down. Unfortunately, he marched with an army that had been fiercely loyal to Maxentius's father, the similarly named Maximian, and they decided to kill Severus and side with Maxentius. It was probably much easier for them to serve Maxentius; they barely had to learn a new name![5]

5. Serious historians will tell you that this is "ludicrous" and "not how it works at

Upon learning of the defeat, Constantine decided to ally with Maxentius and his father to avoid a war he was not confident he could win. Galerius was furious and ejected Constantine from the tetrarchy. Constantine's troops remained loyal to him, and he continued as *de facto* emperor in spite of Galerius. Constantine bided his time, carefully shoring up his power base and attempting to avoid outright conflict.

Unfortunately, Constantine's new allies had not sated their appetite for political intrigue. In 310 AD Maxentius's father declared himself to be an Augustus again in open defiance of Constantine, and Constantine had no recourse except the field of battle. He roundly defeated his aging opponent and continued his reign.

More important for history, however, is that during the battle against Maximian Constantine had a vision. He saw a vision in the sky of a cross and heard a heavenly voice say, "In this sign, conquer." Constantine painted the sign of the cross on his soldiers' shields, won the battle, attributed his victory to the Christian God, and converted to Christianity.

Or at least, that is the version of the story that Constantine would have us believe. The real story is considerably more complex.

Constantine would later say that he had this vision at a different battle that happened two years later, in 312 AD. Moreover, our best evidence indicates that Constantine did have a vision during this conflict, but interpreted it as a sign of favor from Sol Invictus—a Roman god known as the Unconquered Sun. It appears that at this battle Constantine observed some kind of solar phenomenon[6] he interpreted as a sign of favor from Sol Invictus.

Constantine was interested in questions of religion for most of his life. Like many people of the time, Constantine was exposed to a vast array of religions and philosophies that claimed to expound the truths of reality. Not all of these religions were incompatible. For example, a pious Roman could easily worship both Roman and Egyptian gods. Yet many sought to know the "highest God"—that deity that stood above all others as the final primordial principle of the cosmos. Constantine appears to have believed that Sol Invictus might be this highest God in 310 AD. However, his beliefs changed over time. His mother Helena was a devoted Christian and ensured that he knew Christian beliefs from an early age. Constantine appears to

---

all." But if *you* were an ancient Roman soldier, would you rather have to memorize a new boss's name every six months knowing that they were probably going to be killed or displaced in the brutal world of Roman politics, or just follow the guy whose name starts with "Max"?

6. We cannot know exactly what Constantine saw in the sky. It could have been a solar halo, which appears as a ring around the sun and is caused by the way light refracts through ice crystals in clouds.

have moved away from his belief in Sol Invictus to the faith of Jesus of Nazareth. One crucial element of this process occurred in 312 AD, when on the night of a battle Constantine had a dream in which Christ appeared to him, telling him to mark his shields with a symbol of Christ.[7] Constantine won that battle and then retroactively interpreted his solar vision in 310 AD as coming from Christ—which both fit his new theology and explained away the embarrassment to his newfound church that he had been proclaiming the favor of Sol Invictus just two years prior.

Constantine had another motive for massaging his conversion narrative. Before becoming emperor he had spent many years in the court of Galerius, who had continued the Great Persecution after Diocletian's retirement. During this time, Constantine appears to have made no effort to aid the Christian cause. Constantine probably knew that such advocacy would have been political (and possibly literal) suicide; he was not yet an emperor and hence had no power. Yet it would have been awkward to explain to his new Christian brethren that he had known of their God and been sympathetic to their cause but had not lifted a finger to help them in their darkest hour. Constantine avoided awkward questions about his youthful exposure to Christianity by focusing on his adult visions rather than his mother's teachings.

These factors raise one of the ten million dollar questions of the fourth century: just how sincere was Constantine's conversion to Christianity? When dealing with such a masterful propagandist and politician, is it possible to determine if there was any sincerity underneath his public professions of faith?

As is so often the case in ancient history, we are not entirely certain. Constantine left no diary of his private thoughts for us to peruse. However, most of the evidence points toward at least some degree of sincerity. Christians made up only 10 percent of the empire at this point, and many Christians believed that their faith disqualified them from military service, leaving them underrepresented among the empire's most powerful demographic. Christians were not a particularly advantageous group to court for an emperor constantly trying to secure his place in the tetrarchy against his rivals. Moreover, during his reign Constantine pushed policies not just tolerating but favoring Christians. It is difficult to imagine Constantine insisting upon such favors for a minority group if he converted only for political gain. It is true that Constantine was not baptized until his deathbed, which some have seen as evidence of insincerity. However, as we learned in

---

7. Specifically, Constantine was told to paint the chi-rho on his shields. The chi-rho is a combination of the Greek letters chi and rho, which are the first two letters in the Greek word *Christ*.

chapter 1, deathbed baptisms were a common practice in antiquity that usually indicated pious fear rather than lukewarm waffling. While he happily rearranged the details of his life story to suit his needs, Constantine does seem to have believed, at least somewhat, in the faith he took on.

If Constantine was a sincere Christian, his theology was strikingly similar to his politics. Constantine believed in victory through unity. He had come to know Jesus Christ as the one who brought him victory in battle, and he believed that these victories were crucial to preserving imperial unity.

Unity would be in short supply for quite some time, however, as Constantine was busy playing a game of imperial whack-a-mole against his rivals. A very brief summary of the next twelve years of fighting is as follows. Maxentius went to war against Constantine, and holed up in Rome to outlast his rival in a protracted siege battle. But Maxentius had miscalculated his support in Rome, which was fraying under the pressure of heavy taxation he imposed. So Maxentius, in a bid to increase support, went to the Sibylline priestess—a Roman analogue to the oracle of Delphi—who prophesied that the true enemy of Rome would be destroyed in the upcoming battle. Emboldened by this ambivalent prophecy, Maxentius left the protection of Rome to fight Constantine's army at a site known as the Milvian Bridge. Meanwhile, Constantine had his dream of Christ in which Jesus told him to paint a Christian symbol on his soldiers' armor. Constantine's army crushed Maxentius, and in the chaos of the retreat Maxentius fell into the river and drowned. Constantine no doubt rejoiced in the superior specificity of his deity's battle predictions, while Maxentius ruefully reflected on the ambiguous wording of the Sibylline oracle.

Galerius had died during the intervening years, which left only Constantine and his erstwhile colleague Licinius in the imperial college. Together they re-divided the empire between them, with Licinius taking the eastern half of the empire and Constantine the west. Licinius married Constantine's half-sister to cement the deal. Both emperors formally agreed to cease the persecution of Christians begun under Diocletian, bringing the horrors of the Great Persecution to an end. For the first time in imperial history, Christianity was a legal religion. Christians would no longer have to live in fear of the state's persecution.

But Constantine was not satisfied with ruling half the empire. He had ambitions of ruling the entire empire, and he was not about to let Licinius prevent that. We are not completely clear as to his motivations. Naked ambition is, of course, a powerful motivator for rulers in every age. It is also possible that Constantine had seen how much chaos was caused by the tetrarchy and decided it was no good for the empire. There was just no way to prevent four power-hungry emperors from fighting with each other; Rome needed a single emperor calling the shots. Whatever the reason, Constantine found pretexts for war with Licinius that would allow him to bring all of the empire under his rule.

It all came to a head in 324 AD, when Constantine invaded the East on the pretext that Licinius had started persecuting Christians again. While there is little evidence that Licinius had done so, Constantine knew that this pretext would give him popular support. The Great Persecution had not been popular even among pagans, and Constantine's increasingly Christian empire would be keen to avoid a reprise of those bloody days. Constantine began proclaiming himself the liberator of the Christians from Licinius's oppression. Constantine crushed Licinius's armies on the battlefield and trapped him in the city of Byzantium, which he promptly conquered. After briefly fleeing to the nearby city of Nicomedia, Licinius surrendered to Constantine—finally the unchallenged master of the entire Roman world.

Constantine enjoyed his mastery for a few short moments, after which the exiled Licinius drummed up support for a comeback with the help of the Gothic tribes of modern-day Germany. Constantine had already fended off similar betrayals from Maxentius and Maximian. He was in no mood to tolerate a third challenge. Licinius was arrested and hanged in short order. Then Constantine could take a long, deep breath and survey his domain as the truly unchallenged master of the entire Roman world—respected by all, and more importantly, *obeyed* by all.

That desire extended to the church. Ever since his victory over Maximian, Constantine had begun to weigh in on affairs of the church in the West. He had made it very clear that what he wanted above all was *unity*. Unity in worship kept the church, like his army, together. Unity ensured that the one true God would continue to grant him victory. Unity might give a very tired Constantine a chance to rest after almost twenty years of relentless campaigning and politicking.

The church responded to Constantine's demand for unity by engaging in further division and debate. Traumatized by the Great Persecution, elated by Constantine's patronage, and haunted by nagging questions about the nature of the God they worshiped, Roman Christians would be embroiled in an empire-wide controversy within a year of Constantine's final victory. Unbeknownst to all, his exaltation of the church had dried the timbers of long-standing but poorly understood differences within its pews. Those differences would soon explode into a conflagration of rivalries, competing sources of power, and theological controversies. The spark that lit the fire came from the city of Alexandria, where a seemingly ordinary conflict between a priest and his bishop turned into one of the greatest fights in all of church history.

Chapter 4

The Beginnings of a Controversy

THE FOURTH-CENTURY CHURCH WAS no stranger to conflict. In every city of every province in the Roman Empire, faithful Christians disagreed with each other about the best way to praise God. Some of those conflicts erupted into doctrinal wars, with each party declaring the other to have betrayed the true faith. Some of these wars became part of the church's history. The victors were declared to be defenders of the faith, while their opponents were derided as heretics, their names remembered only to warn others away from their teachings.

Even the worst of these conflicts paled in comparison to what was about to explode in Alexandria. Just as Constantine finally brought his last political rivals to heel, the Nicene controversy exploded onto the newly cleared Roman scene, shredding old alliances and disrupting long-standing certainties. Previous church conflicts had been local affairs, and they had stayed local affairs. There was no empire-wide figure with the authority to enforce a universal church decision. That had changed with Constantine's ascension to the imperial purple. Now just such a leader existed—and his power would be put to the test by a seemingly local conflict that captured all of Christendom's attention.

Arius of Alexandria

Few historical figures are as shrouded in myth and legend as Arius of Alexandria. If you have heard of him at all, it is probably either as an archheretic more certainly hellbound than Judas Iscariot, or as a principled and courageous intellectual who happened to fall on the wrong side of the theological majority—the first Constantinian casualty of conscience.

Normally when a figure provokes such polarizing reactions, the truth about them lies somewhere in the middle. In Arius's case, however, the truth lies off the scale altogether. The oral traditions, legends, humors, and hearsay about Arius are far stranger and more fascinating than anything that modern historians have made of him. Ancient traditions report that Arius was a talented composer who wrote hymns promoting his theology set to popular sea shanty tunes. Other rumors report that Arius was stunningly attractive, and other priests in Alexandria complained about how all the young women flocked to Arius's sermons instead of theirs. While looks can be a matter of taste, Arius also enjoyed substantial moral authority as a disciple of the shadowy figure known as Lucian of Antioch. While we know almost nothing about Lucian's life, we do know that he was a martyr of Diocletian's Great Persecution. Martyrs held substantial authority in the early church, and Arius's studies with the great Lucian would have buttressed his own credentials.

If we take all of these rumors together, Arius looks like a sort of theological James Bond: popular with women, talented at any hobby he put his hand to, and mentored by the most honored names in his line of work. Also like James Bond, his name misleads as much as it reveals. For Arius of Alexandria was not actually from Alexandria. He was born, probably to parents of Berber ethnicity, in a Roman region called Cyrenaica, which is in modern-day Eastern Libya and considerably to the west of Alexandria. The reason for his confusing name has to do with the fact that ancient priests and bishops took the name of the city where they served instead of the city where they were born. For example, ordinarily a man named Mark born in Rome would be known as Mark of Rome. If our plucky Mark was called to ordained ministry and was then sent to Antioch to serve there, he would be known as Mark of Antioch. This appears to be precisely what happened to Arius. At some point he left his Libyan roots to serve in the big city of Alexandria. He was no longer Arius of Cyrenaica; now he would take on the pleasingly alliterative name Arius of Alexandria.

Arius had a long career in Alexandria, and was an old man by the standards of the day (fifty to sixty) when the Nicene controversy began. Over the course of his life, Arius built a substantial legacy of sermons and lectures that expounded his view of the Trinity. While most of his works have been lost, a couple of his letters and one fragment of theological poetry have survived. The poetical fragment is called the *Thalia*, and it expresses his view of God quite beautifully:

> So God himself is inexpressible to all beings.
> He alone has none equal to him or like him, none of like glory.
> We call him unbegotten because of the one who by nature is begotten;
> We sing his praises as without beginning because of the one who has a beginning;
> We worship him as eternal because of him who was born in time.
> The one without beginning established the Son as the beginning of all creatures
> And, having fathered such a one, he bore him as a son for himself.
> The Son possesses nothing proper to God, in the real sense of propriety.
> For he is not equal to God, nor yet is he of the same substance.
> I shall say in plain words how the Invisible is seen by the Son—
> It is by the power by which God himself can see, but in his own degree,
> That the Son endures the vision of the Father, as far as is lawful.
> Or again: there exists a trinity in unequal glories, for their hypostases are not mixed with each other
> In their glories, one is more glorious than another in infinite degrees.
> The Father is other than the Son in substance, for He is without beginning.
> ... By God's will the Son is such as he is, by God's will as great as he is,
> From the time when, since the very moment when, he took his subsistence from God,
> Mighty God as he is, he sings the praises of the Higher One with only partial adequacy.
> To put it briefly: God is inexpressible to the Son,
> For he is what he is for himself, and that is unutterable.[1]

The centerpiece of Arius's theology is that there is no being like the Father, not even the Son. Moreover, the Father is perfectly free; the Son is "such as he is" by God's will rather than by his own nature. To put the matter differently, the Son may *look* a lot like the Father—shining gloriously in the transfiguration, displaying immense wisdom and power, helping to create all that is. However, the Son's abilities are a gift of the Father rather than a natural characteristic. To use a superhero analogy, the Father is like Superman. He has his powers by being the kind of being that he is. Kryptonians

---

1. Arius, *Thalia*, 1–9, 12–18, 29–33, in Williams, *Arius*, 101–3.

have the natural ability to draw power from the sun and move faster than a speeding bullet or see through obstacles with their X-ray vision. To Arius, the Son is more like Batman. The only way Batman can move faster than a speeding bullet is by riding in a powered-up Batmobile. He can see through obstacles if he has a pair of X-ray goggles. In other words, Batman does not have his powers by nature. He obtains them through tools, and if you take his tools away then he will lose his powers. Batman is ultimately just an ordinary human (albeit with an extraordinary aversion to mammalian nightlife). Just so with the Son; he is enabled to act in divine ways by the Father's gift, not by his nature. Hence he can act exactly like the Father only "as far as is lawful"—that is, to the extent that the Father allows the Son to do so.

Arius extended this logic even further, making a short argument that drove his opponents insane with fury. It goes like this: If the Father begat the Son, then the Son had a beginning at some point in time. If the Son had a beginning, then there was a time before that beginning; therefore, there was a time when the Son was not. The Son was thus not eternal. Arius's enemies took this to be utter blasphemy, defaming the Son by denying him the eternal existence that all members of the Godhead shared. For Arius it was nothing more than the simple, logical conclusion of the Father-Son relationship. Fathers exist before their sons; that is the nature of being a father. Throughout all of his writings, Arius is incredibly keen to preserve the unique, special character of the Father, even to the point of claiming the Son cannot even really understand the Father fully. Perhaps nothing chilled his enemies more than the claim that the Son can praise the Father with only partial adequacy. If even the Word could not praise God adequately, what hope did the church have of praising God in its worship?

You may be wondering just what the big deal was about the Father being so special. Why did it matter so much that the Father was the only being who was truly eternal, uncaused, and omnipotent? The story is complicated, but it boils down to three basic reasons: tradition, disdain for modalism, and Arius's conception of what it meant to be God. We will discuss each of those reasons in turn.

First, Arius insisted throughout his life that he was doing nothing more than proclaiming the ancient, traditional faith of the church. While his vision of the whole church may have been a bit limited, he probably had reasons for confidence in this point. Throughout the controversy, churches in two provinces of the empire consistently backed his theological vision: his homeland of Cyrenaica and the province of Bithynia, which is up in the northern coast of modern-day Turkey. His ideas also found sympathetic audiences in the province of Caesarea, which is in modern-day Palestine. Arius may well have been taught the doctrines he proclaimed as a child in the Libyan church and found them confirmed during his discipleship with Lucian of Antioch. The agreement he received from others throughout the empire probably convinced him that he was simply expressing the rule of faith as the Libyan church had faithfully received it.

There was also historical precedent for Arius's ideas. Origen of Alexandria was very insistent that the Son and Spirit were subordinate to the Father, occasionally saying they were as beneath the Father as creation was beneath them. In fact, some historians have argued that there is a direct line from Origen to Arius, and that Arius saw himself as continuing Origen's theological school. This particular theory has been pretty thoroughly debunked. For one thing, Origen was very clear that the Son is eternally generated from the Father, which means there was never a time when the Son was not—the exact opposite of Arius's infamous argument. Arius also made it clear that the Son does not know the Father, which would have been anathema to Origen, for whom Christ was the Wisdom of God.

Arius was not a new Origen. But Origen was not the only one to describe the Son as subordinate to the Father. Most theologians of the first few centuries talked about the Son as inferior to the Father in some way, if only because the Father caused the Son's existence. So Arius could reasonably claim to have at least partial backing from Christian tradition.

The second driving force behind Arius's theology was his utter disdain for the heresy of modalism. Arius worried that elevating the Son to equality with the Father made it impossible to differentiate them as two separate entities. In other words, if Father and Son were exactly alike, that meant that one could not really separate them or distinguish them. If they cannot be separated, then they are really just two aspects of the same underlying reality—precisely the conclusion the modalists had reached.

On the other hand, if we say, like Arius, that the Son is inferior to the Father, then he is most definitely different from the Father, and there is no risk of confusing the two as the same entity. Arius affirmed that the Father and Son were two distinct things (two *hypostases*, in Origen's language), and he thought that the differences between them proved their distinction.

You might still be wondering why these distinctions were so important. There are lots of ways for beings to be different, after all. Most differences do not imply being better or worse. The Father and Son might have different favorite colors, or different tastes in music. Or perhaps the Father thinks that mint chocolate chip is the best ice cream flavor, while the Son prefers strawberry. Why did the Son have to be not just different from the Father, but inferior to him?

This brings us to our third reason for Arius's position: common beliefs about what constituted divinity. Virtually every Christian of the fourth century took it as axiomatic that the true God, the one eternal source of all existence and goodness, was utterly unchangeable and uncaused.

The ancients had several reasons for thinking this way, and hundreds of pages have been written evaluating those reasons. I can only give you a very simplified version of one such argument here. God is the ultimate first cause that explains why things are the way they are. Every other cause also requires a cause. For example, if I want to know why I exist, I can say (with gratitude or irritation, depending on my life circumstances and the progress of my therapy) that my parents made me. But this only pushes the question back one step further. My parents are not self-causing beings. They, too, have causes: my grandparents, who are themselves caused to exist by my great-grandparents. On and on we can go, until we find the first human beings, who came to be in a world that itself was caused by the accretion of gasses after a supernova, which was caused by other astronomical events, and so on and so on. If this chain of explanation is ever to end, there must be something that causes other things to be without needing to be caused itself. This self-causing thing is what we call God.

Now, here is the rub. If God can change, we have to ask what the cause of that change is. But if anything in God has a cause, then God is not the first cause anymore. Now there is something *other than God* that explains why God is blue and not red, for example, or being merciful instead of vengeful in one particular moment. Since that thing would be the ultimate cause of God's being a certain way, that thing would be the real God. To be God, in the sense of being a first principle, is to be unchanging.

This line of thinking has come under significant attack in the last few centuries. However, our fourth-century Christians did not have the benefit of reading twentieth- and twenty-first-century books, so for them the arguments for God's unchanging nature stuck. On such a basis, it was difficult for many of them to see the Son as equal to the Father. The Second Person of the Trinity sure seems to undergo change; the Son becomes incarnate, gets crucified, and is resurrected. The Son, therefore, had to be of a lower nature than the Father. To say otherwise would be to assume that the Father was vulnerable to change, which was to say that the Father was not (and could not be) the truest, highest God.

The Father's status as the highest God is the true center of Arius's theology. We know him mostly because he was criticized for "denigrating" the Son in the eyes of his proto-orthodox contemporaries. But Arius did not see himself that way. In fact, Arius spent most of his writing and preaching explaining the Father's nature and characteristics. His teachings on the Son hang off the main body of his work like an appendix. His chief theological worry was that other Christians wound up compromising the glory of the

Father by making him the equal of the Son. It was the theological equivalent of handing an athlete a silver medal for a first-place result, and hardly the praise that the church owed the Father as the highest God.

The motivations behind Arius's theology highlight one of the most important and least-understood aspects of the Nicene controversy: Arius saw himself as theological traditionalist. He couched his own faith in terms of fidelity to past Christian tradition. Arius was concerned to preserve the traditional theology of the Father's utter transcendence and unchangeability. Arius would be the one to reject novel and unbiblical terminology his enemies insisted on applying to God.

Today, many think of heresy as something done only by self-styled theological progressives or liberals. In the parishes I have served, I often hear parishioners describe their more liberal beliefs and say, "I guess I'm just a heretic." Yet for all his traditionalism, Arius went down in the books as a heretic, proving that heresy is an equal opportunity category. Even Tertullian, from whom much of our Trinitarian ideas and vocabulary come, was labeled a heretic in large part because of his affiliation with a schismatic sect called Montanism. Montanism appealed to his nostalgic longing for a simpler, purer, more stringent Christianity from his good old days. Origen of Alexandria would be condemned for heresy centuries after his death despite his prolific and brilliant insights. The question of what makes for heresy is much more complicated and much more interesting than current usage of the word implies.

Alexander

Arius might never have suffered the ignominy of condemnation were it not for the fateful appointment of a new bishop in his city. That bishop's name was Alexander of Alexandria. Some ancient historians tell us that Arius was also a candidate to be named bishop instead of Alexander. No reliable records of the election exist, so we cannot know for certain if Arius and Alexander clashed for the episcopal throne. If they did, poor Arius must have had the worse position based on names alone. Not only did Alexander of Alexandria have as pleasingly alliterative a name as Arius of Alexandria, but Alexandria's more forgetful churchgoers would more easily remember the name of their eponymous bishop.

Whatever the reason, Alexander became bishop and Arius remained a priest. Perhaps Arius could have held his tongue if Alexander's greatest fault was winning an election that Arius had hoped to win. However, Alexander represented a different theological tradition that Arius could not abide. Alexander claimed that the Son and the Father were "of the same substance"—*homoousios* (ho-mo-oo-SEE-os) in Greek.

What does *homoousios* really mean? It is most literally translated as "of the same substance."[2] The prefix *homo* means "same," and *ousia* is translated as "substance"; its Latin equivalent is *substantia*, which Tertullian was fond of using to describe God. Substance is quite literally the stuff out of which one is made, and members of the same species have the same substance. I am quite amazingly of the same substance as musical icon Brandi Carlile and acting legend David Tennant; I am not of the same substance as a red panda or an angel.

To say that the Son was *homoousios* with the Father was to say that the Son has his divine qualities—eternity, glory, omniscience, omnipotence, etc.—because he is fully divine. They are an inevitable consequence of the kind of being that the Son is. Just as a human father and son are similar on the basis of being the same kind of thing, with the same basic powers and weaknesses, so the divine Son and Father are. Just as a son of Superman would inherit all his Kryptonian powers,[3] the Son of the Father would be a fully divine being with access to divine powers by virtue of his natural divinity, not just as a gift from the Father.

Theologians like Alexander used this language because they wanted to emphasize the similarities between Father and Son to the absolute highest degree possible. They loved to emphasize the correlative nature of terms like "Father" and "Son." Of course the Son is generated by the Father in some way. On the other hand, a father does not become a father until the instant he has a son. Each term is defined by their relationship with the other. There is no reason to think, as Arius seemed to, that the Son has to be a different kind of thing than the Father just because the Father causes him. In a particular kind of way, the Son also causes the Father.

Alexander and his theological compadres thought there were good reasons to believe the Son and the Father were very similar. They had several biblical passages they would regularly turn to. Christ is described as being in the "form of God";[4] Jesus states that he and the Father are one,[5] and the beginning of the Fourth Gospel famously states that the Word was God in

---

2. You will also encounter translations such as "of one being" or "consubstantial," which is not so much a translation as a transliteration from Tertullian's Latin.

3. Of course, this analogy assumes that Superman's partner is also a Kryptonian. I have no idea what would happen if Superman and Lois Lane had a child together. In the case of the Father and Son, though, there is only one parent involved, so we do not have to worry about the Son having a non-divine parent.

4. Philippians 2:6.

5. John 10:30.

the beginning.⁶ Beyond these verses, one of the most important passages for understanding Christ's nature was this excerpt from Wisdom 7:⁷

> For she is a breath of the power of God
> and a pure emanation of the glory of the Almighty;
> therefore nothing defiled gains entrance into her.
> For she is a reflection of eternal light,
> a spotless mirror of the working of God,
> and an image of his goodness.
> Although she is but one, she can do all things,
> and while remaining in herself, she renews all things;
> in every generation she passes into holy souls
> and makes them friends of God and prophets.⁸

Remember from chapter 3 that Christians believed that the Bible was meant to be read allegorically. The figure of Wisdom does not seem to have much to do with Jesus on a first reading. For one thing, she is personified as female rather than male. For another, the book of Wisdom is extolling the value of living wisely, not clarifying the roles of various divine entities. It would be an odd thing indeed for it to have Jesus in mind on a literal level. However, as Origen had repeatedly pointed out, the New Testament repeatedly describes Christ as the Wisdom of God.⁹ Origen and other early Christians saw these passages as a key to understanding Old Testament depictions of wisdom. If Christ is Wisdom, then whenever the Bible talks about wisdom, it is talking about Jesus, at least implicitly. How significant, then, that Wisdom 7 describes personified Wisdom (and hence Christ) as a divine figure. She is "a pure emanation of the glory of the Almighty," a "spotless mirror of the working of God," she "can do all things" and "renews all things." Wisdom sounds an awful lot like the Father—and hence, so does the Son.

Alexander and his theological allies wanted to push this similarity as far as possible. One such ally, the impressively named Theognostus of Alexandria, explained the relationship between Father and Son thus:

---

6. John 1:1.

7. Today, many Protestant churches do not include the book of Wisdom in their Bible. It is often classified as part of the "Apocrypha"—a group of Greek writings that were composed after the close of the Old Testament and which Jewish communities do not consider to be part of their Scriptures. Early Christians, however, did include Wisdom in their Bibles. Its canonical status would not come under scrutiny until the Protestant Reformation in the 1500s AD.

8. Wisdom 7:25–27.

9. For example, 1 Corinthians 1:24, Colossians 2:3, and possibly Matthew 11:19.

> The essence (ousia) of the Son is not derived from outside [of the Father's being], nor was he produced out of nothing, but issued from the essence (ousia) of the Father like radiance from light and like vapor from water; for neither the radiance, nor the vapor is the water itself or the sun itself, nor is the one alien to the other, so too [the nature of the Son] is an outflowing of the Father's essence.[10]

Theognostus almost broke language to make his point. While he agreed with Arius's concern to distinguish Father and Son, he attempted to describe them as two things that are not the exact same but are so intimately related to each other that you can never find one without the other. He uses the imagery of flow to accomplish this. Vapor flows from water, brightness flows from light, etc. Tertullian made the same point with psychological metaphors; the Son is the Father's internal dialogue that flows naturally out of his process of thinking. Theognostus's imagery is more earthy, and also more prone to accusations of modalism. After all, water and vapor are just two forms of the exact same thing. Brightness is just one aspect of light. Are these analogies just a resuscitated, warmed-over modalism? Arius would probably say yes and cringe; Theognostus and Alexander would probably say no in indignation, and the modalists would probably plaintively say yes and wonder why no one wanted to associate with them.

The Clash

Alexander, being thoroughly convinced that he was in the right, preached his theology from his pulpit every Sunday. Arius, thoroughly convinced that his bishop was not only wrong but heretical, accused his bishop of modalism and demanded that he repent. This was an extremely bold move. Bishops are overseers. In most churches, the process for resolving a disagreement with your overseer is pretty simple. The overseer tells you to knock it off. You either comply, which ends the disagreement, or the overseer ends your ministry and removes you from the church, which also ends the disagreement. Presumably Alexander attempted to do exactly that to Arius. He was, however, profoundly unsuccessful. Not only did Arius continue to minister, but prominent bishops from across the empire rushed to defend him from Alexander. How did Arius manage to keep preaching his theology and start a disagreement that enveloped the whole Roman Empire when his bishop was telling him to stop?

---

10. Theognostus of Alexandria, *Hypotyposes*, in Hanson, *Search*, 77.

The short answer is that we are not quite certain. Many details of the story have been lost to history. The evidence we *do* have, however, suggests that part of the answer is that bishops of Alexandria tended to have less power than bishops elsewhere in the empire. You may remember how Origen's conflict with his Alexandrine bishop ended: Origen got to travel the world and teach everywhere and when his jealous bishop tried to reel him in, he was laughed off by his fellow bishops. The Alexandrian episcopacy was also rocked by a major schism only a few decades before Arius and Alexander clashed. To make a long story short, Egypt had endured a particularly harsh treatment under the Great Persecution, and many of its Christians became *traditores*. Once the persecution ended, some of these people repented and desired to be readmitted into the church.

The general attitude in the church was that God's forgiveness was for everyone, even traitors, and that these people could be readmitted given appropriate time and reparation. Nevertheless, the wounds of the Great Persecution were deep. Many Christians were not willing to allow *traditores* to sit in the same churches as they did, especially if their friends or family had suffered due to the traitors' cooperation with persecutors. One of these folks was Meletius, bishop of the town of Lycopolis. Lycopolis was only a short distance from Alexandria. During the Great Persecution, the reigning bishop of Alexandria, Peter, went into hiding. Peter probably reasoned that he could not be a very effective pastor and overseer if he was dead. Meletius accused Peter of abandoning his post and ordained priests to serve in churches under Peter's jurisdiction. Among bishops, there are few insults bigger than taking over a colleague's responsibilities without permission. Of course, Meletius meant it as an insult; he was ordaining priests because he thought Peter was not doing his job. After the Persecution ended, Meletius continued to foment discord by criticizing Bishop Peter and refusing to accept back Christians who had betrayed the faith.

This was particularly bold on Meletius's part because Peter, as the bishop of the bigger and more historic city, was presumed to hold authority over him. Peter deposed Meletius from his office as a disturber of the peace. But Meletius was a fairly charismatic fellow. He had also apparently been briefly exiled to do slave labor in the mines during the Great Persecution, and he held all the moral authority that comes with suffering for your faith. So Meletius and his followers, including twenty-eight other bishops, ignored Peter's decree and kept on worshiping. They even called their gathering the Church of the Martyrs, just to drive home which congregation had been faithful during times of strife. This schism continued all throughout Alexander's episcopate, and attempting to reconcile the Meletians with the broader Egyptian church was a constant struggle for him and his successors.

As is often the case in the church, you only have as much power as others think you have, and the fact that there was a vocal minority of Christians loudly insisting that Alexander, like Peter before him, was a terrible bishop with no authority did little to burnish his credentials when disciplining rogue clergy.

The bishop of Alexandria was in a very unusual place. Perhaps more than in any other city of the time, Alexandria's bishop claimed authority to oversee and even appoint bishops of the outlying towns. When other bishops accepted his authority, they addressed Alexander as their "papa"—the same word that was eventually applied to the Roman pope. When they did not, they rebelled and challenged his authority with astounding success. At the same time, priests within Alexandria itself appear to have seen the bishop as just the first among equals. They viewed the bishop as a convener, but not as a teacher or authority figure.[11] When they believed him to be in the wrong, they would tell him so, and would expect to be treated as equals rather than subordinates.

Perhaps more important than any of the political details was the legacy of trauma that overshadowed the players in the controversy. Arius, Alexander, and all their allies had endured the Great Persecution. They almost certainly had friends who had suffered and even died for the faith. Both sides could claim the legacy of the martyrs. On the one hand, Christianity had been illegal in the first place because Christians only believed in one God, the Father. For Arius, to elevate the Son to the Father's glory was to create a second God, thereby turning Christians into polytheists. It mocked the monotheism that his friends had died for. On the other hand, Christians had been persecuted for taking the name of Jesus Christ. They died for their fidelity to his gospel, with prayers addressed to his name on their lips. To denigrate Christ's divinity was to invalidate the faith of the martyrs—not to mention Jesus Christ himself, the very first martyr. Religion stirs up strong feelings in even the most peaceful of times. The fourth century was far from the most peaceful of times, and even seemingly arcane theological terminology became an occasion for the church to relive its traumas.

These dynamics turned a minor theological brushfire into a roaring conflagration. After Arius denounced his bishop, Alexander told him to knock it off. Arius refused. Alexander denounced Arius as a heretic, and

---

11. Some historians think that the bishop of Alexandria was elected in an unusual way that contributed to this dynamic. It is possible that the bishop of Alexandria was elected by the priests of the city. Most other prominent cities chose their bishop by calling together a council of nearby bishops to elect a new one—or, after Constantine's rise, by accepting the candidate that the Roman bureaucracy endorsed. Alexandrine priests might have reasoned that, as the bishop's electors, they had ultimate authority over him.

convened a small council of bishops close to Alexandria to confirm his decision. The council agreed with Alexander, and Arius was removed from ministry.

Arius then appears to have relied on his charisma to outlast his boss. First, he tried to ignore Alexander by staying in the city and setting up rogue churches with like-minded clergy and laypeople. After a while, Arius was persuaded to leave the city (whether by force or persuasion is uncertain). As a charismatic and well-connected teacher, he probably had deep support networks throughout the empire. He wrote to several influential bishops throughout the church, including Eusebius of Caesarea and Eusebius of Nicomedia. His requests for support were granted, and from there things escalated further. A council of bishops in Palestine concluded that Arius was *perfectly* orthodox and Alexander was in the wrong. Alexander responded with a lengthy tome refuting their accusations. Meanwhile, Arius's new allies wrote their own letters to supporters, stirring up help for Arius and his cause. A synod in Bithynia, Eusebius of Nicomedia's home court, further consolidated support for Arius and his theology. Bishop Alexander responded with another letter, usually referred to as the *henos somatos,* in which he told Arius's supporters exactly what he thought of them:

> In our diocese lawless and anti-Christian men have recently arisen, teaching an apostasy which one might reasonably consider and label the forerunner of the Antichrist. I wished indeed to treat this matter with silence, that if possible the evil might be confined to its supporters alone, and not spread into other regions and contaminate the ears of innocent people. But Eusebius, now bishop in Nicomedia, thinks that the affairs of the church lay under his control; after abandoning his office at Beirut and coveting the church at Nicomedia without being punished for it, he has now established himself at the head of these apostates, daring even to write letters in all directions in support of them, hoping to drag down some of the ignorant into this shameful and anti-Christian heresy. Thus, since I know what is written in the law, I could no longer keep silent, but I had to inform you of all of these things, so that you would be made aware of which people have fallen into apostasy and also of the terrible threats caused by their heresy, and pay no attention to anything that Eusebius writes to you.[12]

Alexander has made several serious accusations in this letter. He accused Eusebius of dereliction of duty, ambition (never an admired trait in

---

12. Alexander of Alexandria, *Henos somatos* 3–5, in *NPNF* 2:2, 3–5.

a Christian leader), and even of being a harbinger of the Antichrist! Yet the very fact that bishop Alexander had to write such a letter is proof controversy is no longer between Alexander and Arius; now it is between Alexander and Eusebius of Nicomedia, two bishops with different jurisdictions who each think the other a disgrace to his office.

The Nicene conflict was now underway as different power brokers lined up behind each side of what appeared to be a minor regional conflict. Yet even this was not new in the Christian world. Bishops had disagreed with each other before, and had occasionally done so vociferously. Most of the time, the church had shrugged and moved on. The Roman Empire was a big place, and opposing bishops often lived in different regions, so they could mostly ignore each other and let the controversy fizzle out. The Nicene controversy was different for one crucial reason: the presence of the first Christian emperor, who believed that unity in the church was necessary for peace and unity in the empire.

In a few short months, Constantine seized the reins from these quarreling bishops and gave the church its first universal council. We have been living in the aftermath of his choice ever since.

Chapter 5

The Council to Settle It All (Or Not)

By 325 AD, the great Emperor Constantine was very, very tired.

He had just spent the better part of two decades unifying the Roman Empire in the face of political intrigue, rebellions, wars, and new rebellions from previously defeated enemies. He was more than ready to settle down and enjoy a period of unchallenged rule and empire-wide unity. He had one more obstacle in his way: the ecclesiastical rebellion that gripped the Christian church. Alexander, Arius, and Eusebius of Nicomedia were drawing the faithful into a massive conflict that Constantine feared would become a circular firing squad. Bishops were gathering in local councils all across the empire and issuing conflicting rulings on the matter of Arius. They even began to excommunicate those with whom they disagreed, effectively ruling other Christians to be outside of the church. As bishops began to declare each other *persona non grata,* Constantine looked on with worry. Remember from chapter 3 that Constantine believed that unity in worship was necessary for unity in the empire. Just as Constantine had enforced military unity through his wars, now he wished to enforce theological unity so that the Christians of his empire could worship God with one voice. God would in turn bless Constantine's newly Christianized empire and assure him of future success on the battlefield.

To that end, Constantine did something that had not been done since the time of the book of Acts. Constantine summoned every single bishop in the empire to attend a grand gathering in the town of Nicaea, just a few miles away from his newly minted imperial capital in Constantinople (modern-day Istanbul, Turkey). He offered to pay the costs of their transportation and lodging to the destination to ensure maximum attendance. He hoped the bishops would hammer out the points of debate, settle all their differences, and walk away perfectly unified in the confession of their faith.

Setting the Guest List

Constantine's hopes would crash against reality soon enough. Before we proceed further, though, you might be wondering why Constantine only invited the bishops to this council. There were other Christian leaders who held significant authority in the church. Why were no charismatic teachers or early monastic leaders invited?[1]

There were several reasons for Constantine's reluctance to bring non-bishops into the fold. First, teachers and monks were not terribly easy to corral. Charismatic and brilliant teachers were few and far between, and there were hardly enough of them to populate a council. While monasticism had begun by 325 AD, it was still a fairly new movement, and many of its greatest leaders had yet to emerge. Moreover, monks who abandon all worldly possessions to live lives of poverty, silence, and solitude in the desert are not typically keen to attend massive meetings full of imperial grandeur, discussion, debate, and general human interaction. Since bishops were in possession of full-time jobs and could be found in their home church every Sunday, they were far easier to corral. Beyond the logistical challenges posed by inviting other groups, bishops were already used to having the final say in matters of church politics. They were the overseers of the church, after all, and they believed that gave them ultimate authority to adjudicate matters of faith. It just so happened that councils were the bishops' usual means of exercising that authority—and had been for at least a century. While no one had ever summoned all the bishops together before, groups of bishops in a region would occasionally convene councils to settle conflicts in their area. Constantine expanded the Christian council, but he certainly did not invent it.

Constantine's choice to summon the bishops of the empire was not merely a matter of convenience, however. Throughout his reign, Constantine consistently empowered bishops and augmented their religious authority with civil powers. He allowed bishops to judge certain types of legal cases, and they were allowed to preside over some state ceremonies such as

---

1. There was one other important source of authority in the church: martyrs. Each side of the Nicene conflict would attempt to claim the martyrs' legacy as their own. However, since one must die to become a martyr, they were conspicuously absent from the council. Apparently none of them decided that their idea of eternal bliss was leaving the heavenly choir to sit in on a very long church council.

the freeing of a slave. When Constantine made his expected donations to the poor of the empire,[2] he did not give them personally. He funneled the donations through bishops, and especially the bishops of the major cities of the empire. For example, a bishop might receive grain or tunics to be given to the poor of the city. Usually it was the emperor's job to decide how to distribute these sorts of gifts. Constantine deputized the bishops to serve in that role. In so doing, he made the citizenry personally dependent on their bishop's largesse. A bishop who gave money and gifts wisely could enjoy immense goodwill from the citizens of his city. A bishop who squandered the gifts was likely to arouse their ire.

The bishops' response to their newfound powers depended on who the bishop in question was and where they were. Bishops living a smaller, provincial life probably didn't notice or enjoy many of the benefits their metropolitan colleagues did. However, many of the most influential bishops were quite enamored of their new powers. The great historian Peter Brown wrote, tongue firmly in cheek:

> If God helps those who help themselves, then no group deserved the miracle of the "conversion" of Constantine in 312 than did the Christians. For the Christian leaders seized their opportunity astonishing pertinacity and intelligence . . . and, when Constantine finally conquered the eastern provinces in 324, he was greeted by [Bishop] Eusebius of Caesarea, who placed his pen at the emperor's disposal with a skill and enthusiasm such as no traditional Greek [rhetorician] had seemed able to summon for Constantine's grim and old-fashioned predecessors.[3]

Eusebius of Caesarea is one of the clearest examples of what a bishop eager to seize the reins of power could do with Constantine's blessing. Eusebius had inherited the vast library that Origen had left at Caesarea, and he put that library to good use writing scholarly texts. His most important work was a book called *The Ecclesiastical History*, a comprehensive history of the church from the end of the book of Acts until Eusebius's own day. Modern-day scholars still use the *Ecclesiastical History* as a guide to the early church, albeit with a healthy awareness of Eusebius's own biases. Eusebius expanded Origen's *Hexapla,* wrote a history of the world called the *Chronicon,* and produced a massive and massively complimentary biography of Constantine.

---

2. Roman emperors had long been expected to personally care for the empire's poor via donations from the imperial treasury.

3. Brown, *World of Late Antiquity,* 82.

Eusebius believed that a closer relationship between church and emperor would serve both parties. He praised Constantine for establishing the worship of the true Christian God throughout the empire and ending the persecution of Christians. He reminded other politicians of the blessings God had bestowed upon Constantine due to his faith, impressing upon them the importance of continuing the new Christian empire that Constantine had initiated. He insisted that only a Christian emperor was fit to rule because only an emperor ruled by God could rule the empire. Eusebius hoped that support for the new emperor would ensure that the church remained in Constantine's good graces.

Eusebius was in significant need of the emperor's good graces at the time the Council of Nicaea was called. He had been condemned as a heretic, and needed to clear his orthodoxy. Eusebius had been a participant in a recent council of Antioch. It was one of several local councils that had been called to address the ongoing controversy between Arius and Alexander, and it roundly sided with Alexander against Arius. Eusebius was excommunicated from the Syrian church at the council's conclusion for failing to agree to its statement of faith.

This excommunication had no practical effect on Eusebius. He was the bishop of Caesarea in the Roman province of Palestine. None of the other bishops at the council had any power over him, and he could continue his ministry without any problems. Yet for a bishop who flaunted his connections to the emperor and hoped for the expansion of the newly Christianized regime, being excommunicated by one of the largest cities in the empire was not good optics. Eusebius was looking for a chance to clear his name in front of the whole empire. The Council of Nicaea was the perfect venue for Eusebius and other bishops like him who had been caught in the crossfire of controversy.

The Council's Attendees

So it was that in May 325 AD, bishops from across the empire arrived in Nicaea with a mix of trepidation and excitement to embark on the church's first ecumenical council. "Ecumenical" is a ten-dollar theological word that simply means "universal." Because Constantine invited every single bishop in the empire, the council was considered to be universal in scope. However, that does not mean that every bishop in the empire accepted Constantine's invitation. Of the approximately 1,800 bishops invited, somewhere between 200 and 318 attended. Of those who did attend, almost all of them were from the eastern half of the empire. A few prominent Western bishops were too ill to attend, including the bishop of Rome, who sent a few delegates to attend in his place. The Roman delegates were joined by about ten other Western bishops. The other 790 bishops in the West apparently decided that the commute was too long, and sent their regrets back to the most powerful man in the empire. Although they were thrilled that the emperor shared their faith, the bishops of the empire did not automatically assume that he had the authority to command them. They were the overseers of the church, and they answered to God, not the emperor. If Jesus called the council of Nicaea, they would all attend. Constantine would have to be content with a more modest head count. Thus the church's first universal council began with at most one-sixth of its invitees in attendance—and that does not count the bishops who lived outside of the Roman Empire and were never invited at all!

But the council, blessedly existing before the notion of a quorum, was not to be deterred by minor inconveniences like 80 percent of the eligible members not being present. All the major episcopal players were there. Bishop Alexander of Alexandria was in attendance, along with his plucky young secretary named Athanasius. Athanasius would become one of the most tenacious defenders of the council in the years to come, but in 325 AD he was an observer of the fracas and nothing more. Eusebius of Caesarea was jockeying for influence and looking for an opportunity to clear his name of heresy charges. Eusebius of Nicomedia was there rallying his supporters and probably enjoying the fact that this great and holy council had been assembled so very close to his own diocese. Noticeably absent, however, was Arius himself. There is no record that he was at the council. As a mere priest and not a bishop, he would not have been included in the general invitation. While some stories report that he was in attendance, we have no evidence to that effect. If anyone felt it odd that the controversy would be resolved with only one of its two litigants in attendance, they did not mention this in their writings about it.

Most importantly, the Emperor Constantine himself attended the council. He was present for its opening proceedings, glittering with purple and gold regalia. In a gracious show of humility, he let the bishops sit down before him, then gave an opening speech to the council and started the proceedings. We do not know if Constantine was present for the whole council or if he merely made an impression at the opening ceremony and then left. Since Nicaea was so close to the new capital, Constantine may have split his time between working in his capital and herding quarrelsome bishops when necessary. Whatever his involvement, Constantine was simply too busy to run the council every day. He delegated the day-to-day operations of the council to a senior bishop, and the proceedings began.

The Council's Work

We are not entirely certain how the council proceeded. It is a tragedy of church history that no one thought to take meeting minutes at the very first ecumenical council. However, several of the attendees described the events of the council in writings after the fact, and from their recollections we know two important things occurred.

The first is that Eusebius of Caesarea was able to clear himself of any charges of heresy. Eusebius wrote that he presented his church's rule of faith to Emperor Constantine himself, and Constantine personally affirmed the bishop's orthodoxy. Supposedly Constantine told Eusebius that his creed was perfectly orthodox, and he merely needed to say the Son was *homoousios* with the Father in order to be cleared of all charges. This Eusebius did, and hence was vindicated against his enemies.

Eusebius's story has given rise to an urban legend that Constantine ran the Council of Nicaea himself, personally deciding what theologies were orthodox and which were heretical. If Eusebius's account is true, then there would be much truth to that rumor. However, you should trust Eusebius's account about as far as you can throw him. Eusebius has a reputation for stretching the truth when it suits him,[4] and no other accounts of the council mention Constantine doing anything like this. Eusebius was anxious to secure his own orthodoxy, and suggesting that Constantine, the great hero of Christians across the empire, had personally vindicated him would help Eusebius secure his authority. Moreover, if the emperor himself had personally endorsed the phrase *homoousios*, bishop Alexander and his allies would have mentioned that fact. Their silence on the matter is good evidence that Eusebius's story is exaggerated. The more likely story is that most of the assembled bishops agreed that Eusebius was orthodox and Constantine rubber-stamped the verdict, relieved to have one more conflict settled.

We know very little about the sort of debates that Eusebius might have endured while proving his orthodoxy. There is one legend about those debates that is too interesting not to include. The bishop Nicholas of Myra was a passionate advocate of the Son's full divinity and a fervent ally of Alexander. He also happens to be the historical inspiration for the figure of Santa Claus due to his penchant for throwing bags of gold through the windows of impoverished Christians' homes. (Nicholas of Myra knew how to use the

---

4. Eusebius is especially quick to exaggerate his closeness with Constantine. Eusebius occasionally implies that he and Constantine have met for long, detailed, personal chats. The historical record suggests that they met four times at most, and always in group settings rather than one-on-one conversations. Eusebius may call himself Constantine's friend; at most, he was a distant acquaintance.

gifts Constantine gave him!) One popular myth about the Council of Nicaea is that Nicholas attended and was so enraged at Arius's blasphemous arguments that he walked across the council floor and punched Arius in the face. That particular myth has not made it into many Christmas carols. Fortunately for the history of religious violence and unfortunately for church history nerds, there is no truth to this legend. There is no evidence that Nicholas or Arius attended the council, and the account of their one-sided boxing match comes from an unreliable document written centuries after the council. Nevertheless, it is fun to imagine Eusebius sweating with relief after his reinstatement, grateful to have escaped the fury of Santa Claus's devastating uppercut.

Eusebius's readmission would have important consequences in the years after the council. However, the bishops at the time thought of it as a minor point of order to be completed before the main work of settling the controversy between Alexander and Arius. That work turned out to be fairly straightforward. As the council proceeded, it became clear that Alexander's party and their friends had the upper hand. Arius's theological allies had a distinct minority share of the vote, and they were steadily peeled off, one by one, as Alexander and his allies patiently explained their position. One of the minority's chief reservations was that *homoousios* could imply that the Son and Father were material entities. Words like *ousia* could imply a sort of ooze-like, materialistic substance, and bishops wanted to be clear that the God they worshiped was not some cosmic ooze. Once Alexander and his allies made it clear they did *not* mean that, most dissent melted away. And so the Council of Nicea came up with the following creed:

> We believe in one God, the Father almighty,
> maker of all things visible and invisible;
> And in one Lord, Jesus Christ, the Son of God,
> begotten from the Father, only-begotten,
> that is, from the substance of the Father,
> God from God, light from light,
> true God from true God, begotten not made,
> of one substance with the Father,
> through Whom all things came into being,
> things in heaven and things on earth,
> Who because of us men and because of our salvation came down,
> and became incarnate and became man, and suffered,
> and rose again on the third day, and ascended to the heavens,
> and will come to judge the living and dead,
> And in the Holy Spirit.

> But as for those who say, There was when He was not,
> and, Before being born He was not,
> and that He came into existence out of nothing,
> or who assert that the Son of God is of a different hypostasis or substance,
> or created, or is subject to alteration or change
> —these the Catholic and apostolic church anathematizes.

This creed is putting Arius squarely in its crosshairs. It uses his hated word *homoousios*, translated in this version as "of one substance with the Father." It anathematizes his famous statement that there was a time when the Son was not and that he came into being out of nothing.

When Arius was presented with the creed, he refused to sign it. Few others joined him.

They would soon feel the weight of their dissent. Constantine had called this council to enforce unity in the church, and he was not about to let the dissenters continue to sow discord in his empire. Arius, two Libyan bishops who had stuck with him to the end, and a handful of other supporters were exiled from the Roman Empire on Constantine's orders. Eusebius of Nicomedia, Arius's primary supporter among the bishops, would join them in exile a few months later. He tried to have his cake and eat it too by signing the creed but continuing to permit priests who contradicted it to practice. Constantine would not stand for any dissent.

This was not the first time that a Christian had been exiled from the empire for their beliefs. Back in the third century, a group of bishops had petitioned the pagan emperor Aurelius to exile Paul of Samosata, a notorious modalist. Aurelius did not care who the church deemed a heretic, but he saw that there seemed to be more people opposed to Paul than for him, so he decided to exile him just to resolve the controversy. Constantine's exiles were different. For him, the success and unity of the empire depended on the unity of the church. In his empire, there was no way to be a religious criminal without being a political criminal too. To be a heretic is to automatically be a political dissident. Arius was the first target of this new ecclesial-political alliance, but he was far from the last.

Consolidating the Hierarchy

The assembled bishops were not content to condemn Arius's theology, however. They also took steps to prevent another charismatic heretic from engulfing all Christendom in conflict. The bishops drafted and passed a set of canons (a ten-dollar word for "church laws") that would be binding across the empire. Many of these canons are still observed in the Roman Catholic, Eastern Orthodox, and Coptic Orthodox churches today. The council was determined to reinforce the authority of bishops in general, and the bishop of Alexandria in particular. It did so by standardizing several important procedures. The council standardized a response to the Christians who had lapsed during the Great Persecution. Previously each bishop had the authority to decide how to treat the *traditores* on their own. Now, they were bound to act according to the council's decree. Lapsed Christians could be readmitted to the church as catechumens and would observe a twelve-year period of repentance before they could be fully restored. They were not allowed to be ordained under any circumstance. These canons supported Alexander's approach rather than those of his rival Meletius, further marginalizing the movement that had weakened the eponymous Alexandrine patriarch. The council also standardized the selection of bishops. A bishop would be elected by the other bishops in his province. If Alexandrine priests imagined themselves to be the bishop's equals, this new canon would quickly dispel their illusions. Moreover, the council explicitly declared the bishop of Alexandria to be in charge of the rest of Egypt and several other parts of North Africa, reinforcing his authority in the face of other challengers.

The council of Nicaea was concerned to ensure that no one would usurp the bishop of Alexandria's prerogatives to oversee the region in his care. Ironically, they did so in a way that many have read as reinforcing the power of the bishop of Rome. The canon describing the bishop of Alexandria's authority reads: "Let the ancient customs in Egypt, Libya and Pentapolis prevail, that the Bishop of Alexandria have jurisdiction in all these, since the like is customary for the Bishop of Rome also."[5]

This canon reinforces the authority of the Metropolitan of Alexandria by referencing the custom of Rome. Many Roman Catholics will point to this as evidence of the primacy of the bishop of Rome in the church. It appears that the church is resolving its conflict by seeing what Rome does and copying its approach. Non-Romans dispute this, of course. For one thing, the canon references the ancient traditions in Egypt, Libya, and Pentapolis as the basis for its authority, not Rome. Second, the canon seems to be saying that the bishop of Alexandria will have the exact same authority as the bishop of Rome. He is not subordinate to the Roman pope.

In either case, authority clearly lies with bishops. Bishops decide who gets ordained, bishops of large cities control outlying provinces, and bishops control who is in the church and who is excommunicated. Seen in this way, one of the legacies of Nicaea is the general triumph of bishops over other

---

5. *Canons of the Council of Nicaea*, Canon 6, in *NPNF* 2:14, 15–16.

models of authority. Arius was a charismatic teacher who attempted to assert his authority. He fought with his bishop, left to find a more agreeable supervisor, and continued to correct his errant foe from afar. Just a century before, Origen had done almost exactly the same thing and was hailed as one of the greatest authorities of the age. By contrast, Arius got excommunicated and exiled, and the council outlawed the methods he had used to contest his banishment. With Constantine firmly behind their cause, the bishops were keen to bring order to the chaotic dissents and disagreements that had marked the church.

The story might well have ended here. Constantine and his bishop allies could have serenely continued rolling out their vision for Christendom, convincing the persuadable and exiling the incorrigible. It was not to be, however. For though the participants of the council could not see it, storm clouds were already gathering on the horizon. Some of the bishops who had signed on to the creed were none too happy about it, including the powerful and newly-rehabilitated Eusebius of Caesarea. A few of the pro-Nicenes would not prove adept in navigating the turbulent waters of imperial politics. Within a few years, the most celebrated proponents of Nicaea would be either removed from power or dead, and the council's findings would be condemned as heretical. Generational change, simmering theological questions, imperial intrigue, and the world's most poorly-timed insult were about to bring the Nicene conflict to new heights.

The Council of Nicaea was designed to end a christological conflict. Though the bishops could not have known it as the council adjourned, the conflict had only just begun.

PART 2

Chapter 6

The Eusebii Strike Back

INSTEAD OF THE ORDERLY march to political and ecclesial unity that Constantine envisioned, the years after the Council of Nicaea more closely resemble a chaotic free-for-all of semantic confusion, political schemes, and recalcitrant bishops refusing to acknowledge the results of the emperor's grand council. If you find yourself confused by the twists and turns described in this chapter, you are not alone. The events that followed Nicaea confused the ancient church at least as much as they do readers today.

The Return of the Exiles

The person most responsible for the chaos and confusion was Constantine himself. After initially punishing all heretics and dissidents with exile, within a few years Constantine had reversed himself entirely and readmitted virtually all of Nicaea's critics to the empire. Foremost among these returning exiles was Arius himself. After suffering banishment, Arius wrote a letter to Constantine that requested reinstatement as a priest and included a new statement of faith Arius had written personally. In the statement, Arius affirmed that he believed in the Son and the Father while saying nothing about the relationship between them. Instead, Arius begged the emperor to avoid "superfluous questions"[1]—in other words, to ignore all of the controversial teachings that Arius had just been exiled for and accept him back into the empire. You might imagine that Constantine, having just spent the better part of two decades putting down rebellious enemies and quarrelsome

---

1. Socrates, *Historia Ecclesiastica* 1.26, in *NPNF* 2.2.

officials, was not about to let a clearly unrepentant and powerful heretic back into the empire. Yet Constantine readily accepted Arius and instructed bishops to readmit him to the church.

However, Bishop Alexander defied Constantine's request. This was a very bold thing to do. Fortunately, Alexander also had the good sense to die of natural causes shortly after defying the emperor, thus avoiding any potential punishment. He was succeeded by Athanasius, that plucky young priest who had been his secretary at Nicaea a few years before. Showing the kind of brash resolve that defined his career, Athanasius upheld the ban on Arius's ministry. Arius was now in limbo. Several sympathetic bishops had obeyed Constantine and readmitted him, but he could not minister under them. The Nicene Canons prohibited a priest from transferring from one diocese to another without their original bishop's consent—consent the bishop of Alexandria would not give. After a few years of frustration, Arius wrote to Constantine again. In his frustration, however, he made a mistake. Arius mentioned in his letter that many Christians in Libya missed him, and he hoped aloud that they would not be too angry at his continued excommunication. Constantine interpreted Arius's words as a threat of riot or rebellion. He responded with cold fury. Constantine refused to intervene and ordered all of Arius's writings burned for good measure.

Imperial tempers change quickly, however, and Constantine once again changed his mind. About a year after ordering the man's books consigned to the flames, Constantine sent another letter to Arius. This letter was far more cheerful in tone and invited him to present his theology to a large council of bishops due to meet in Jerusalem. We have no idea why Constantine changed his mind so frequently. Perhaps Constantine's desire for unity was so strong that he was willing to overlook virtually anything else in pursuit of it. As long as the book burning had set Arius straight about who was in charge, Constantine would happily readmit the heretic and claim a victory for the church.

Arius died before the hoped-for reconciliation. Although Arius was vindicated by the council in Jerusalem, he died en route to see the bishop who was due to welcome him back to ministry. Many of his opponents saw Arius's death as a divine vindication of their position. They believed God had prevented the arch-heretic from slipping back into the church, still unrepentant and unremorseful, at his last hour. Still, it is hard not to see some tragedy in Arius's story. Arius was unapologetic in his theological commitments, and he persisted in them even when rebuked by the most powerful men in the empire. Yet he was hardly the only one to have such commitments. He was simply in the unfortunate position of being the most prominent and least powerful of his allies. Many of his theological compatriots held important and powerful bishoprics with all the privileges those entailed. Arius was profoundly charismatic and intellectually gifted, but he had no institutional power vis-a-vis the church's overseers—not to mention the Roman emperor. And so the consequences of the controversy fell disproportionately on his shoulders. He died alone and separated from the church he had served all his life.

Other Nicene-skeptical clerics fared substantially better than Arius in the years after Nicaea. Eusebius of Nicomedia, exiled for allowing anti-Nicene priests to minister under his authority, was permitted to return around the same time as Arius and took up his episcopal post. Eusebius also saw a considerable rise in his fortunes and influence as a bishop—ironically enough, probably as a result of Nicaea. As you know from the previous chapter, Nicene canons dictated that bishops in major metropolitan cities, like Rome and Alexandria, had seniority over bishops in their surrounding area. Nicomedia just happened to be very close to the rapidly growing imperial capital in Constantinople, and Eusebius of Nicomedia just happened to be very good at currying favor with Constantine. Eventually, Constantine appointed Eusebius to be the bishop of Constantinople, further expanding his influence. When the emperor Constantine was on his deathbed, it was Eusebius who baptized him.

As one Eusebius gained power in the imperial capital, another Eusebius was also busy consolidating his influence. Eusebius of Caesarea, rehabilitated and vindicated at the Council of Nicaea, ingratiated himself with Constantine and began to flex his ecclesial muscles. It turns out that Eusebius of Caesarea was not nearly as excited about the Nicene Creed as his descriptions of the council might have implied. According to some of his critics, Eusebius of Caesarea made his ambivalence everyone's problem. Within a few years of its creation, the strongest proponents of the Nicene Creed were removed from their posts and replaced with bishops far more in line with the outlook of the two ascendant Eusebii.

The Fall of the Nicenes

Marcellus of Ancyra was one of the first bishops to suffer deposition and replacement. You will learn more about Marcellus in chapter 8. For now, you just need to know that he had a unique way of speaking about the Trinity that sounded like modalism to almost everyone else. He was tried for heresy at a church council and summarily deposed from his position. While he was a fervent proponent of the Nicene Creed, most of its other proponents found him to be an embarrassment and political liability for their position. Hence they made little fuss when he was removed.

The next victim was much more politically significant: Eustathius, bishop of the important city of Antioch in modern-day Syria. He had been one of the fiercest defenders of *homoousios* language even before the council. He had even presided over the council that condemned Eusebius of Caesarea as a heretic for his Trinitarian doctrine.

Now the shoe was on the other foot.

Eusebius participated in a new council, in which he accused Eustathius of modalism. The two bishops took the floor and argued with each other for days in a discussion that seems to have generated more heat than light. One rather befuddled attendee noted that the two bishops appeared to agree with each other, but acted as though they were mortal enemies.[2]

The tide had definitively turned against Eustathius and in favor of Eusebius of Caesarea. There are probably several reasons for the change in fortune, but one of the most consequential was that Eustathius had accidentally insulted the emperor's beloved mother at a recent banquet. Constantine was not particularly happy with Eustathius at the trial's outset. Add to that a few scandalous charges made by a powerful and persuasive opponent like Eusebius of Caesarea, and most of the gathered bishops saw an opportunity to get rid of a man who had become an embarrassment to his allies and a villain to his enemies. Eustathius was declared a heretic by the council and stripped of his position as bishop of Antioch. Emperor Constantine personally confirmed the deposition.

The final major player at Nicaea was Bishop Alexander of Alexandria. However, since he had cleverly managed to die shortly after the council, he avoided any attempts to remove him from power. That burden would fall upon his predecessor, Athanasius. He was a natural successor to Bishop Alexander. They shared the same theology, which is unsurprising since Bishop Alexander had been his adoptive father. Athanasius was orphaned at an early age and Bishop Alexander took him in, making sure he had a good education and raising him in the church.

When the time came, Athanasius was elected as bishop of Alexandria and succeeded his adoptive father in God. He would have great difficulty holding onto his seat. Athanasius was throughout his episcopal career burdened with political machinations designed to remove him from his powerful position. They started shortly after his election and went on for almost the entirety of his life. Nor were his opponents content to accuse him of

---

2. A confusing meeting consisting of two powerful leaders yelling angrily at each other without really understanding each other—who says the ancient world was so different from our own?

heresy. Shortly after his election, Athanasius was accused of murdering a fellow bishop and cutting off his hand to use in a black magic ritual. Several bishops who happened to be skeptical of Nicaea called a council to determine if Athanasius was killing people. Presiding over that council was none other than Eusebius of Caesarea, fresh from his successful campaign against Eustathius of Antioch.

Athanasius, showing the exact level of sass and pluck that would serve him well throughout his episcopacy, prepared no grand defense for his trial. Instead, he brought along a very special guest. That special guest was the person who he had been accused of murdering. It turns out that the man was alive and well and living close to the location of the trial, with both of his hands still quite firmly attached to his wrists. Athanasius simply presented this man to the council as the evidence of his innocence. The murder charges were quickly dropped.

Athanasius was not off the hook yet, though. His opponents also brought charges that he had threatened to cut off grain shipments from the Alexandrine ports. While to us modern readers this might seem like a ludicrous charge, it was a real possibility in the fourth century. For centuries, Alexandria had been the linchpin of the Roman food supply. Alexandria sat on the banks of the Nile River, which has extremely regular and predictable flooding cycles. Egyptian farmers knew exactly how to exploit these predictable floods to produce immense harvests—so immense that Alexandria became the breadbasket of the empire. While a few decades earlier a bishop would have had no influence over the commercial shipping of Alexandria, that had changed with Constantine. You will recall from chapter 3 that Constantine made bishops civil administrators, giving them large amounts of money and goods to distribute to the local population as they saw fit. That gave them influence, and they could theoretically use that influence to get local farmers and dockworkers to do their bidding. So the charge that Athanasius was threatening the empire's food supply was credible—and if true, was tantamount to treason.

Constantine did not take any chances. After the council sent him their findings, he exiled Athanasius from the city of Alexandria, ordering him never to return. (It turns out Athanasius *would* return, many times, as he would be exiled and recalled from exile a grand total of five times over the course of his heartburn-inducing ministry.) With Athanasius's departure, the three most prominent centers of support for the Nicene Creed had lost their bishops. Athanasius knew exactly who to blame. In his mind, the Eusebii were striking back after their frustrating defeat. Eusebius of Nicomedia had helped to depose Eustathius, whose downfall Eusebius of Caesarea had orchestrated. Eusebius of Caesarea had also presided over Athanasius's trial and removal. Modern scholars are less convinced of Eusebian malice. Both Eusebii were very powerful bishops who presided over a lot of church functions, and Athanasius had plenty of other enemies closer to home. The followers of the schismatic Bishop Meletius saw Athanasius as just the next stooge in a long line of too-tolerant bishops who had abandoned the faith of the martyrs and cozied up to traitors instead. They also happened to hate the council of Nicaea because its canons had inhibited their churches. Perhaps it was the Meletians who engineered Athanasius's exile; perhaps they entered into an alliance of convenience with the Eusebii. Whatever the truth, the result was the same: Athanasius and the other Nicene stalwarts went into exile, and those skeptical of the council ascended to even greater heights of power.

A Vacant Throne

The situation was about to become even more confusing. For all of his political acumen and sheer force of will, Constantine had one fatal flaw as a leader: he was mortal. In 337 AD, Constantine died, and left the empire in the hands of his three surviving sons and two nephews. Constantine's three sons were, in predictable Roman fashion, named Constantius II, Constantine II, and Constans. Many historians regard Constantine's inheritance decisions as a major mistake. He had seen how unstable four emperors could be; now Constantine was attempting to divide it between five emperors! Constantine's sons agreed that the plan was a mistake. Their two cousins were assassinated a few months after the emperor's death in a scheme probably, but not provably, orchestrated by Constantius II. Then, other branches of the Constantinian family tree were mysteriously pruned of male relatives. These sorts of purges were rather common in ancient Rome; since imperial titles were passed down through heredity, getting rid of one's family was a great way to remove potential rivals for the throne. Once the purge was done, Constantine's three sons met to divide up the empire: Constantine II would rule the westernmost third, which included Gaul (modern-day France), Britain, Spain; Constans would take Italy, North Africa, and a province called "Illyrica" that included modern-day Croatia and Slovenia; and Constantius II would take everything to the east of that.

The division of the empire was going to become bad news for everyone, as the three brothers would not really be able to share power and would begin a massive civil war within three years. The church, now married to the imperial structure, would inevitably be caught up in this strife. However, the division was very good news for Athanasius. He spent the last years of

Constantine's reign trying to run his churches from afar, writing letters and offering what counsel he could while in exile. After the old emperor's death, Athanasius was allowed to return home with a letter of permission from Constantine II, in whose territory Athanasius had been living.

Athanasius was overjoyed to return to his diocese and city. Constantius II, however, was considerably less overjoyed. Alexandria was in his jurisdiction, and he did not appreciate his brother lobbing estranged bishops back into his territory as if they were just stray episcopal baseballs that he could simply toss back from the neighbor's yard. Constantius II tolerated Athanasius's presence for about a year, then ordered Athanasius back into exile. Eusebius of Nicomedia, who was now bishop of Constantinople,[3] was all too happy to pile on. He called a council that declared Athanasius removed as bishop of Alexandria and named a more malleable candidate named George of Cappadocia to be bishop instead. Athanasius, defiant in the face of his powerful enemies, refused to recognize the authority of the council or the emperor to remove him. And so it was that in Easter of 339 AD, a group of armed soldiers arrived in Alexandria to kick Athanasius out by force. He briefly took refuge in a nearby church, performed a few baptisms, and then fled by boat to the city of Rome, which was under the friendlier reign of Constans.

The use of force against Athanasius did not go unnoticed. Riots broke out across the city, and soldiers were called in to stop the violence. Nor was Athanasius the only bishop whose departure provoked riots. Eusebius of Nicomedia was able to become bishop of Constantinople because its previous bishop had been exiled by Constantine. Eusebius passed away several years later, and his predecessor returned to the city to take up his title again. Constantius II was displeased at the return of this other exile, and called in soldiers to remove him. Just as in Alexandria, citizens of Constantinople rioted in protest.

We will spend some time reflecting on the relationship between religion and violence in Part 3 of this book. For now, you just need to know that riots were not terribly uncommon in this time period. Unless they were aristocrats, denizens of the Roman Empire had no say in their government, and when events became intolerable they had no recourse except to riot. It was rare for the removal of a bishop to occasion a riot before Constantine's reign, since it was by definition a local matter handled by the regional church. However, when Constantine assigned bishops responsibilities for

---

3. Now that he is bishop of Constantinople, Eusebius of Nicomedia should technically be called Eusebius of Constantinople. However, since we already have enough names (and enough Eusebii) to keep track of in this book, I am going to keep referring to him as Eusebius of Nicomedia to minimize confusion.

distributing food and money to their cities, he made them the direct patrons of many of the city's most vulnerable. Those citizens understood that a change in the bishop could result in a change in the distribution of those goods—and they would fight to stop it. Moreover, it is important to remember that the Nicene controversy was not an arcane matter for theologians. Arius taught his theology to ordinary dockworkers via song; while his opponents were not as musically gifted, they also proclaimed their theologies to the masses. Ordinary Christians cared deeply about the Nicene controversy; they loved Jesus, and the way they praised Jesus mattered to them. When distant powers removed a bishop whose theology they loved, they replied with anger.

Too Many Words, Too Many Councils

The church's confusion and conflict was not limited to its interactions with emperors, armies, and criminal trials. All across the world, bishops attempted to resolve the continuing controversy regarding the nature of the Son. Despite the putative success of Nicaea, the five-sixths of the bishops who had not been in attendance did not believe the matter had been settled and continued to argue with each other. They found very little agreement. One of the major reasons for their continued frustration was the lack of a common vocabulary within which to debate. Back in chapter 4, I introduced you to the word *ousia,* which is usually translated "substance." *Ousia* is, of course, the root word from which *homoousios* is derived. We also discussed the word *hypostasis,* which references an independently existing thing. Ousia is the stuff of which things are made, and a hypostasis is an individual thing that can exist on its own. Two hypostases—say, like two people—can share one common substance.

Great theologians of past generations had used these words to describe God in the way I have described. However, not every bishop had bothered to read those great theologians.

During this time period, many writers thought of *hypostasis* and *ousia* as synonyms. This caused a lot of unnecessary confusion, especially because the Nicene Creed says that the Father and Son are *homoousios*—in other words, the same substance. If "substance" is synonymous with "independently existing thing," then it sounded like the creed was saying that the Father and Son were actually only one independently existing thing, which is modalism. In fact, a notorious modalist of the third century had used *homoousios* in precisely this modalistic sense and had been condemned for it. Of course the bishops of 325 AD did not have a modalistic meaning in mind, but it was hard to get this point across when the most notorious heretic of the last generation was using the same vocabulary as them. Nobody wanted to be a modalist, but this semantic confusion made it seem like you had to be a modalist if you wanted to affirm Nicaea.

Other potential candidate words, like *prosopon* (PRO-so-pon), which means "person" in Greek, unfortunately carried similarly modalistic connotations. There is another linguistic controversy that continues to confound even plucky present-day church history lovers. In Greek, there are two words that potentially describe the Son: *agenetos* (ah-GEN-uh-tos) and *agennetos* (ah-GEN-uh-tos). In addition to being homophones distinguished only by a single "n," the two words are almost synonymous in definition. *Agenetos* means something like "having never not existed" with a connotation of "immortal, intransient, and immutable." *Agennetos* means something like "ungenerated" or "unbegotten." For most people, those two definitions were interchangeable, and hence the words were synonymous. Others, however, wanted to insist on a distinction between them.

We can see the distinction beginning in Origen, who thought the Son was certainly *agenetos* but generally did not call the Son *agennetos*. Because Origen thought the Son was eternally generated, the Son was intransient and eternal. Since he was a Son, however, he was clearly begotten of the Father and hence not *agennetos*. That's what being a Son means. Other people said otherwise. In one spectacularly stupefying argument, Athanasius argued the Son was *agennetos*—in other words, unbegotten. While it might seem contradictory to claim that a Son was never begotten, Athanasius insisted that the Son had to be *agennetos* to be the image of the Father. Since the Father is *agennetos,* if the Son is *agenetos* then he is not the image of the Father unless he is *agennetos* too. If you had trouble following that argument, fear not—so did everybody else. I am going to try to spare you the details of how this particular argument played out. Just know that, in the years following Nicaea, a whole bunch of the argument consisted of people sitting around and trying to figure out which of two homophones their opponent had used.

When they were not busy discerning which of two homophones their opponents had used, the bishops of the empire were busy attempting to work out their theological differences in the midst of changing political alliances. Their efforts often led to further confusion and division within the church.

Take, for example, the Council of Rome in 341 AD. Julius, the current bishop of Rome, was playing host to two famous Nicene exiles: Athanasius and Marcellus of Ancyra. Julius took the opportunity to make his own pronouncement on the question of the Nicene Creed. He called a small council of bishops around Rome to gather together and investigate the theologies of the two exiles. The council found them perfectly orthodox in belief,[4] and wrote a letter summarizing their findings and excoriating the theology and practices of the Eusebii and their allies. The letter found much to complain about, but perhaps most significant of all was that the Eusebii and the councils they led had not consulted the bishop of Rome before deciding who should be the bishop of cities like Alexandria and Ancyra.

This argument would have come as a surprise to the Eastern bishops for any number of reasons. First and foremost, none of those bishops had asked the bishop of Rome's opinion as to who got to be the bishop of cities hundreds of miles away from Rome for at least a hundred years. If the bishop of Rome really had such authority, it was odd that he had not used it for a hundred years until Julius decided to complain about not being asked. Second, the canons of the Council of Nicaea only said that ancient cities like Alexandria had the same authority as Rome, not that they were subordinate to Rome for picking or evaluating their bishops. The bishop of Rome clearly believed himself to have the final say in matters of church governance, as Roman Catholics hold even today. The Eusebii, along with most bishops of the East, were unconvinced.

Bishops were not the only figures in the East to object to Julius's council. Constantius II was also less than thrilled to hear of it. For the boundary lines of the empire were shifting, and not in his favor.

The Strife of the Sons

About a year earlier, Constantine II decided that he was tired of only having a third of the empire to rule. As the oldest son of Constantine, he thought he deserved a bigger share of the empire. So he declared war on his brother Constans and moved to take over his territory. Constantine II suffered a humiliating military defeat and was quickly killed. Constans took over Constantine II's third of the empire, making him the more powerful of the two remaining brothers.

Constantius II did not love that his brother suddenly had twice the territory that he did, and he hated the idea that the bishop of Rome, his brother's capital city, was trying to boss all the bishops in his territory around. This was not just a matter of spiritual authority; since bishops held civic powers, any loyalty to a bishop outside of his territory was a threat to Constantius II's authority. Imagine, for example, how the president of

---

4. The fact that this council found Marcellus to be perfectly orthodox is evidence of how strong support for the Nicene Creed was in Rome. There are few other councils that would have viewed him as orthodox!

Mexico might react upon learning that all Mexican lawyers were required to obey the dictates of a Canadian judge. Constantius II's reaction was much the same.

An opportunity for the emperor and his bishops to retort would soon present itself. For it just so happened that later in 341 AD there was a dedication ceremony for a new church in Antioch. Bishops from all over the eastern third of the empire were present, as was Constantius II himself. So they decided to have a council right then and there to respond to the matter.

In the inimitable style of councils assumed to be a smooth ride, the council of 341 AD would kick-start one of the most perilous and difficult periods in the entire controversy for anyone trying to understand it. While church historians have yet to settle on a name for this period, it could easily be called the Era of Too Many Creeds. During this period bishops kept meeting, often at the same place, kept making up more creeds for us to hold in our minds, and kept angrily repeating the same theological lines in the sand that they had drawn for years.

I will not subject you to a punishingly detailed analysis of these many creeds, because that would be counterproductive.[5] Instead, let me present a very brief summary of the back-and-forth over these tumultuous years.

First was the aforementioned Council of Antioch in 341 AD, usually referred to as the "dedication council" since it occurred at the dedication of a church. This council produced four separate creeds to counter Julius's criticism. It emphasized that the Eusebii and their allies had never been followers of Arius because Arius was a priest and they were bishops. It also criticized Marcellus of Ancyra's theology and emphasized the orthodoxy of the Eusebii and their allies. Most interestingly, one of the creeds describes the Father, Son, and Spirit as three hypostases that are "one in agreement," which sounds a little bit like the Father, Son, and Spirit created the Trinity out of some kind of especially firm handshake. In actuality, it is a reference to the language of Origen, who occasionally described the Trinity in exactly this way. The creed also condemned the Arian proposition that there was a time when the Son did not exist, but continued to endorse other planks of the Arian platform.

Emissaries from Constantius II's territory presented the creed to Constans in the West, who ignored it for two years before deciding to call a council of bishops from the East and West to finally resolve all their differences. In 343 AD, bishops convened in the town of Serdica (modern-day Sofia, Bulgaria) to resolve all their differences. In this goal they failed spectacularly, but they did succeed in creating exciting new differences

---

5. Also, my editor won't let me.

to argue about. For starters, the delegates from the East refused to begin the council until Athanasius was expelled. Delegates from the West were largely in favor of Athanasius and refused to begin the council *unless* he was present. The bishops continued to meet in separate groups and argue about whether they could actually have a council for about a year, at which point they disbanded and the Western bishops wrote a long and embarrassingly confusing statement of their theological position. It used the terms *ousia* and *hypostasis* interchangeably, which caused them to sound like modalists to the Eusebii and their allies. The Western bishops thought that in saying there is one hypostasis in God they were saying that there is one common substance (*ousia*) that Father, Son, and Spirit share. But Eusebian bishops heard instead that there is only one *thing* in the Trinity, which is modalism. The creed also made the odd statement that the Holy Spirit did not suffer in the incarnation, but the man he put on in the incarnation did, implying that the Son simply is the Spirit incarnated—a classic example of modalism. The Eusebii and their allies were utterly verklempt at this statement of faith. Even Athanasius was so embarrassed by his defenders' declaration that he found ways to studiously ignore the document throughout his life.

These abortive attempts at church unity only increased the bishops' desire to find a consensus solution. Constans began to press Constantius II to allow Athanasius to return to Alexandria, to which the Eastern emperor consented. Meanwhile, groups of Nicene-skeptical bishops continued to work on a creed they hoped could unite the empire. Mindful of past leaders and utterly unmindful of future generations of church history nerds who would have to keep all of their creeds apart, the bishops met at Antioch and produced a document referred to as the Macrostitch Creed—the fifth creed in four years to be produced in the city of Antioch. The Macrostitch Creed attempted to say the bare minimum necessary for reconciliation. Like the Dedication Creed, it rejected Arius's inflammatory statement that there was a time when the Son was not. It even went as far as to say that the Son was not something "alien to" the Father. In other words, there was *some* likeness between Father and Son, although the creed would not attempt to say exactly what. Yet there were also clear limits; the council rejected Athanasius's position that the Son is unbegotten (*agennetos*) and condemned Marcellus of Ancyra for heresy. In short, the Macrostitch Creed was an attempt at peace through moderation. If bishops who endorsed the Nicene Creed would abandon the "extreme" positions of Athanasius and Marcellus, then those more skeptical of the council would reject the most "extreme" tenets of Arius. The strategy is a common one in any kind of negotiation. Leaders often believe that if the loudest, most problematic voices on both sides of a dispute are silenced, the peace-loving, reasonable folks in the ideological center will find a solution.

Unfortunately, the pragmatic solution was not to be achieved. A delegation brought the Macrostitch Creed to the council of Milan, but the council refused to even consider it until the delegation condemned Arius as a heretic. The delegation, insulted at being treated with such suspicion, refused. They returned home with the creed unsigned.

At this point, you may be despairing that unity will ever be achieved in the Nicene controversy. No matter how they tried, the bishops seemed unable to find a way of expressing God's being that the majority of churches could accept. Even attempts at peacemaking proved abortive, especially with the imperial brothers Constans and Constantius II regularly eyeing each other with suspicion. Nonetheless, progress was made during the hectic Era of Too Many Creeds. As the bishops fought and argued, the best thinkers on each side of the dispute began to refine their ideas and terminology. Schools of thought began to coalesce around a single word that both sides could agree summed up the debate. The confusion generated by so many dueling creeds appears to have motivated theologians to find a better way through the impasse. They built new systems of thought and forged new theological-political alliances to expound their ideals. In the next two chapters, we will explore those theological alliances in detail: their concerns, contributions, innovations, and embarrassments.

Chapter 7

Who Needs the Homoousios?
Anti-Nicene Theologies

LIKE MOST OF US, the Nicene Creed had a rough first twenty-five years.

After a honeymoon period dramatically cut short by the Eusebii's revenge, Athanasius's exiles, and the utter inability of all parties involved to be normal about anything, the church's first council had strikingly few proponents to its name. Athanasius wrote tirelessly in its defense, but even those unopposed to the Nicene Creed were hesitant to ally with an exiled bishop who could be a tremendous political liability.

When churches did discuss the creed, it was mostly to complain about that strange word it used to describe the relationship between the Father and the Son: *homoousios*.

Funnily enough, the bishops gathered at Nicaea had not thought very much about the word *homoousios*. Athanasius recalled that the council thought its most important contribution was to describe the Son as "from the substance of the Father." Calling the Son *homoousios* was just a logical consequence; if the Son is from the Father's substance, then the Son can only have the same substance as the Father. In this new era, however, the term *homoousios* was to become the focal point of a decades-long, multi-party debate. Even in the midst of profound disagreement, everyone came to agree on one thing: the phrase *homoousios* summed up everything the pro-Nicenes thought important about the council of 325, and everything the anti-Nicenes feared.

Thus *homoousios* had the very salutary effect of focusing the conversation around a set of theological issues. Throughout the first quarter-century

Who Needs the Homoousios?

of the creed's life, the issues dividing the church were as often personal—about, say, the orthodoxy of Marcellus or the guilt of Athanasius—as they were theological. When bishops did attempt a genuine theological discussion, they often misunderstood or purposely mischaracterized each other. The linguistic divide in the Roman Empire did little to improve understanding. Eastern and Western bishops had been trained in different schools and used different expressions to describe the mystery of God. Only when everyone began to focus on a single question—"Is the Son *homoousios* with the Father or not?"—was regular, productive debate possible.

You might think that question has only two possible answers: either the Son is *homoousios* with the Father, or he is not. Fortunately for intellectual history and unfortunately for any hopes of finishing this chapter quickly, that is not the case. If there is one thing that ancient bishops and theologians can be trusted to do, it is to give multifaceted and complex answers to a seemingly simple question. In this chapter, we're going to examine the figures who rejected the Nicene Creed and the *homoousios* with it. They managed to create no fewer than four distinct schools of thought, each of which gave its own description of the Father-Son relationship.

Before we dive into those schools, you need to know one thing: Arius has gone more out of style than shag carpet. By the year 350 AD, no one cited him as an authority and his writings were quickly lost to history due to the paucity of thinkers willing to read and engage with him. Many of the anti-Nicenes agreed with Arius's basic theological tenets; some of them even went further in their subordination of the Son. When they agreed with him, however, they did so quietly. Arius had died as a convicted heretic outside the bounds of the church. No pious cleric was going to claim affinity for the theology of a heretic—even if they quietly suspected his condemnation had been unjust. Perhaps even more importantly, the leaders of each of the four anti-Nicene groups were bishops, and Arius had been a mere priest. Bishops were the overseers of the church, and (at least in their own minds) were the preeminent teachers of doctrine. It was therefore inappropriate for bishops to be instructed in the faith by those of lower ecclesiastical rank. Prominent teachers of the faith might disagree with this view of episcopal authority, but with the new power that bishops held in a post-Constantinian church, it was increasingly difficult to challenge their intellectual hegemony no matter how brilliant or charismatic one was. Taken together, these two considerations allowed anti-Nicene bishops to dismiss the theology of Arius while quietly advancing an agenda similar to his own. When facing accusations of Arianism, anti-Nicene bishops simply claimed to be above the influence of a mere priest. If their theology happened to be similar to his, then it was only because their superior knowledge of Scripture had allowed them to express its truths with more clarity than Arius had been able to.

The Heteroousians

With the memory of Arius gone, new theologians could rise to occupy a central place in the controversy. None did so more effectively than the members of the first school of anti-Nicene thought, often referred to as the Heteroousian party. As you can probably guess from the name (*hetero* means "different" in Greek), these thinkers were committed to the thoroughly anti-Nicene belief that the Father and Son possessed different substances. Some sources refer to this group as the Anomian school, naming them after the Greek word for unlikeness. The main figures in this party insisted that the Father and Son were not just different, but utterly unlike one another. Most other parties of the time viewed the Heteroousians as radicals because of this stance, and the defenders of Nicaea would write most of their best works in critique of the Heteroousian position.

There are two main thinkers who define the approach: Aetius of Antioch and Eunomius of Cyzicus. Aetius was the earlier of the two, and his personal and intellectual reputation defined the school for decades. Aetius was a remarkable character. Almost certainly raised as a pagan, Aetius converted to Christianity as a young man and began to gain renown as a teacher. He was trained in the theological tradition of the Eusebii and friends, and he had a reputation even among *them* for being a hardcore subordinationist. His radical teachings on the Son's unlikeness to the Father began to earn him notoriety and scorn in equal measure across the empire. Controversial teachers tend to make enemies even if they have the best of personalities. Aetius did not have the best of personalities. In fact, he was almost as famous for his theology as he was for being a massive jerk. He managed to earn banishment from his home at *least* four times over the course of his life. In one particularly embarrassing incident, the city authorities demanded he leave Antioch despite having the personal favor of the bishop because he preached a sermon so incendiary that its hearers rioted in protest. At the end of his life, Aetius was summoned to the court of the emperor to explain his teachings. Aetius took this as an opportunity to correct what he saw as the emperor's rather foolish misunderstandings of his position. The emperor, irritated at Aetius's condescension, expelled Aetius from the imperial capital and ordered him never to return.

Despite all his warts, Aetius managed to project a powerful charisma that drew a certain kind of person to him. Many of his students were willing to risk death decades after he had passed for the sake of Aetius's memory. It's hard to know exactly where his charisma came from, but there is no doubting that Aetius had it.

Many of Aetius's teachings are lost to history. However, we do know the basic thrust of his Heteroousian theology. Aetius argued that the Son must be of a fundamentally different substance than the Father.

His argument basically went as follows. It was assumed in those days that the Father was utterly simple. In this context "simplicity" is not a synonym for stupidity; they were not saying that God the Father had to repeat his pre-Algebra class every year. Rather "simple" meant "not compounded" or "lacking parts." The Father was not made up of any smaller, more fundamental components. The Father was the first, after all; where would God's constituent components have come from?

Everyone would have agreed with Aetius up to this point. Then, Aetius made his radical claim: no simple being can generate another being of the same substance. His argument may strike you as odd. It certainly struck most of his contemporaries as odd. After all, most Christians believe God is omnipotent and can do anything. It sounds as though Aetius is placing a restriction on the Father's power. Aetius saw the matter differently, though. Unfortunately, none of Aetius's works have survived to the present day, so we don't know exactly how he argued for his conclusion. We do know, however, that there were some common beliefs at the time that may have made Aetius's argument seem logical. Many ancient thinkers believed that an effect preexisted in its cause. For example, as the first human Adam was the ancestor of all people, and so all people were said to exist "in" Adam in some way. This is why Paul can write that in Adam all people have died.[1] Similarly, if the Father begets the Son, then the Son must "preexist" in the Father in some way. If so, then the Father is not simple anymore, for the Father has at least two parts: his essential and unchanging Fatherhood, and the Son preexisting inside of himself. There is another way of getting to this conclusion. If the Father and Son share the same substance, then we can distinguish between their common substance and the traits that make them themselves and not another. Once again, the Father must have at least two parts: the substance he shares with the Son, and his own essential Fatherhood—that secret combination of traits that distinguishes him from all other entities. Aetius thinks that the Father must be simple, and therefore the Father clearly did not generate a *homoousios* Son. Instead, the Father must have made the Son by willing into existence a lesser, unlike being.

---

1. 1 Corinthians 15:22.

Aetius did not spell out how the Father might have gone about this. His student, Eunomius of Cyzicus, would attempt to fill in this logical gap while intensifying and further clarifying his teacher's arguments.

Unlike his star-studded teacher, Eunomius had a privileged but relatively obscure upbringing. He was born in a small Cappadocian city called Oltiseris on the border of Cappadocia and Galatia. He was born to a family of aristocrats, although they were probably towards the bottom of their social class. Eunomius had a pronounced lisp as an adult. His lisp may have been due to a speech impediment, but it might also have been caused by ancient Roman prejudices. Cappadocia was the butt of many Roman jokes. Ancient aristocrats saw Cappadocia as a wasteland and its residents as uneducated hillbillies; there was a common joke that you were as likely to hear a Cappadocian speak well as you were to see a pig fly. Having a Cappadocian accent was a badge of shame among the elite. As he began his education Eunomius might have tried to rid himself of his ancestral accent with limited success, resulting in the lisp.

Eunomius's family was wealthy enough to send him away to school to learn a trade. Eunomius spent his early years studying the principles of writing shorthand—a very lucrative skill that could easily lead to a career in the church, the academy, or the court. After completing this course of study, Eunomius apparently wanted more. He sought out a rhetorical education for himself in the imperial capital of Constantinople. As he progressed, he left the capital for Alexandria, the major center of learning in the East. It was here that he met Aetius and learned his Heteroousian model of the Trinity.

Eunomius's star would continue to rise—even at his teacher's expense. After Aetius was expelled from Constantinople, a group of sympathetic bishops needed a new ally in the region and proceeded to install Eunomius as the bishop of the city of Cyzicus just a short boat ride away from Constantinople.

Eunomius also gained fame through his association with a network of wonder-working Heteroousian bishops. Many of the clerics in Eunomius's circle were rumored to be capable of miraculous deeds. Some of Eunomius's followers saw him in the same supernatural light as his friends. Eunomius encouraged his followers' wonder, relating extraordinary dreams he had that seemed to impart special revelation. Empowered by an august reputation, Eunomius seemed poised to reach even greater heights of notoriety.

Unfortunately, Eunomius appears to have learned all the wrong lessons from Aetius about how to win friends and influence people. Shortly after taking up his post, Eunomius preached an Epiphany sermon in which he shared with the congregation his opinion that Mary, the mother of Jesus, had not remained a virgin after his birth. Most preachers have learned that sharing your unsolicited opinions with your congregation is an excellent way to generate complaints about your sermons, and Eunomius was no different. Some of his congregants took exception to his views and complained to the emperor. While Eunomius held onto his seat, he wisely left town for awhile to let tempers cool. He would not be so lucky in future controversies. In the aftermath of one of the rebellions that swept through the empire with worrying regularity, Eunomius fell under suspicion of siding with the rebel forces. That suspicion was probably unfounded, but the emperor was unwilling to take chances and declared Eunomius exiled to the island of Naxos. Fortunately the emperor rescinded his exile before it began, but a few years later the pro-Nicene emperor Theodosius would exile him again, this time for good.

You are probably getting the impression by now that Eunomius was not a particularly good bishop. He appears to have done pretty much zero administrative or pastoral work, and he had a knack for irritating just about everyone that should not be irritated. While he undoubtedly had some influence, it's hard not to read his story and think of him as a man pushed about by the tides of ecclesiastical currents that he couldn't really control —or even manage. In that way, perhaps his exiles were a blessing. They got him away from all of that stuff he wasn't very good at and allowed him to concentrate on what he *was* good at: explaining why his theology was the right one, and why everyone else was wrong.

Eunomius's writings enthusiastically repeat Aetius's arguments before adding on a few of his own. Eunomius goes even further than his teacher; he describes the Father as "ingenerate" and claims this is definitive of the Father's very essence. The Father's lack of being generated is, in other words, precisely what makes him the Father. And if that's the case, then by definition the Son can't have the same substance as the Father, since being generated is at the core of the Son's distinct identity.

Eunomius's enemies criticized him for hanging so much of his argument on a single word—and a word that does not even appear in the Bible! For Eunomius, however, words had a special power. Eunomius believed that every single thing in the universe had a true name, given to it by God, that described its very essence. If we pay attention to these true names, which come from God, then we can know the truth of each thing. Eunomius points to the creation narrative in Genesis. Adam gives *each animal its name;* Eunomius apparently takes this to mean that God gave Adam the true name of each animal, which is how Adam came to know what that animal was. Furthermore God used names to create things themselves. God said, "Let there be light," and there was light.

Eunomius had a fascinating philosophy of language. Even if most human speech cannot describe the reality of the world, *certain* words, given to us by God, can pierce the veil of mystery and illuminate reality—even the reality of God. Eunomius thought that "ingenerate" was the true name of the Father and thus signified his essence with perfect clarity. If the Father was ingenerate by definition, then the Son could not be one with the Father by that very definition.

Of course, his argument raises the question of how exactly the Son is made if the Father doesn't generate him. The only other option at the time was to say that the Son was created, just like other beings—and even the Heteroousians were not willing to go that far. Eunomius answered the dilemma by identifying a special kind of production in between generation and creation. He names this middle production "energy." Nowadays the word "energy" is so vague that it could mean almost anything. Perhaps Eunomius was arguing about the kind of fossil fuel the Father consumed to produce the Son's energy, or maybe we imagine him as a fourth-century yoga instructor, carefully arranging his healing crystals and reminding you to open your heart chakras so divine energy could flow through you as you performed your Son salutations. Of course, "energy" meant something different in Eunomius's day. He appears to have been looking for something to indicate the activities that we do simply by being what we are, even when those activities are not part of our essence. While Eunomius doesn't explain further, I suspect that he has in mind something like the way the sun produces light. A sun produces light simply by being the kind of thing that it is, and as long as the sun exists, it will produce light. But light is not the same thing as the sun. They are categorically different things, different in substance and power. Or perhaps we could think of the way that human beings will have a heartbeat simply by being human. We do not try to produce a heartbeat; it simply happens by virtue of us being the kind of thing that we are. Just so, Eunomius claimed, with the Son. He is produced from the Father in a special way, unlike any creature, but also in a way that did not make him like the Father.

From this brief description, you can already guess that the Heteroousians are not going to carry the day. But they have more staying power than it may seem. When Eunomius of Cyzicus loses the day, he and his allies set up a slew of "Eunomian" churches that are in communion with him and not the rest of the church. These churches would persist well into the fifth century, testifying to the depth of loyalty that this theology commanded.

The Homoiousians

Although they commanded deep loyalty among their followers, the Heteroousians were theologically radioactive to the majority of fourth-century Christians. Even those uncomfortable with the Nicene Creed recoiled at the suggestion that the Father and Son were unlike each other. Jesus had revealed the Father to us; if he was so radically unlike the Father, it seemed impossible for Jesus to know the Father, let alone reveal him to us.

Thus several moderate schools emerged, attempting to chart a middle ground between the Nicene Creed and its Heteroousian detractors. The most politically significant of those groups is referred to as the Homoiousian party. The Greek prefix *homoi* means similar, which is rather ironically similar to the prefix for same, *homo*. The only difference between the two prefixes is the single "i" (or iota, in Greek) at the end. There is a running joke among scholars of the period that the difference between truth and falsehood came down to a single iota. The popular saying "one iota of difference"—as in, "it does not make one iota of difference to me whether we order pizza or hamburgers for dinner"—comes from this controversy. Yet if the alphabetical difference between the two positions was so small, the theological differences were so much larger.

The brightest light in the Homoiousian party was Basil of Ancyra. Basil had a particular interest in charting a middle course because he had replaced Marcellus as bishop of Ancyra after the infamous theologian was deposed following the council of Nicea. Stepping into the chair of the man who had just been condemned for a pro-Nicene theology so strong it bordered on modalism, Basil was determined not to make the same mistakes. He also knew that he could not throw in his lot with the Heteroousian school. The Son could not simply be totally different from the Father; if the Son was to reveal the Father's heart to us, the Son had to be similar to him.

Basil began his theology with an explanation of the point of theology. The church teaches doctrine to help us form the most appropriate conceptions of God. Forming an appropriate conception of God is a tricky matter. On the one hand, God is infinite and transcendent. Our finite minds cannot hope to comprehend God in all the divine fullness. On the other hand, we cannot simply throw up our hands and claim ignorance of God. For God has used the Bible to reveal some aspects of divinity to us. If we claim not to know anything about God, then we are invalidating the revelation that God has provided. Church doctrine, therefore, must honor both that there are things we are bound to say about God and matters in which we are bound to admit our ignorance. Simply put, we need to know what we know, and to know what we don't know. The theologian does this by reading

Scripture carefully, paying attention to those patterns and concepts that recur throughout its pages. The patterns that emerge from these readings shape what we can say about God—and what we must not say.

In the midst of the Nicene controversy, Basil saw that there is one repeated pattern of imagery that the Bible uses over and over again: that of Father and Son. Basil then proceeds to make the preeminently sensible point that everyone, Homoousian, Heterousian, or otherwise, needed to quit arguing so much over a few inconclusive prooftexts and focus instead on the broad sweep of the biblical story. Basil argued, for instance, that whether Proverbs 8:22 describes the Word as a creature or not, the fact of the matter is that the vast majority of passages refer to him as a Son. Therefore we should think of him as a Son rather than a creature.

Up until now, Basil has sounded very much like the pro-Nicene party. Athanasius probably read his work to this point with delight. Athanasius was *less* pleased, however, with the rest of Basil's thought. Since we can't know the Father directly, we can't know anything about the relationship between Father and Son. All we can do is say that they *are* Father and Son, and therefore they must be similar in substance—*homoiousios*. Even in that assertion, Basil was attempting to be cautious. He wanted to claim that the Son is similar in substance to the Father in order to prevent any suspicion that the Son is actually a creature. How exactly the Son is similar to the Father is beyond our ability to know. We must simply affirm the truth of their similarity and leave it there.

Basil of Ancyra proposed to solve the problem of Nicea by essentially declaring certain topics off-limits. He was hardly alone in proposing this strategy; as we shall see, most theologians will declare certain difficult questions to be unanswerable by human minds. Basil, however, had an unfortunate habit of attempting to have his cake and eat it, too. Basil claimed that we do have some grounds for thinking the Son is like the Father. Like Athanasius, he made use of the ancient maxim that likeness in activities implies a likeness in substances—in other words, similar beings do similar things. Jesus does similar things to the Father; both save humanity, both proclaim divine truth to the world, and both are involved in its creation. Basil went even further in saying that the Son has all the divine properties like wisdom, life, goodness, power, etc. and has them in exactly the same way that the Father does! He concluded by saying that the Son has "everything according to essence and absolutely as does the Father."[2] This is, of course, exactly what a pro-Nicene might say. More to the point, Basil appears to have broken his rule about speculating on the relationship between the Son

---

2. Ayres, *Nicaea and Its Legacy*, 152.

and the Father. There is no biblical text or image to suggest the level of similarity Basil envisions.

Like many compromise solutions, the Homoiousian approach ended up not being ideologically stable. Under pressure, Basil could sound like a pro-Nicene one minute and an anti-Nicene the next. Moreover, his sensible-sounding theological approach raised questions as many questions as it answers. An image like a father-son relationship can raise all sorts of possible implications. We might imagine a similarity in substance, or we might imagine an identical substance, since human fathers and sons share the same substance of humanity. A Heteroousian might be quick to point out that fathers were greater and more authoritative than sons (a common belief in the ancient world); should we not take this image to be a sign of the Son's inferiority rather than equality? A modern reader might imagine the Father taking the Son out for ice cream or teaching him how to play various kinds of sports. Whose inferences are valid? And even more importantly, who gets to decide which inferences are valid and which are beyond the pale of theological speculation?

Each party in the dispute would answer these questions differently, which ultimately prevented the Homoiousian school from winning universal allegiance. Nevertheless, its compromise formulation proved attractive to many bishops, and it enjoyed a brief period as the regnant theology of the Empire.

The Homoians

Ironically, the Homoiousian school would fall out of favor when it was displaced by a *second* compromise position, referred to as the Homoian school. Using the same prefix *homoi-* as Basil of Ancyra, the Homoians took his theological caution one step further. The notion of substance had already caused far more trouble than it was worth. Even worse, the term itself never appeared in the Bible! The Homoian solution to the endless debates over whether the Father and Son's *ousia* were the same, different, or similar was simple: just stop talking about it altogether. Since everyone, even the Heteroousians, agreed that the Son was like the Father in at least some respects (goodness, life-giving power, etc.), the Homoians recommended writing a creed that said this much and no more. Their logic of conformity was appealing to many with backing in the imperial power structure, including Emperor Constantius himself, who awarded the Homoians his imperial favor.

Roman emperors are usually a practical sort of people, and perhaps Constantius II liked the Homoians simply because they promised a viable solution to stop all of the bishops' angry arguments and thereby make Constantius's life easier. Alas, convenience is not a valid theological reason to reject a creed, and so the Homoians were obligated to advance theological reasons for their position. They had several objections to *ousia* language. The first was its materialistic connotations, as talk of "substance" was apt to make God sound like a physical being. The second was that the language was unknown "to the people"—that is, to the average people sitting in the pews who didn't have time for fancy theological training. Ordinary people weren't sitting around thinking about the substance of God; why should the church make arguments when none were there before? Finally, and probably most importantly, the Homoians pointed out that the Bible never talks about the substance of God at all. Most of the Nicene Creed was based on straightforward quotations or paraphrases of Scripture; the Homoians simply proposed tossing out the unbiblical bits that had crept in.

The leading luminary of this school of thought was Acacius of Caesarea, who had succeeded Eusebius of Caesarea in his role. This lineage gave Athanasius no small amount of ammunition, since he could point out that Eusebius *signed* the Nicene Creed, and even wrote a letter about how the creed was orthodox. Now that his successor was in power, he seemed to be attempting to remove the creed altogether—an embarrassing situation for the church of Caesarea.

Athanasius's critique would often fall on deaf ears given the Nicene Creed's unpopularity. In an era when many bishops were desperately searching for a new creedal formulation that could unify the church, they were willing to overlook the occasional historical inconsistency in the pursuit of that unity. The Homoians would be the darlings of the empire for years before they, too, would fall out of favor.

The Pneumatomachoi

As the Homoiousians and Homoians jockeyed for imperial favor, yet another theological school was beginning to form. This group raised a crucial question that had somehow gone almost overlooked throughout the entire conflict thus far: what about the Holy Spirit?

The Third Person of the Trinity has been tragically overlooked throughout most of the Nicene saga. Even the creed itself left the Spirit mostly untouched, with the bare-bones clause "We believe also in the Holy Spirit" being all it had to say about the matter. Perhaps it was inevitable that, as people investigated the Son's divinity, some would eventually begin to ask similar questions about the Spirit.

The historical origins of one such group are somewhat mysterious, but it appears to have strong links to Constantinople. The story begins with poor Paul of Constantinople, the erstwhile bishop of Constantinople who endured numerous exiles at the hands of his enemies. Macedonius, the priest who had accused Paul of criminal activity and kick-started his first exile, became bishop in his stead. (So much for priestly loyalty!) Macedonius apparently taught that the Spirit was less than fully divine, and developed a sizable audience for his view. His followers became known by several names. They were occasionally called Macedonians after their founder, but the name that has most endured is *pneumatomachoi* (noo-mah-toe-MAH-koi). This Greek phrase most literally translates to "Spirit-fighters," which sounds like the rejected name of a school pep club. But for the ancients, the term meant something different: it described the Macedonians as fighters against the Spirit and its key role in the plan of salvation.

Now the Pneumatomachoi held to all different beliefs about the Son's relationship to the Father. They might have been Homoians or Homoiousians; a few might even have affirmed that the Son was *homoousios* with the Father. What united them was their belief that the Spirit was not of the same substance as the Father. Some identified the Holy Spirit with one of the angels that surrounded the throne of God.

It is difficult to evaluate the Pneumatomachoian theology of the 350s because very few of their texts have survived to the present day. Fortunately, their beliefs are described in some detail by their opponents, especially Athanasius. We can understand their beliefs by investigating how Athanasius responded them.

The Pneumatomachoi argued against the Spirit's divinity on the basis of several scriptural texts. Just like Arians had used Proverbs 8:22 to argue that the Son was a created being, so the Pneumatomachoi cited Amos 4:13. Most of the fourth-century biblical translations rendered that verse something like this: "I am the one who establishes thunder and creates spirit and declares to the people his Christ." The Pneumatomachoi declared that when God "creates spirit" he is referencing the creation of the Holy Spirit. If the Holy Spirit is created, then it is a creature and not divine. Now if you look this passage up in your Bible today, you are likely to be very confused by this argument. Based on modern scholarship, Amos 4:13 reads as something more like, "He who forms the mountains, who creates the wind, and who reveals his thoughts to mankind" (NIV). There is no reference to spirits at all, let alone the Holy Spirit. Part of the confusion comes from the fact that both in both Hebrew and Greek, the word for "spirit" is the same as the word for "breath" or "wind." Ancient authorities were aware of this fact, and Athanasius will savage the Pneumatomachoi for poor textual analysis; Amos 4:13 is not necessarily discussing spirit at all, and even if it is, there is no indication that it is referring to the Holy Spirit rather than human spirits.

The Pneumatomachoi have another argument up their sleeve, however, and one that is trickier to refute. The Bible calls the Son the "only-begotten" of the Father in John 1:14, 1:18, 3:16, 3:18, and 1 John 4:9, among others. The Son's begottenness or generation from the Father is a key part of the pro-Nicene argument. When something is begotten, it is of the same substance as that which begets. Just as human fathers and mothers beget human children, so the Father begets a divine Son. However, if the Son is only-begotten, then nothing else can be begotten of the Father. Thus the Spirit cannot be begotten of the Father. Surely, then, the Spirit cannot also be *homoousios* with the Father! He lacks the appropriate form of origin, and therefore must have been created rather than begotten.

It turns out this argument will be rather difficult for its opponents to handle. It is one of the main reasons why the final version of the Nicene Creed will state that the Spirit proceeds from the Father, rather than saying he is begotten by the Father—that term is reserved for the Son alone. Even though they did not carry the day, the Pneumatomachoi have left their mark on the creed—and as we shall see in later chapters, they won far more victories than is often remembered.

Conclusion

The anti-Nicene thinkers of the fourth century were not a monolith. They disagreed with each other just as often as they disagreed with the pro-Nicenes, and they often fought with each other for power and influence in the newly Christian empire. All they agreed on was that the Son was definitely not *homoousios* with the Father. The Nicene Creed was an inadequate statement of faith. The church needed to do better, and the thinkers described in this chapter were determined to help it do so.

Perhaps the most remarkable thing about the Nicene Creed is that it managed to inspire such passionate criticism. (It inspired passionate loyalty too, but that is a topic for our next chapter.) To understand why requires us to see beyond the particular arguments and positions of each school. Every thinker has certain core beliefs about the world, humanity's place in it, and the nature of God that shape their theology. While the anti-Nicene thinkers did not always agree with each other, they often shared these underlying core beliefs. Understanding their core beliefs reveals why the Nicene Creed was so unacceptable to each of these groups.

The first core belief that anti-Nicenes tended to share was that the Father was utterly unique. No other entity, not even the Son, could share the place the Father held or even be the same kind of being the Father was. They may have differed on the degree of separation—Basil and the Homoiousians admitted the Son was of similar substance, while Eunomius saw the Father as so superior that he was the "God" of the Son—but all agreed that there had to be at least some distance between the two. Moreover, everyone agreed that the distance between Father and Son was the only way that the Christian faith could make any sense. After all, Jesus often described himself in a subordinate role, stating that the Father was "greater" than him[3] and referred to him as "[his] God."[4] Anti-Nicenes believed there was no way to make sense of Christ's statements except that he was a lesser kind of being than the Father—perhaps divine, but only a second divinity at best. A clear delineation between Father and Son also helped these Christians explain how they worshiped only one God. If the Father was the utterly unique supreme being, then the Father alone was truly God. While the Son might share in some of the Father's divine qualities—always willing what is good, having the power to save, receiving the desperate prayers of sports fans when their team is losing, etc.—he does not have them due to his own nature. He has been given them "on loan" by the Father, in whom they truly and properly reside. Thus Christians might pay homage to the Son, but ultimately acknowledge only the Father as the one God of all that is.

The belief in the Father's utter uniqueness led to a second core belief: that there was a special bond between the Son and the created world. After all, the Bible states that "by [the Word] all things were made."[5] Many anti-Nicenes took this passage to mean that the Word created the world because the world could not have survived the Father's direct creation. The Father was so great, powerful, and holy that created things could not survive his presence; they would melt away into nonexistence. So the Father created the Son as a lesser divinity that could have contact with the world without destroying it. Eunomius would say that the Son was the "God of this world," while the Father was the "God of the Son."

If the Son and the world had a special bond, then that led to a third core belief: that the world was saved through the work of its creator, who was not the Father. The Son became incarnate, suffered, died, and rose again

3. John 14:28.
4. John 20:17.
5. John 1:3.

because he saw the tragic plight of his creation due to sin. While the Father empowered the Son for this mission, the Father's relationship to the work of salvation was a much more distant one. After all, the Father could not have direct contact with creation without destroying it. He could only work through the Son. That meant that salvation restored human beings to communion with the Son. Humanity's relationship to the Father, however, was harder to place. As creatures, we have no real relationship with the Father since we rely on the Son as a mediating figure. Eunomius claimed that our relationship to the Father is only intellectual. When we consider the Son's glory as the one who is generated from the Father, we can imagine the Father's ungenerated, uncreated glory. We can have some understanding of the Father's essence, then, but any further relationship does not seem to be possible.

These three core beliefs create a picture of the world divided into three layers: that of the Father, that of the Son (and possibly the Spirit), and that of human beings, angels, and other things made by the Son. For anti-Nicenes, the primary location of the Christian story is between the second and third layers of the story. The Father remains a remote, unapproachable figure who sets events in motion through his intermediaries and then watches the proceedings from his inaccessible light. The good Christian should give thanks for the distant illumination we receive from the Father, but should not expect to approach it. Instead, Christians must content themselves for the reflection of glory we see in Jesus Christ—the moon to the Father's sun.

This picture of the world proved powerful and alluring for many Christians of the fourth century. For many others, however, it was not only repugnant, but blasphemous. The anti-Nicenes had not only defamed the glory of the only-begotten Son, they had cut Christians off from the greatest hope of the faith: full communion with the very essence of divinity itself. The Council of Nicaea had expressed far more than a bare-bones statement of Trinitarian doctrine. It carried the astounding good news that in Jesus Christ we encounter the very heart of the Father himself. This core conviction led the various pro-Nicene parties of the period to write their own works in defense of the creed. It is to those plucky defenders of the creed that we now turn.

Chapter 8

We Need the Homoousios!
Pro-Nicene Theologies

WITH THE DIVERSE THEOLOGIES of the anti-Nicenes behind us, it is now time to discuss the other side of the theological coin: those individuals who championed the theology of the Nicene Creed and led the party often referred to as the Homoousians.

Unlike the figures of chapter 7 who were united only by their antipathy towards the language of *homoousios*, the pro-Nicene theologians we study in this chapter agreed not only about the importance of the creed, but about the vital significance of defending their cause against its skeptics. You might think they would be united in their theologies. After all, when attempting to achieve a political result, it helps to have a unified platform and a single message for all of your allies to reinforce. However, it turns out that each of the creed's primary defenders had their own unique rationales and perspectives. Sometimes their theologies complemented each other, and sometimes they contradicted each other. Nicaea's defenders were no more willing to lose to the anti-Nicenes in word count than they were in church councils. We will have to examine each thinker in turn to understand the Nicene Creed's eventual success.

The Original Nicene: Athanasius of Alexandria

If there is one figure whose entire life is defined by the Nicene Creed, it is Athanasius of Alexandria. As the adoptive son of Bishop Alexander and a five-time recipient of exilic sentences due to his Homoousian theology, no one could claim the mantle of a pro-Nicene quite like Athanasius. We will delve into his theological writings to understand exactly why his opponents found his thought so dangerous—and why Athanasius thought the Council of Nicaea worth the enormous personal trials he suffered for its sake.

Athanasius set down his thoughts in several writings that are still required reading for many seminary students today. His most famous work is *On the Incarnation,* in which he attempted to argue that the Homoousian position is the only one that makes sense in light of God's plan of salvation. In short, Athanasius insisted that *who* Christ is—the only-begotten Son of God, *homoousios* with the Father—is intimately connected with *what* Christ came to do.

Athanasius sees two interrelated problems with humanity that Christ came to fix. The first is the fact that all human beings eventually die. While God did decree that death is a punishment for sin, mortality is not merely a punishment devised by a God who is angry that humans do not follow his rules. It is the natural consequence of human beings turning away from God. One of the most fascinating parts of Athanasius's thought is that he conceived of human beings as fundamentally nothing at all. Athanasius did not mean that people are worthless. He meant that God created everything, including human beings, from nothing. Without God's creative act, human beings would not exist. We have nothing inside us that does not come from God, and without God we would not exist. To put it simply, humans are quite literally nothing without God. When created beings turn away from God or disconnect themselves from God's will, they return to their natural state of nonbeing in the same way that a fan will stop spinning once you unplug it from its power source.

This situation causes quite a dilemma for God. On the one hand, it is in the nature of things that sin causes death. Human beings are not the sort of creatures who can survive sinning forever. Even if God forgives all human sin, humanity will still die if they do not repent and return to God. Moreover, God is the ruler of the universe, and it is not fitting for God to let the human race go on harming each other and destroying the natural order without consequences. That would mean that God's good plans for creation were thwarted. On the other hand, God created the human race, loves it, and destined it for complete happiness. If the human race were simply abandoned to self-destruction, then God's plans would also have been thwarted. Neither option is fitting for a God who is omnipotent, all-good, and rules the whole universe. If humanity is not saved, the devil wins.

God solved this problem by taking a human body to himself and offering it up to the Father through his death. Since all humanity died in Christ's crucifixion, the law that death follows sin was fulfilled. Yet because Christ is God, a natural source of life and being, all human beings who are united with Christ in baptism are united with his divine life.[1] Since his life is immortal, Jesus succeeds in his mission to save us from death and destruction. In a truly lovely turn of phrase, Athanasius describes Christ's work as "by the grace of his resurrection banishing death from them as straw from the fire."[2] Crucially, this plan only works if Christ is truly God, *homoousios* with the Father. The life of a created divinity, no matter how glorious or impressive, would have the same problem as humanity's life: it would be nothing in itself. Humanity needed contact with the Father's uncreated and self-sustaining life to be saved. Only a Savior with that kind of divine life could fit the bill.

Thus only a Son *homoousios* with the Father solves the first dilemma. The second dilemma concerns human knowledge. One of the effects of sin is that we lose our knowledge of God. Human beings were made in the image of God, but that image is obscured by sin. Since we cannot recognize God in the world, we cannot recognize the image of God in ourselves or in others.

How can God restore the knowledge that we have lost? It is not fitting for God's image to be effaced any more than it is for God's creations to be destroyed. For Athanasius, the answer was that sinful humans must see the Word of God, who is both the perfect image of the Father and the one in whose image they were made. Only thus will humans be restored to the knowledge of God. Athanasius compares Christ's work to a painter; when a portrait has been damaged or destroyed, you can only recreate it by having the original subject sit for a new painting. By coming to us in a

---

1. Athanasius's assumption raises some interesting questions for modern readers. Foremost among them is why, exactly, the death and resurrection of *one* man should have implications for the rest of us. Athanasius is making a very bold claim here: that the power of death has been broken over every single human being, and that there is something fundamentally different about every single human and human body because of Christ's life, death, and resurrection. Particularly in the individualistic West, we might question how that could be. How can what happens in one human body affect what happens in another body and soul? While this already-too-long footnote is not the place to answer the question entirely, I can tell you that Athanasius assumes that there is such a natural solidarity between members of the human race that what happens to one human affects all of us. He gives the example of a king visiting a city. The king doesn't have to enter every single house in the city in order for them to be honored. Even just visiting one house affords the whole city a greater honor and dignity, not to mention royal protection. So it is, Athanasius says, with humanity. For Athanasius, we are already more closely united to each other's fate than Western audiences assume.

2. Athanasius, *On the Incarnation* 2.8.

flesh-and-blood body, the Word of God gave us the most concrete possible view of the one true God.

Athanasius was able to expound his own theology at length in *On the Incarnation*. However, he did not always have the luxury of setting out his own views without worrying about what his opponents might say. The political winds blew against Athanasius for much of his life, and he was forced to refute the views of other, more influential clerics. Nowhere is Athanasius's capacity for dialectic and debate more evident than in his *Orations Against the Arians*.

The most innovative aspect of Athanasius's work was its title. You will often hear the word "Arian" used to describe those who hold similar views to Arius. As you saw in the last chapter, none of the anti-Nicene leaders believed they were following in the tradition of the condemned heretic Arius. Most of the participants in the controversy were bishops, who were not keen to be seen as following a lowly priest. Athanasius was the first to consistently use the word "Arian" as a handy moniker for all those with whom he disagreed. When especially peeved, Athanasius referred to his enemies as "Ariomaniacs"—people who have literally gone mad in their admiration of Arius.

Athanasius did not simply use these terms for rhetorical purposes. He thought there was real theological significance in them. The *Orations Against the Arians* opens by talking about how the heresy of Arius is the absolute worst. In fact, Athanasius refers to it as the harbinger of the antichrist. It is uncertain whether Athanasius meant that Arius's teachings signaled the literal, imminent end of the world, or whether they were the harbinger of the antichrist because Arius quite literally denied Christ, claiming that the Creating Word was but a mere creature. In either case, Athanasius believes that all those who deny the *homoousios* are committing the same error as Arius by failing to honor Jesus appropriately. They are thus dangerously misguided at best and antichrists at worst.

The depth of Athanasius's feeling is clear from his punishingly intricate defense against Arian accusations. Athanasius left no stone unturned in his defense of the Son, piling up biblical evidence and philosophical argumentation to make his point. I would love to walk you through every argument that he made, but this section is already getting long in the tooth and I have editors to assuage. We will have to content ourselves with covering a few of the main ideas Athanasius expounds.

Athanasius's first idea is this: the Bible uses the same sorts of names to describe Father and Son. If the Father and Son are described in the same ways, then we should assume that they are the same in terms of *ousia*. Here is a non-exhaustive list of examples Athanasius supplies: the Father is described as a "fountain of living water" in Jeremiah 2:13; the Son is described as "the Life" in John 14:6 and like a spring that never fails in Isaiah 58:11. The Son is called "Wisdom" in Proverbs 8, Psalm 104, and many other places besides, while the Father is referred to as a fountain of wisdom in Baruch 3:12. The reason for this overlap in names, Athanasius says, is because the Son is like the Father in every possible way—except for the fact that the Father begets and the Son is begotten. In certain parts of the world, you are likely to hear someone say, "If it looks like a duck, walks like a duck, and quacks like a duck, it's probably a duck." Athanasius's version of this folksy aphorism would probably go, "If it is named like God, it is probably God."

Athanasius expanded his notion of biblical names with two other ideas: the Son's perfect knowledge of the Father, and the Son's status as the perfect image of the Father. These two ideas are closely connected. Remember that the incarnation of the Son saves humanity by bringing us into contact with the grade-A, bona fide, life-generating divinity of the Father. If the Son is going to connect us to the Father, then the Son has to know the Father. After all, Jesus cannot share with us those aspects of God that he is not privy to. A Christ who can only praise God with "partial adequacy," as Arius's *Thalia* had claimed, could only offer a partial salvation. Only a Son who is *homoousios* with the infinite Father could possibly understand the Father fully—and this, Athanasius thought, is precisely what the Bible was telling us. The Bible described the Son as Wisdom (even as the Wisdom of God) to reassure Christians that Christ really did have the Father's wisdom, and hence could really, fully save them.

For salvation to occur, the Son must not only know the Father. The Son must also be able to communicate the Father to us. This is where Athanasius's idea of a perfect image comes in. As anyone who has ever taken a low-quality smartphone photo knows, there are various degrees of image quality. An untrained artist (or a smudged smartphone lens, in our digital age) will take a picture that conveys some general sense of the image but misses significant details. Better images will convey more of the original subject. The best picture would be one which perfectly conveys the original subject. Athanasius takes this simple concept and adds a twist. The *best* image of something is not a picture at all. It is the same sort of thing as its subject.

Think of it this way: the best image shares as many properties as possible with its subject. Pictures are two-dimensional; persons are three-dimensional. Pictures are made of pixels or ink and cannot reason, will, or remember. When posted on social media, pictures can obtain likes and reactions and, no matter what social media wants you to think, just because someone likes or fails to like a photo of you doesn't mean they like or dislike *you*.³ No picture can be a perfect image of a living being. The best image of one person is going to be another person who looks just like the first person. So it is with the Father and Son. The best image of the Father is another divine being *homoousios* with him.

Because the Son is the perfect image of the Father, Athanasius also insisted that the Son is "proper" to the Father. Athanasius does not mean that the Son always wears a top hat in the Father's presence, or only speaks in the thees and thous of Elizabethan English. The Greek word translated as "proper" is *idios,* and it is related to our English word "idiom." A person's idiom is their characteristic mode of expression. If someone makes jokes all the time, or constantly inverts their sentence structures, or always pauses at the end of their statements, then that is part of their idiom. Athanasius said that the Son is part of the Father's idiom—the very means of the Father's self-communication to the world, and hence of the very same stuff as the Father. One can hear the echoes of Tertullian's psychological analogy wherein the Son is the Father's mode of dialogue—and with good reason. One of the reasons Athanasius was so worried about the Arian approach is that, by separating the Son from the Father, it winds up unable to explain how the Father communicates with creation at all.

Throughout his career, Athanasius expounded these arguments against Nicaea's opponents. He was stubborn and persistent in his arguments no matter the opposition he faced. He was also not above a scalding insult of his opponents. Athanasius breezily opened one speech against the Arians by expressing surprise they had not been overcome by the force of his arguments and were instead replying to him and compared them to dogs consuming their own vomit.⁴ He thought the stakes were high enough to justify such harsh language. In attempting to praise God for redeeming the world, the Arians had instead spoken in such a way as to imply that God could not even communicate with the world. Athanasius would not allow this to stand in Christ's church, and he was convinced that Nicaea's *homoousios* language was the best way to refute such errors.

---

3. Saint Athanasius, living in the 300s AD, was of course blissfully ignorant of social media, but I like to think he would agree with the general point.

4. Athanasius, *Orations Against the Arians,* 2.1. The reference to dogs returning to vomit is not arbitrary; it is an allusion to Proverbs 26:11. After this insult, Athanasius describes how the anti-Nicenes have misunderstood Proverbs, so his insult is a very stylized bit of literary cleverness. It is still pretty mean by modern standards, though.

The Original Embarrassment: Marcellus of Ancyra

Unfortunately, Athanasius had severe difficulties getting the rest of the church on board with his theological program. One of the main reasons for his difficulty was another supporter of the Council of Nicaea: Marcellus of Ancyra.

Little is known about Marcellus's early life. We know that he was the bishop of Ancyra (modern-day Ankara in Turkey) for some time and demolished pagan temples during his tenure. He was also responsible for one of the notable theological movements of his day. It was mostly notable because everyone else hated it. Marcellus promoted a way of speaking about the Trinity that almost all his contemporaries found to be modalistic. Marcellus furiously denied the charges of modalism, but had immense difficulty convincing anyone else that he was right. He was eventually deposed and exiled for his trouble.

Marcellus claimed that God was one *hypostasis,* that is, only one independent thing (you can probably imagine the anti-modalist alarm bells ringing in other Christian's heads at that statement alone). To buttress this claim, Marcellus drew on Tertullian's idea that the Word is God's faculty of reasoning and speaking. Unlike Tertullian, Marcellus did not claim that the Father and Son are two distinct *hypostases* (the plural of *hypostasis*). Instead, the Son is a faculty of God, like memory or logic are faculties of the human mind. Marcellus seems to have thought that the faculties of the mind—emotions, intellect, will, memory, etc.—are real things that exist within the greater whole of the mind. They are not *hypostases* because they have no real existence. If I dropped out of existence, my will and intellect would stop existing too. They are, however, distinct things from one another. Marcellus likely thought this was a good way to express that the Father and the Son are distinct things while still arguing that there is only one God, one *hypostasis*. Everyone else disagreed with him, but the plucky bishop was not about to let something as trivial as universal rejection change his theologizing. Instead, he cheerfully talked about how these faculty-gods interacted with each other. The Son "goes out" from God in creation alongside the Spirit. Marcellus originally said that the Son and Spirit would "go back in" to the Father at the end of time, just like they were before creation. At this point, the Son's kingdom would end and all would be handed over to the Father, just like 1 Corinthians 15:24 said.

If the idea of the Son and Spirit "going out from" and "going back into" the Father sounds vague to you, you are not alone. Marcellus is one of the hardest early Christian thinkers to follow. He tended to write using dramatic rhetorical flourishes that he was clearly very proud of having thought of, but which make it even harder to understand him. For example, he seems to have thought that the Trinity is three when acting but one otherwise. He communicated this by describing God as "the monad which expands to form a triad while in no way allowing itself to be divided."[5] Perhaps Marcellus enjoyed this sentence; other readers were more worried that it was nonsensical. Of course you can divide a triad. That is what makes it a triad! So Marcellus was forced to clarify this by saying the Godhead expands "in energy alone," which clarified almost nothing. To modern readers it sounds like Marcellus wanted God to expand by opening a blocked chakra. To ancient readers, it sounded modalistic.

Marcellus enthusiastically embraced the theology of Nicaea. If the Son was simply a thing within the mind of the Father that exited and entered him, then of course they were of the same substance. Unfortunately for other pro-Nicenes, Marcellus became a weight around their neck. When asked to explain their own theologies, they were constantly forced to distance themselves from Marcellus's vague, modalist-adjacent speculations. He played a similar role for the pro-Nicenes as Eunomius and Asterius played for the anti-Nicenes. All three were controversial figures with a small, dedicated following who alienated all those outside of their camps. Anti-Nicene writers would make their position seem reasonable by comparing it to Marcellus's excesses; pro-Nicene writers would play the same game with Eunomius and Asterius.

Interestingly enough, Marcellus struck up a friendship with Athanasius toward the end of his life. During one of his many exiles from Alexandria, Athanasius found his way to Rome and met Marcellus, who was still in the middle of his very long exile. The two expats met and talked theology, and Athanasius apparently came to appreciate Marcellus's devotion to the Nicene cause (if not his theology). It is easy to imagine the scene: two of Nicaea's great defenders at a local watering hole, sipping a fine Italian vintage while complaining about anti-Nicene trickery and comparing each other's exiles to see who had gotten the worse deal. Marcellus may have a strange place in the pro-Nicene camp, but there can be no denying he deserves his spot.

The Cappadocians Emerge

While Marcellus and Athanasius may have carried the Nicene torch at the beginning, they would not be the ones to bring it to its destination. Both men died before the whole fifty-six years of controversy played out.

5. Marcellus of Ancyra, *Fragment* 67.

However, Athanasius's theology fired the minds of a younger generation of thinkers who would successfully bring the controversy to its resolution.[6] Usually referred to as "the Cappadocians" after the region of their birth, this next generation of thinkers are still among the most celebrated figures in all of Christianity. They also happen to have shared deep bonds with each other; two were brothers, and the other was a close family friend. Even more fittingly, there were three of them. Who better to defend the three-in-oneness of God than a "trinity" of Cappadocian friends and family?

Before continuing, however, there are a few caveats to make. In a book like this, I cannot give a complete summary of any thinker's arguments. That is doubly true for the Cappadocians, who are among the most well-studied and voluminous thinkers Christianity has produced. There are all kinds of different understandings of what one particular Cappadocian meant by one particular term or how exactly they understood the Trinity. We simply do not have the time to get into those debates. However, I will not make the opposite error of oversimplifying them. Some thinkers present the Cappadocians as having the exact same theology, which is called the "Cappadocian solution" or the "Cappadocian settlement."[7] That is just not true.[8] While the Cappadocians agree on many points (and even repeat the same arguments), they also have significant disagreements about the Trinity, especially when it comes to the divinity of the Holy Spirit. I will attempt to split the difference by highlighting the distinctive arguments of each. Just know that many of the arguments I describe are common to all three thinkers. I will note which arguments would have caused disagreement among them.

The Tireless Uniter: Basil the Great

The first of these three figures is Basil of Caesarea, often known as Basil the Great. Basil was born to a minor aristocratic family just on the edge of the Black Sea in modern-day Turkey. His family was a powerhouse of Christian superstars. As you will learn later in this chapter, his younger brother Gregory would go on to be a world-class theologian in his own right. His sister Macrina was a celebrated ascetic and teacher. His parents were both devout Christians who traced their spiritual lineage back to Origen of Alexandria. During the Great Persecution, Basil's family withdrew to the desert

---

6. Marcellus's theology may have fired the minds of some people, too, but only with rage and confusion, so his influence mostly ended with his death.

7. For example, Lienhard, "Cappadocian Settlement."

8. Even if it *was* true, we should find a better name for it than "the Cappadocian solution," which sounds like a Turkish liquor.

and lived as hunter-gatherers to escape their persecutors. The plan worked. Once the Great Persecution ended, the family resumed its prominent position in the community. By the time Basil came along, several decades had passed since that horrific persecution, but his family's unwavering commitment to the faith had not.

Basil's family was also deeply committed to education. As Basil began to show his prodigious academic talents, his family sent him to Athens to study with the finest minds of the age. Basil learned rapidly and well at Athens. But he found himself dissatisfied by the school climate. Gangs of students would attach themselves to one particular teacher and aggressively recruit new students to study exclusively with their teacher, often using violence to persuade them—an ancient version of *West Side Story*, but if the Sharks and the Jets were arguing over whom you should take English literature with. Basil came to appreciate asceticism as the true marker of a Christian education, rather than the rowdy jockeying of his classmates.

While in Athens, Basil would make one of the most consequential friendships of his life with a fellow student, later known to history as Gregory of Nazianzus. The two of them began to live a quasi-monastic life. The two met with a group of students for regular prayer and practiced the same kinds of fasting and vigils as the monks they admired. Basil eventually left his studies and was drawn to Eustathius of Sebaste, a charismatic Homoiousian bishop often associated with the infamous Pneumatomachoi. While Eustathius was not a monk, he adopted many of the same ascetic practices that monks did. Basil was so impressed by the man that he decided to forsake the wealthy life his education could have purchased and henceforth to serve only God's aims.

Basil was ordained a priest and then became bishop of the important province of Caesarea. From his powerful perch, Basil advanced the pro-Nicene cause in every way he could. He worked to install allies in nearby dioceses. He countered the hegemony of an increasingly skeptical imperial court. He forged alliances with those who could be persuaded of the Nicene Creed's truth—or at least were not opposed to it. Most importantly to this chapter, Basil wrote numerous works expounding his own view of the Trinity and attacking the views of the anti-Nicenes.

Basil's two most prominent Trinitarian works are *Against Eunomius* and *On the Holy Spirit*. *Against Eunomius* is (as you might imagine) a refutation of the views of Eunomius, the infamous Heteroousian we met in chapter 7. While Eunomius had insisted that the Father, being unbegotten, could not share a common substance with the begotten Son, Basil argued otherwise. Basil made several arguments against Eunomius that his fellow Cappadocians would repeat. The first was to insist on God's utter incomprehensibility. By defining God as pure and simple unbegottenness, Eunomius essentially claimed that he had a complete knowledge of the divine substance, and was therefore in a position to say what God could and could not do. This was not only prideful, but impossible. The depths of God's being cannot be fully known by anyone or anything but God.

Basil refused to prioritize any one biblical description of God above all others. Each adjective or metaphor gives us some facet of God's character. Taken together, they give us a well-rounded picture of God insofar as humans can comprehend. When, for example, Jesus called himself bread, he was not saying that God's body is glutinous, or that he is best consumed with a hefty slice of butter. When we look at the Bible as a whole, we see God nourishing people and realize Jesus was saying that he nourishes the soul. Ditto with all the other terms applied to Christ and/or the Father: living vine, light of the world, life, wisdom, strength, goodness, truth, etc. Athanasius had said that if the Son is described the same way as the Father, then he probably is the same in substance as the Father. Eunomius had countered that this was impossible, as the Son and Father were different in at least one respect: the Son was begotten and the Father was not. Basil broke the impasse by pointing out that our descriptions of God are never perfectly accurate anyway. To latch on to any one description of God and treat it as absolute is to miss the orthodox forest for the heretical trees.

Moreover, Eunomius's favored Greek term for the Son, usually rendered as "something begotten," is nowhere found in the Bible to describe Jesus. Or as Basil delightfully puts it:

> *For a child is begotten to us, and a son is given to us. And his name is called*—not "something begotten"—but *the angel of great counsel* . . . Furthermore, Peter . . . did not say: "you are something begotten," but rather: *You are the Christ, the Son of the living God.* And no passage can be found in which Paul, who filled all his writings with the designation "Son," mentions "something begotten"—the very term which Eunomius proposes with great boldness, as if he took it from the divine instruction.[9]

If you are sympathetic to Eunomius, you might think Basil has been overly harsh. After all, a Son is begotten by definition. Is it really such a stretch for us to apply the term "begotten" to the Son? In Basil's view, the answer was an unequivocal yes. He did not think we should make a habit of adding descriptions to God beyond those revealed in the Scriptures. After all, God's being is incomprehensible to us. We cannot be certain that divine being works the way human being does. Thus what might be true of human

---

9. Basil of Caesarea, *Against Eunomius*, 1.1.

beings might not be true of God. Think of this as similar to how compound words work. If I know what the English words "standing" and "under" mean, I can put them together to say that I am standing under a bridge. That is a perfectly logical thing to say. But perhaps I want to get creative with my sentence structure, and I swap the order of my words. Instead of saying I am standing under a bridge, I say I am understanding a bridge—and in doing so I have completely changed the meaning and connotations of my sentence without realizing it. Basil argued that this is precisely what Eunomius does by calling the Son "something begotten." That particular term is only used pejoratively in the Bible—hardly an appropriate description for the redeemer of the world!

In the middle of his argument, Basil gave a simple formula to answer a question that has bedeviled Christians for millennia: how is there only one God when Father, Son, and Spirit are three persons? Basil said that if Father and Son are *homoousios,* then anything we say of the Father's substance must be true of the Son's and *vice versa.* If we describe the Father as light, then the Son is also light. If the Son is the living bread, then so is the Father. The oneness of the Trinity comes from the fact that Father, Son, and Spirit are so intimately related that whatever is true of the being (*ousia*) of one must be true of the being of the others.

Or at least the Son and Father are so related.

For while Basil is hailed as a great defender of the divinity of the Son, his track record on the Holy Spirit is viewed with far more suspicion. Unlike his erstwhile friend and fellow pro-Nicene Gregory of Nazianzus, Basil never described the Holy Spirit as *homoousios* with the Father or Son. Basil did argue for the Spirit's divinity, and did so powerfully. However, to be divine was not the same thing as to be *homoousios* with the Father. Even Arius said the Son and Spirit were divine, just of a lesser divinity than the Father. Some Pneumatomachoi would have made much the same claim about the Spirit. And Basil's reticence is particularly noteworthy given his short discipleship under Eustathius of Sebaste, who appears to have been Homoiousian.

Basil may well have seen his reserve as a strength rather than a weakness. Throughout his career, Basil routinely built alliances with those who were generally sympathetic to his theology, even if they were not in complete agreement. Basil may well have believed that it was worth making some concessions to the Pneumatomachoi if it gave him allies against the radical Heteroousians and their ilk. Furthermore, the Holy Spirit is never directly called God in the Bible, unlike the Son. If the Bible was mum on this topic, Basil may well have decided to do likewise for the sake of building alliances. His famous book *On the Holy Spirit* appears to have been intended as a peace offering to the Pneumatomachoi, setting down a theology of the Spirit that both parties could agree on for the sake of their common worship.

Even if Basil never used the word *homoousios* to describe the Spirit, he still provided powerful arguments for its divinity and affiliation with the other divine persons. The reason the Spirit is equal to the Father and Son is because the Spirit is inseparable from them in all their works. People proclaim God's words through prophetic speech by listening to the Holy Spirit. In fact, when a prophecy is true, we know it was given by the Holy Spirit. If the Spirit is the guarantee that a prophet has spoken with God, then the Spirit must be divine. The Spirit is involved in creation just like the Father and Son, hovering over the waters in Genesis 1:2. Just as we conclude the Son's equal divinity from the similar ways the Bible describes him and the Father, so too we conclude that the Spirit is divine from the fact that the Spirit is always present when the Father and Son are acting. The Spirit also understands the mind of God[10]—which no created thing can do. Thus the Spirit must be divine.

Basil's energetic contributions to Trinitarian theology helped pave the way for the final resolution of the Nicene controversy. It is a testament to the brilliance of his friends and colleagues that his theology is the least studied of the three of them. Basil was a genius, but his greatest legacy to the church was as a reformer and master bishop. He was deeply involved in his city, and undertook a massive fundraising effort to create a building that offered care to the sick and shelter for the homeless. It was one of the first charities of its kind—and Basil could be seen at the clinic, taking time from his duties to bandage wounds and feed the hungry personally. He built a network of influence and alliances that were crucial to the eventual resolution of the controversy. Basil did all of this despite chronic illnesses that hounded him throughout his life and led to his early death at the age of forty-nine.[11] Yet when it comes to theology, the extraordinary contributions of his brother and his Athenian confrere have received far more attention. These two not only shared a common cause and social circle, but the same name. Just as two bishops named Eusebius led the charge against the Nicene Creed, two bishops named Gregory engineered its ultimate triumph.

---

10. 1 Corinthians 2:11.

11. You may think that forty-nine is an old age for someone living in the fourth century. That is not true. High infant mortality rates skew the data for an average Roman's life expectancy. Many infants did indeed die before reaching the age of five. However, a Roman man who lived to age five was likely to live into his sixties.

The Brilliant Brother: Gregory of Nyssa

The next figure to discuss is Basil's younger brother, Gregory of Nyssa. We know less about his life than his brother's. Gregory was substantially younger than Basil and appears to have looked up to him. When Eunomius wrote a reply to Basil's *Against Eunomius*, Gregory indignantly interceded by writing his own book refuting Eunomius's refutation. This spared his big brother the trouble of responding to Eunomius himself. Basil, having recently died, probably appreciated Gregory's help. As far as we know, Gregory was not sent off to Athens for the same classical education as Basil. The family recognized that Gregory was brilliant, decided to educate him at home, and assigned Basil to be his tutor. Gregory learned prodigiously. His writings display a first-rate knowledge of Greek literature, language, and logic that could rival the smartest graduate of the academy at Athens.

Gregory had a profound "conversion experience" that transformed him from a strong but contented Christian layman into a passionate priest and theologian. Gregory had a dream in which forty martyrs came to him and expressed their disappointment in his loose living. The somnolescent martyrs had rather high standards, as Gregory's "loose living" consisted of being a churchgoing teacher of public speaking and a devoted husband to his wife.[12] Nevertheless, Gregory was convicted and got into ecclesiastical business alongside his brother. When Basil began his campaign to install pro-Nicene bishops in positions of power, Gregory was high on his list.

Gregory was not as successful a bishop as his brother. He did not understand how to win friends and influence people. In 371 AD, Basil and his uncle got into a huge fight and were not on speaking terms. Gregory was so bothered by the family rift that he forged a letter from his uncle to Basil. Gregory hoped the letter would cause the two of them to start talking again. His brother and uncle discovered the ruse and were not amused. There is something of a parable in this small incident. Throughout his career as bishop, Gregory tried to reconcile those estranged from the church: first some followers of Marcellus of Ancyra, then later a group of schismatic Christians in Antioch. Both attempts failed. Basil considered sending Gregory on a

---

12. Gregory's marriage was no inhibition to his joining the clergy. In this time period clerical marriages were not the norm, but there was no canon law on the books forbidding it. We know only two things about Gregory's marriage to his wife. First, it produced a son. Second, Gregory's very first written work was titled *On Virginity*, and in the work Gregory described marriage as a regrettable institution, a concession made by God to human weakness after the fall. Gregory claimed that had there been no fall we would have all lived as perpetual virgins and never gotten married. We have no word as to how his wife received this book, but I have to imagine it made for some awkward conversation at the dinner table.

diplomatic mission to the West but felt he did not have enough good sense for such a sensitive assignment. Gregory's aptitude for politics and diplomacy was so poor that he was exiled after a group of anti-Nicene bishops accused him of misusing church funds and he was unable to make a defense. Gregory's heart was in the right place, but his foot was often in his mouth.

If Gregory's church plans frequently went awry, his theological writings almost always succeeded. Gregory of Nyssa is regarded today as one of the most brilliant thinkers Christianity has ever produced, and theologians in the twenty-first century continue to read Gregory for inspiration. He also has the distinction of being one of the first Christian writers to call for the complete abolition of slavery. Gregory set out his Trinitarian theology in two works: *Against Eunomius* and a letter addressed to a fellow Christian named Ablabius. The letter is usually called *On Not Three Gods*, and rather predictably explains why Christians do not worship three gods even though they acknowledge three divine persons.

Gregory repeatedly expanded on the arguments of his predecessors to advance the pro-Nicene cause. Gregory had a knack for finding logical arguments for the Homoousian position. The divine essence was infinitely good. Eunomius had claimed the Son was divine, but not as much so as the Father. In other words, Eunomius said the Son was still infinitely good, but less so than the Father. Gregory pointed out that this was absurd. Any lack of goodness is evil by definition. So if the Son was less good than the Father, the Son would be partially evil. It did not matter if the Son still had infinite goodness. If he lacked any of the Father's goodness, then there was evil in him, and he could not be divine if he was even partially evil. Eunomius's claim that the Son was less divine than the Father was logically incoherent.

Interestingly, Athanasius made a similar claim in his *Orations Against the Arians*. Athanasius asserted that the Word could either be God or a creature, but that he could not be a lesser God; there was no category of being in between full divinity and creaturehood. Gregory has here given us a very compact, simple way of arguing for Athanasius's insight. His vision is not always different from those who came before. But he brings a clarity of argument that few possess.

Gregory's penchant for logical clarity was particularly apparent when attempting to explain the knotty question of why Homoousians worship only one God when there are three divine persons. Gregory appeals to several strategies to achieve this end. First, Gregory turned the tables by arguing that his position is the *only* one that can plausibly claim to worship one God. For Eunomius and his ilk, the Father, Son, and Spirit are of different substances. How on earth could offering worship to three separate beings be monotheism? Second, to speak of the Father, Son, and Spirit as a united Trinity is merely to follow the Bible's lead. For example, the Son is all-powerful because the Bible speaks of him as having authority over all, the same as the Father has authority over all. Thus the reverent thing to do is to follow Scripture's lead and describe the two as unified.

Gregory was not just content to attack Eunomius's argument, of course. He also wanted to build up his own positive account of the Trinity. First, he made many of the same interpretive moves as Basil, including appealing to the common *ousia* of the three *hypostases*[13] as that which allows for unity. Second, we describe the three of them as unified because Scripture speaks of them as unified. Third, Gregory pointed out that Christians are taught to baptize in the name of the Father, Son, and Holy Spirit. That is by itself nothing new. Basil made the same argument. But Gregory picked up on the difference in number: the biblical command is to baptize in one *singular* name, but that singular name is three names that signify the relationships among the divine persons: Father, Son, and Holy Spirit. The Bible gives us a three-in-one name for God!

Gregory had many similarly provocative arguments throughout his text. However, by far his most controversial line of thinking was to explain the Trinity by reference to a common nature. Gregory frequently described the three persons of the Trinity as sharing a common substance (*ousia*), or a common *physis* (FOO-sis) that united them. The word *physis* is usually translated as "nature," and in this context it specifically referred to one's character and traits. It is common for people to talk about "human nature"; Gregory used *physis* to refer to God's divine nature. Just as three people all share a common human nature, Gregory said, so too all three persons of the Trinity share a common divine nature.

Scholars will often refer to this account as the "generic" account of the Trinity. They do not mean that the argument itself is generic, like some kind of grocery store cereal brand. They mean that Gregory turns the oneness of God into a category (or a genre) that individual beings (*hypostases*) participate in. This creates substantial problems. For starters, it is difficult to see how God is meaningfully one. I can point to my two colleagues who work in my office and say that we are one in virtue of our common humanity, but if the three of us were (heaven forbid) to be worshiped, no one would say they were only worshiping one person. A second, and arguably even trickier problem, is that Gregory has created a fourth thing in the Trinity: the divine nature itself. Now the Trinity is not just the three persons found in the Bible; it also includes this divine nature that Gregory describes but is nowhere

---

13. This formula—that God is one *ousia* and three *hypostases*—is the much-vaunted "Cappadocian solution" to the problem of the Trinity.

found in Scripture. In his defense, Gregory is not the only one to use the generic account. Basil has a similar strategy, and it is arguable that Gregory of Nazianzus occasionally uses the generic account as well.

Gregory of Nyssa attempted to reply to these critiques in *On Not Three Gods*. He argued that the divine nature was different from created natures. When we observe three humans acting, the most unity they can achieve is to do the same thing three times. Three lawyers can give the same speech simultaneously; three artisans can repair three different parts of the same machinery. But when the Father, Son, and Spirit do one thing, they do not repeat each other. We are not saved three times. We are saved once, by three persons. The members of the Trinity do not each do a part of the work, but the whole of it. We were not created in three parts, with each Person doing one third of the work. Instead, the persons do one literal thing. We are not created three times; we are created once with all three persons' involvement. We are not saved three times; we are saved once, with the involvement of all three persons. Each action of God "originates in the Father, is implemented by the Son, and is perfected by the Spirit."[14]

The generic account remains controversial today, and we will have reason to reexamine the Nyssen's account of divine unity in later chapters. For now, we must turn to the final member of this new Homoousian trio: Gregory of Nazianzus.

The Theologian: Gregory of Nazianzus

We know more about Gregory of Nazianzus than any other figure in the Nicene controversy, with the possible exception of Athanasius. The reason we know so much about Gregory of Nazianzus is Gregory of Nazianzus. At the end of his life, Gregory wrote an autobiographical poem that recounted his story in exquisite detail. Gregory was a masterful writer and his poem is full of his heartfelt feelings about the events of the Nicene controversy. It also contains detailed descriptions of all the ways that people wronged him (in his mind, at least). Gregory of Nazianzus was a rather dramatic fellow. He was also a profoundly pious man, and both characteristics would shape his life and the life of the Nicene Creed.

Like the other two Cappadocians, Gregory of Nazianzus was born into a minor aristocratic family. They were the most important people in his hometown, which was a small provincial city in the province. Being the most important citizen of a Cappadocian city was a bit like being the tallest of Snow White's seven dwarves—even the tallest of them was still pretty

14. Gregory of Nyssa, *Letter to Ablabius*, in *NPNF* 5.

short by others' standards. Most other aristocrats would have dismissed him as a redneck, but Gregory's aristocratic upbringing affected him deeply. He internalized the important responsibilities that his parents shouldered in society—and the many privileges that their rank afforded them. He carried a vision of himself as an aristocrat his whole life. It shaped his expectations and his sense of his own responsibility.

Once he was of appropriate age, Gregory was shipped off to school to learn all of the things that a fourth-century gentleman was supposed to know. He began his studies in Caesarea, where he encountered the writings of Origen of Alexandria. Gregory found in Origen a lifelong teacher and theological inspiration. After Caesarea, Gregory spent time in Alexandria before heading to the largest educational center in the East: Athens. Athens was the home of many of the greatest teachers of the age, especially in the arts of literature and rhetoric. It was there that Gregory would learn the skills that would equip him for any career his brilliant young mind set itself to.

There was one spiritually significant hitch: Gregory had to get to Athens first. Travel across the Mediterranean was normally smooth, but storms could arise with alarming rapidity and smash a ship to pieces. Gregory's ship was caught in a storm for twenty long days. That is a long time for anybody to be stuck in a storm. Even the most experienced sailors began to succumb to terror. With no way of escaping the storm, they turned to prayer. Even the least religious of the crew began to pray to Jesus for deliverance—which was thankfully granted.

Most terrified of all was poor Gregory. After the storm passed, everybody else got up, thanked God for answering their prayers, and got on with their day. Gregory remained prone on the floor of the ship, garments torn in terror, praying to God for safety and pledging his life to God's service. His belief that God had intervened was dramatically confirmed. One of Gregory's servants had a vision of Gregory's mother appearing through the mists and rain and dragging the boat to safety on the shore single-handedly. Gregory later talked with his mother and learned she had a dream about the storm at the exact time it was raging. Gregory took this miraculous intervention as a message from God, and spent the rest of his life serving God in the church and living an ascetic life.

Gregory studied in Athens at the same time as several other important people, including the future emperor Julian. Gregory and Julian were never friends, but Gregory reported meeting the future emperor and being deeply distressed by his impiety and lack of character. Gregory would be a fierce critic of Julian during his brief reign; Julian appears never to have thought about Gregory. Julian was part of more elite circles than Gregory would ever have frequented.

Far more influential for Gregory's life was the close friendship he came to share with Basil. It is easy to see why Basil and Gregory got along so well. They were two young men, about the same age, from the same scorned province of the empire, both passionately committed to their Christian faith. The two of them fell in with a larger group of Christian students who gathered to pray, socialize, and study.

Gregory's awe of Basil is evident when he writes about this period of his life, as is the intensity of their friendship. This only made it hurt all the more when Basil decided to leave his studies. Some students, Gregory among them, begged Basil to stay. Basil ultimately refused. Gregory thought about going along with Basil, but eventually his other friends convinced him to stay at school. He had more to learn, and few careers would have been open to him had he left. Still, the parting was heartbreaking. Basil was so incredibly important to Gregory, and he had chosen a path that Gregory would not follow.

When Gregory's studies came to an end, he returned to his hometown in Nazianzus where he decided to become a productive member of society by living in his parents' house, praying, and writing poetry. For some odd reason, the important people in his life did not find this acceptable, and Gregory was promptly pressured into ordination. First his father, who had become the bishop of the town, forced him to be ordained a priest. Ever the dramatic soul, Gregory responded by leaving town to live with a community of monks before he could even preach his first sermon. One of the members of that community happened to be his old friend Basil. He lived there in happy seclusion before being forced to return home to save his father from accusations of heresy. Gregory's father, who was not theologically educated, had apparently signed on to one of the many anti-Nicene Creeds floating about the empire in the 360s AD. Gregory returned home to restore the peace between his father and the local pro-Nicene forces. While his flock was suspicious of a priest who had left town before bothering to preach a single sermon, Gregory's exceptional skills as an orator and diplomat won their trust. Gregory also put his skills to work for Basil, and played a crucial role in Basil's election as the next bishop of Caesarea. Though Basil's departure from Athens had hurt him, the Nazianzen believed in Basil's abilities and supported his increasing prominence in the church.

That is where the trouble between them began.

Basil's newfound authority to push the Nicene cause was cut off at the knees when the emperor Valens (whom we will meet in a future chapter) split up the province of Caesarea, drastically limiting his sphere of influence.

To compensate, Basil began to create new dioceses and staffed them with clerics who would be faithful to the Nicene cause and loyal to him. Basil asked Gregory to be one such bishop. Gregory refused. Then Basil pulled some strings and pressured Gregory's father to make Gregory a bishop. Gregory agreed, though he had little choice in the matter. His father was his bishop, and he owed obedience to him. His father, in turn, was bound to Basil as the bishop of the closest metropolitan city. Their command that he become a bishop was not something that could be canonically disobeyed.

Gregory responded as he usually did: dramatically. His very first sermon as bishop criticized Basil and his father for pressuring him into this job. He preached it with both men sitting in the church. He included a few subtle digs at Basil over a big point of theological difference between them—the divinity of the Spirit. Remember that throughout his long career, Basil never used the word *homoousios* to describe the relationship between the Spirit and the Father. Gregory, on the other hand, loudly and proudly asserted that the Spirit is *homoousios* with the Father and Son from day one. And in his sermon, he made sure to mention the problems caused by the Pneumatomachoi and suggested that the church needed courageous truth-tellers to affirm the full divinity of the Spirit. Hint, hint. Basil could force him to be a bishop, but Basil could not force Gregory of Nazianzus to agree with him.

Neither could Basil force Gregory to travel to the town where he was supposed to be a bishop. The small town Basil had picked out for his friend had little to offer Gregory of Nazianzus in terms of learning, culture, or ministry opportunities. It also happened to be right on the border of Basil's territory and another bishop's. The other bishop sent hired mercenaries to seize the tithe meant for Basil and bring it to him instead. Gregory had no interest in fighting Basil's battles, and instead retreated to a monastic community to live in seclusion. Basil sent Gregory a series of increasingly angry letters demanding that he do the job he had been ordained to do; Gregory sent a series of curt replies dismissing his old friend. His father then recalled him to serve as a bishop in his hometown of Nazianzus. Gregory duly obeyed, but when his father died he told his priests that he would be going away and expected them to function in his absence. He returned to a monastic life, writing and praying.

There Gregory would have stayed, a bishop-monastic in exile, praying and nursing his hurt feelings, if he had not received a very interesting invitation. Gregory had relatives in Constantinople who procured an invitation for him to come and minister in the heart of the city. This was a daunting challenge. Ever since Eusebius of Nicomedia had come to the capital, the bishop's seat had been passed from anti-Nicene to anti-Nicene. Anti-Nicene theology was assumed to be orthodoxy by the city's religious elite. Gregory would be perceived as a radical bishop from the outlying provinces pushing a strange heretical theology on the city. He would be completely on his own.

Gregory accepted the offer and planted a small pro-Nicene church in the city that he named The Church of the Resurrection. He ministered to his parish faithfully and guided them through the scorn and persecution of the anti-Nicene majority. One Easter Sunday, tensions were so high that a mob gathered outside of Gregory's church and began to hurl stones at the congregants inside. While no one was killed, many were injured and the church itself was nearly destroyed. Gregory of Nazianzus was hauled into court and accused of fomenting the riot. He acquitted himself admirably, but it is not difficult to imagine the tension he must have felt. His theological enemies could inflict violence on him and threaten him with prison to boot. Even though Gregory avoided all legal repercussions this time, there was no guarantee that even his impressive persuasive skills would succeed in the future.

Gregory's greatest gift to the church was a set of sermons that he preached on the topic of the Trinity. Today, these sermons are known as the *Five Theological Orations,* or the *Orations* for short. They are considered to be one of the masterworks of fourth-century theology. In the Eastern Orthodox Church, Gregory of Nazianzus is honored with the title of "The Theologian," implying that he is the standard by which all other theologians are measured. These five sermons are the cornerstone of this honor.

Many of Gregory's arguments in the *Orations* are similar to those of the other Homoousians. Like them, his primary target is Eunomius, the standard-bearer for extreme anti-Nicene theology. Like them, he asserted that Eunomius erred by not respecting the limits of human knowledge about God. By doing so, Eunomius treated theology as though it were a discipline of mere logic, with rules that could be picked up and used by anyone just like one can learn the rules of addition or division. Gregory insisted that true theologians must be prepared spiritually as well as intellectually. Only by knowing God through prayer and self-denial can one hope to glimpse the truth. Interestingly enough, one common rumor about Eunomius was that he attended lavish banquets and indulged in fine foods. Gregory of Nazianzus drew an implicit contrast between his own humble life and the luxury that Eunomius enjoyed. On Gregory's standards, Eunomius's manner of life would be disqualifying for a theologian.

Gregory made several classic statements of Trinitarian theology in the *Orations*. First, Gregory attempted to answer the thorny question of how pro-Nicenes can be said to worship one God. The Nazianzen replies that monotheism does not mean that only one person is divine. The Greek word that is often translated as monotheism is *monarchia,* from which the word "monarchy" is derived. For Gregory, monotheism means there is only one *arche* (source, principle, ruler) at the heart of creation who has no rivals or superiors. Christians are not monotheists because they think that three is equal to one. Christians are monotheists because they affirm the unity, harmony, and identity of action that unites the three persons of the Trinity. Because Father, Son, and Spirit always act in perfect harmony and union with each other, God has no rivals. God's actions are always one and undivided.

Gregory states his doctrine of the Trinity as such: the Father is parent of the Son and originator of the Spirit in a "serene, non-temporal, and incorporeal way."[15] Gregory chose these adjectives to defend himself against the inevitable anti-Nicene counterarguments about the Son's begetting that we covered in the last chapter. He compared the three persons of the Trinity to three stars who produce single light between them. Just as there is one single light in between all three stars, there is one will, one power, in between the members of the Trinity.

Crucially, Gregory was clear throughout his work that the will and power that the members of the Trinity share are the Father's will and power. This is an interesting change of emphasis from Basil and Gregory of Nyssa, where the emphasis was on the generic account of divine essence or substance being the point of unity among the three persons. Gregory of Nazianzus instead emphasized that the source of unity is the Father, who generates both Son and Spirit and gives them every bit of his own power, will, and goodness. Gregory of Nazianzus's account parallels the psychological analogy we first encountered in Tertullian. In the psychological analogy, the Son was treated as the Father's self-expression that was itself a substance. In a similar way, the Nazianzen emphasized that the Son and Spirit come from the Father and are thus inseparable from him, even though they are distinct beings. While they may be three beings, they do not have separate wills from the Father. How could they? They are part of the Father's self-expression. They can no more disagree with the Father than my inner monologue can produce a thought that does not ultimately come from me.

Gregory of Nazianzus also sharpened the Homoousian account of Jesus Christ. We have already seen that one major point of contention in the Nicene controversy had to do with the different ways the Bible describes Jesus. On the one hand, Jesus talks about himself as being eternal: "Before Abraham was, I AM."[16] But on the other hand, the Bible also describes Jesus as being born of the Virgin Mary in Bethlehem at a very specific time. Gregory created a simple rule to interpret such difficulties. When you see

---

15. Gregory of Nazianzus, *Five Theological Orations*, 29.1.
16. John 8:58.

the "higher" or "loftier" titles, you apply them to Christ's divinity. When you see the "lower" or more human descriptions, those should apply to Christ as he is in the incarnation. In this case you would say that the Logos, the Second Person of the Trinity, has indeed existed from all eternity. Meanwhile, the human body and soul that were united *with* the Logos did indeed begin around December 25, 0 AD in Bethlehem.

Gregory was not content to leave this matter as a dry theological rule. Ever the poet, he burst out into praise of the wondrous mysteries of the incarnation:

> He whom presently you scorn was once transcendent, over even you. He who is presently human was incomposite. He remained what he was; what he was not, he assumed. No "because" is required for his existence in the beginning, for what could account for the existence of God? . . . Man and God blended. They became a single whole, the stronger side predominating, in order that I might be made God to the same extent that he was made man.[17]

Gregory of Nazianzus has not just given us beautiful poetry in this excerpt. He has also made a substantial advance in how we think of Christ. For Gregory, the purpose of the incarnation is not just to save humanity from hellfire. He said that humans are to be made God in exactly the way that Christ was made man. Gregory took this theme from Athanasius, who famously said God became man so that man might become god. Importantly, Gregory and Athanasius did not think that we become members of the Trinity when this happens. However, they did think that we share in God's goodness, power, and joy to such an extent that we become godlike—"divinized."

Gregory later took Athanasius's doctrine one step further by casting it into the form of a classic maxim on the incarnation: "What is not assumed is not redeemed." What Gregory meant was that in order for the incarnation to save us, Jesus had to take on every aspect of our humanity except for sin. If Jesus did not take on some part of ourselves, then that part would not be divinized. Athanasius had argued that Jesus saved us by recasting the divine image within the human being. Gregory pointed out that in order for this to work, Jesus had to be an entire human being. If Jesus had incarnated, for example, without possessing a human mind, then he would be unable

---

17. Gregory of Nazianzus, *Five Theological Orations*, 29.19. Gregory's reference to "the stronger side prevailing" is a reference to Christ's divinity controlling the destiny of Christ's life. Gregory insisted that Christ was fully human, but his divinity prevented him from falling prey to sin as other humans are wont to do.

to heal our minds. Only that which Christ has can he redeem. This rule would continue to guide christological reflections for many centuries after Gregory's death—even to the present day.

Gregory's preaching has inspired believers throughout the centuries. It did not, however, increase the size of his church. His flock remained small but faithful, hoping for the days when pro-Nicene theology might rise in the city. Their hope was difficult to hold on to, especially because they had endured an especially aggressive anti-Nicene emperor. While the pro-Nicene faction would eventually triumph, they would do so only after enduring the trials foisted upon them by the emperor Valens. To see how they fared, we must resume the historical narrative and see how this new generation navigated an increasingly hostile political terrain.

Chapter 9

Homoousian Struggle and the Blasphemy of Sirmium

As theological controversy roiled the empire, multitudes of theologians arose to solve the problems raised by the Council of Nicaea. It turns out that a seemingly simple question—is the Son *homoousios* with the Father or not?—has at least ten different answers. The Homoousians all had different rationales for their beliefs and slightly different visions of the Trinity. Anti-Nicene groups did not have a common model of the Trinity in mind at all; they were united only by their dissatisfaction with the Nicene Creed.

If your brain is tired and your eyes are weary from reading page after page of intricate theological distinctions, you are not alone. In fact, there was one person in the fourth century even more tired of all the arguing than you: the emperor Constantius II. Having endured years of ecclesiastical interference from his brothers and constantly keeping watch on the Persian armies worryingly poised on his eastern border, Constantius II was more than ready for the church's quarrels to be over. He had also recently come into possession of the whole empire. His brother Constans had been overthrown by one of his ambitious generals, and Constantius II had in turn defeated that general in battle, securing his universal dominance over the Roman Empire. Now with every bishop answerable to him, Constantius II put his thumb on the scales firmly in favor of the Homoian position.

The First Council of Sirmium

Constantius II began his attempt at imperially enforced unity in the Roman city of Sirmium, which is at the very southern tip of modern-day Serbia. The bishops chose to show their unity by repeating business that had already been settled at previous councils. (Some church tactics are eternal.) The bishops tried a notorious modalist named Photius for heresy. Photius had already been convicted four times, so it was little surprise when he was once again declared a heretic. Constantius II exiled him, presumably so that the assembled bishops would stop wasting time by re-convicting him and get on with actually productive business.

The bishops duly continued on with the next item on the agenda, which was writing yet another creed in the hopes that the other bishops of the world would accept. Their solution was to re-adopt the milquetoast fourth creed of the council of Antioch in 341 AD. In an effort to make the creed more useful, the council appended twenty-seven anathemas that had a little bit more bite. An anathema is a formal condemnation of a theological position by the church. The Greek word *anathema* (uh-NAH-thee-ma) can be translated as "accursed." Anathemas were serious business; it was the council's way of telling someone that their beliefs were not just wrong, but heretical, and that holding them would doom a person to hellfire. Some creeds in this time period (including the original Nicene Creed) began to include lists of anathemas, which were usually included at the end of the document. Typically, anathemas were written like this: "But whoever teaches X, let him be anathema." This allowed a council not merely to say what they believed, but also to clearly define what positions they found unacceptable.

The anathemas of the council of Sirmium can be divided into several varieties. Some of them just repeated the old anxieties about the materialistic connotations of *ousia* language that the Homoousians have been renouncing for thirty-six years straight. The second set of anathemas condemned certain interpretations of biblical passages that had become popular for heretics to cite in support of their position. These anathemas went a step beyond the usual protocol by not only condemning beliefs, but by condemning particular ways of reading the Bible. This did not mean that any random layperson who suggested one of these interpretations at their local Bible study was going to be excommunicated. But the anathemas did prohibit clergy from setting out certain kinds of interpretations in church.

The third type of anathema was directed at modalist theologians including Marcellus of Ancyra, that ever-useful punching bag for Nicaea's opponents. His belief that the Godhead could expand and contract was duly anathematized. Then there is the fourth type of anathema, which appears to be directed toward Athanasius. The council's creed condemned those that taught that the Son was begotten without the Father's willing to do so and those that taught the Son was *agennetos*. His theological opponents associated both these positions with Athanasius. Athanasius's insistence that the Son is proper to the Father—that the Father is not himself without the Son—could be taken to imply that the begetting of the Son was automatic and unwilling on the Father's part. And of course, the fact that Athanasius so often compared the generation of the Son to natural and automatic processes—like light coming from a star—did not help. Athanasius also had a very strong account of the Son being ingenerate like the Father. The council thought he had gone too far. They claimed Athanasius had made the Son *so* much like the Father as to make the Son *independent* of the Father—begotten from him without so much as the Father's awareness, let alone consent.

While that creed did not become the rallying cry of church unity that the council had hoped, it did signal that bishops were ready to move away from the Nicene Creed if they could find a creed that more bishops would agree with. Constantius II was all too eager to effect that unity, and began to strong-arm the bishops of the West, newly under his control, into signing some kind of doctrinal statement. While we are not quite certain what this doctrinal statement said (it is one of the vast majority of ancient documents annoyingly lost to history), it was probably in line with what the Homoian party would have liked: a short affirmation that the Son and the Father are alike with no mention of their substances. Constantius thought this simple document could unite the empire—and was prepared to exile any bishop who refused to sign onto it.

Imperial Pressure and Episcopal Spite

All of this came to a head in incredibly dramatic fashion in Milan in 355 AD. Constantius II, now reliably established as the emperor of the whole Roman Empire and enjoying a brief period of peace, gathered all the Roman clergy in another council. He presented the bishops with a single task: to sign a condemnation of Athanasius of Alexandria. Constantius II had finally had enough of the old Homoousian troublemaker and was ready to not only exile him, but cut off his base of support in Rome. With the wily old Alexandrine out of the way, Constantius II would have removed one of the most prominent opponents of his desired doctrinal solution.

He might have gotten away with it, too, if he had known about Robert's Rules of Order.

Robert's Rules of Order is a set of instructions for running meetings that is as helpful as it is painfully boring to read. Robert's Rules are used to run everything from the United States House of Representatives to church council meetings. One of the most important principles of Robert's Rules is a limit on the number of people who are allowed to bring up new business for the meeting to consider.

Unfortunately for this frustrated emperor, he had not considered implementing Robert's Rules of Order in his church councils, probably because they were not invented until 1,500 years after his death. It cost him dearly. Constantius II's attempts to strong-arm bishops had made him some enemies. One of those enemies was about to exploit the fact that he was allowed to bring up new business.

A particularly spiteful bishop[1] took the floor of the council and agreed to condemn Athanasius, on one little condition. After all, there were heretics afoot, and the faith needed to be protected. He then presented a copy of the Nicene Creed and asked everyone present to sign it. Once they were all on the same page about their own theological commitments, they could deal with the matter of Athanasius. The assembled bishops, who were mostly pro-Nicene, duly lined up to sign the Nicene Creed until one Heteroousian bishop dove across the stage, knocked the pen out of the signing bishop's hand, and yelled, "You can't do that here!"

The situation devolved from there.

After much shouting and many breaches of decorum, the bishops eventually went to the imperial palace to get the emperor's word on the matter. The emperor reminded the bishops that their job was to condemn Athanasius without getting distracted by other matters. If they would just sign the condemnation, they were free to go. If not, he had an order of exile prepared for each and every one of them that he was happy to sign. By and large, the bishops caved to his pressure. Athanasius was condemned by the majority, and the small minority that had refused to condemn him were exiled, including the bishop who had begun the commotion.

Constantius II's actions represent the height of imperial meddling in church affairs thus far in the Nicene saga. There is a popular myth that Constantine was the great meddler in church affairs. As we have already seen, that is not true. While Constantine called the Council of Nicaea, he did

---

1. The bishop in question was Lucifer of Cagliari, who hated Constantius II for his support of anti-Nicene theologies, even calling him the antichrist! Amazingly, Constantius II did not exile Lucifer for this slander. Lucifer continued to write against Constantius II, and even wrote a book called *On Apostate Kings* directed against the emperor and written with a level of vitriol that would make sociopaths blush. If talk therapy had been invented, Lucifer would have been a prime candidate for it.

not personally insist that the word *homoousios* be used, and he recalled its detractors from exile on the flimsiest of pretexts. Constantius II was much more interested in picking theological winners and losers, and exiled many more bishops than his father. Moreover, he intervened almost exclusively in favor of the anti-Nicenes. Whatever the reasons the Nicene Creed eventually won out, it is not because it enjoyed more imperial favor than its rivals. Its most successful interpreters are those who persisted in spite of imperial opposition.

Alexandria Riots Again

With Athanasius officially condemned, the next step was his removal from Alexandria. This would not be easy. Athanasius was hugely popular with the citizens of Alexandria. He had been a fixture of the Alexandrine church for almost five decades at this point. His people loved him as a pastor, and the poor of the city relied on his generosity with the imperial gifts to sustain themselves. Neither did it hurt that Athanasius was on very good terms with the Egyptian monks, who had their own ascetic charisma. So when Constantius II sent a notary to remove him from the city, matters became rather complicated. Notaries are typically not a forceful bunch, and this particular notary only had a handful of troops with him. He tried to attack Athanasius at the church where he was working. However, Athanasius's parishioners delayed the troops long enough for the old bishop to escape.

Next, the regional governor showed up to enforce the order. He had more than enough troops to get the job done, and the bishop fled the city. But if he had to leave, the Alexandrines were not leaving his memory behind. They occupied churches and resisted the governor's forces for six months. The regional governor was removed,[2] and a new governor was appointed who brought even more troops to Alexandria and kicked the local resisters out of their churches. These were dark days. The new troops began a reign of terror and abused the populace with impunity. In response to this, Alexandrines sympathetic to Athanasius attacked the new, imperially-appointed bishop during worship. He escaped, successfully avoiding becoming the next victim of religious violence in the Nicene saga.

Having become something of an expert at living in exile, Athanasius decided to wait out his most recent one with the monks in the Egyptian desert. When an emperor has sent a whole army to find and capture you, it

---

2. Probably for his complete inability to take control of his capital city and force a bunch of angry parishioners out of their churches. The hapless villains of the *Home Alone* movie series would have done better.

really helps to have a bunch of friends who can offer you their desert cave as a hideout. It also helps when those friends have a reputation for holiness and miracle-working such that the average Roman soldier might be nervous about attacking them. Perhaps Constantius II was content to let Athanasius remain in hiding so long as he was exiled; perhaps he had no knowledge of his whereabouts. Either way, Athanasius was able to survive this exile as he had his previous ones.

The Blasphemy

He would not survive it comfortably, however. For the next year would bring a second council of Sirmium, attended by a smaller group of Nicene-skeptical bishops attempting to produce a creed to replace its hated Nicene antecedent. The Homoousians would come to refer to this council's creed as the blasphemy of Sirmium. The blasphemy read as follows:

> Therefore there is one God of all, as the apostle taught, and the rest [of the Scriptures] agree and can contain no ambiguity. But as for the fact that some, or many, are concerned about substance, which is called ousia in Greek, that is, to speak more explicitly, homoousion[3] . . . there should be no mention of it whatsoever, nor should anyone preach it. And this is the cause and reason, that it is not included in the divine Scriptures, and it is beyond man's knowledge, nor can anyone declare the birth of the Son, as it is written on this subject (Isaiah 53:8). For it is clear that only the Father knows how he begot his Son, and the Son how he was begotten by the Father. There is no uncertainty about the Father being greater: it cannot be doubted by anyone that the Father is greater in honor, in dignity, in glory, in majesty in the very name of "Father," for he himself witnesses. And nobody is unaware that this is catholic doctrine, that there are two Persons of the Father and the Son, and that the Father is greater, and the Son is subjected in common with all the things which the Father subjected to him; that the Father has no beginning, is invisible, immortal and impassible; but that the Son is born from the Father, God from God, Light from Light, whose generation as Son, as has been said already, no one knows except

---

3. You may notice that this creed refers to *homoousion* rather than *homoousios*. They are the same word. In Greek, the endings of a word change to indicate its role in a sentence; think of how we might say, "who gave this gift?" and "to whom should I give this gift?" The concept is the same in Greek. Whether you see *homoousion* or *homoousios,* just know that they are referring to the same thing.

the Father; and that the Son of God himself our Lord and God, as it is said, assumed flesh or body, that is man from the womb of the Virgin Mary, as the angel foretold.[4]

The blasphemy of Sirmium proved to be a turning point in the Nicene controversy. It was the apex of the Homoian school's power, and emblematic of Constantius II's attempts to resolve the controversy by short-circuiting the endless *ousia* debates. In the blasphemy of Sirmium, bishops declared that they were simply not going to talk about the *ousia* of God. God's very being would be off-limits for the faithful attempting to praise God in the churches. They should confine themselves to biblical language in worship, acknowledge the Son was glorious but inferior to the Father, and move on.

The Homoousians would not move on, however. The blasphemy of Sirmium became a rallying cry for their side. The creed of Sirmium denigrated the Son by all but denying his substantial equality with the Father. Moreover, the Homoousians believed that the Bible had revealed the Word to be *homoousios* with the Father. For overseers of the church to ignore those statements and instead go on and on about how the Word is inferior to the Father was insulting—blasphemous, even. There is also a political reason why Sirmium was such a rallying cry for the Homoousians. It was the first time in the controversy that a council had directly contradicted Nicaea's creed. Other creeds had been critical of Nicaea, but that they expressed that criticism through conspicuous silence and quiet avoidance of *ousia* language. The blasphemy of Sirmium was the first to say that *homoousios* was an outright mistake. They were not just blaspheming God; they were disregarding the wisdom of the bishops who had met just one generation before them.

In the wreckage of their defeat at Sirmium, the Homoousians began to formulate an idea that would survive for seventeen centuries and counting—that Nicaea itself was the decisive council at which the bishops had attained unity. The job of the present bishops was to respect that consensus. For the pro-Nicenes, the consensus the church sought was to be found in the past, not the future. Bishops did not have to call a council to create a new, perfect creed. They merely needed to gather and declare fealty to the creed that had already been set forth. Many churches today regard assent to the Nicene Creed as a requirement for true Christianity, and that idea began here.

The Homoousians were not the only ones outraged by the council at Sirmium. Many Nicene-skeptical bishops felt that it went too far in its subjection of the Son to the Father. Constantius II reasoned that if he could

---

4. "Second Creed of Sirmium," *NPNF* 2:446.

broker a compromise between the Homoians of Sirmium and the Nicene-skeptical bishops, he could finally resolve the issue. In practice, that meant that he mostly courted Homoiousians. Radical Heteroousians like Aetius and Eunomius would never compromise, but their disapproval seemed an acceptable price to pay. Athanasius and the other Homoousians were unlikely to come around, but given that Constantius II had just chased their senior spokesperson into exile in a desert, he seems not to have been overly concerned about their opinions.

The Drama of the Dated Creed

Having now tried and failed to impose creedal uniformity on the church multiple times, Constantius II decided that he needed to try again, but with more planning. So he called a "pre-council" in 359 AD composed of theological experts to draft a creed that everyone could agree to. This creed is called the Dated Creed, because it was the only creed that actually included its date in the title. It was much more moderate in its eschewal of *ousia* language than the blasphemy of Sirmium. The assembled bishops thought this would be acceptable to most parties, and so the emperor, who must have been very tired at this point, called a pair of councils, one in the East and one in the West, to ratify the Dated Creed.

Neither went according to plan.

The council of Seleucia, in modern-day south-central Turkey, was riven with controversy from the start. It was actually supposed to be held in Nicomedia, but a massive earthquake had recently hit the city, destroying multiple churches and killing a few clergy in the area. Those are not the kinds of acts of God that church staff like to precede their meetings, so they moved to Seleucia. In their new environment, an earthquake would be the least of their problems. Some bishops wanted to write a new creed instead of using the Dated Creed; some got into fights over who could be seated at the council while trials against them were ongoing; and all of them fought over the turbulent question of *ousia* language. Eventually the council dissolved itself without coming to any conclusions. Two quarreling sets of deputies were sent to the emperor, who must have been wondering if there was *any* force on earth that could get these bishops to agree.

He would soon have a chance to try. The Council of Ariminum (modern-day Rimini, Italy) in the West ran longer. There were about four hundred bishops in total, at least eighty of which were firmly in favor of the Dated Creed. They were unable to persuade the rest of the conference to agree with them, however, and so the emperor's prized creed was rejected by the majority. Proving that sore losers are not a modern phenomenon, the minority simply refused to agree that the majority had carried the day. Both groups commissioned sets of delegates to go tell emperor Constantius II that their side had won.

The emperor was not happy. He had called two councils to achieve one unanimous decision. Now he had four quarreling parties at his doorstep. It was time for him to put his hand on the scale more decisively. After receiving the pro-Nicene delegation, Constantius II moved them to a small town called Nike.[5] As a final gambit for unity, Constantius II concocted a master plan that apparently hinged on the fact that Nike sounds like Nicaea.

As much as that last sentence sounds like something I made up, I promise you it is not. Constantius II's master plan went something like this. Once the pro-Nicene delegation got to Nike, he then sent a delegate to the main council at Ariminum to persuade them to just sign the Dated Creed like the emperor wanted. Meanwhile, Constantius II cornered the pro-Nicene delegation at Nike and got them to sign the Dated Creed. Of course the Dated Creed was anti-Nicene, but since they were signing it at Nike, Constantius II advertised it as a "Nicene" creed and hoped that the crowd would assume he meant the creed of 325 AD. It was a way of giving the pro-Nicene bishops a chance to get onboard with his program while maintaining plausible deniability. The bait and switch would not have passed muster with anyone even halfway informed about the controversy. However, Constantius II was also making it very clear that those who would not sign on were likely to get exiled. Slowly, the threat of exile got everyone onboard: first the Nike delegation, then the council at Ariminum, and then finally the council at Seleucia.

At least, that is how it seemed to the untrained observer. The councils did indeed pass the Dated Creed, but with a few key modifications. The Dated Creed described the Son as being like the Father in all respects, which satisfied the Homoiousians. After all, if the Son and Father are alike in all respects, then that includes their *ousia*. However, this crucial clause was not included in the modified Dated Creed passed by one of the councils. Of course, the modification caused significant confusion in the empire when multiple versions of the same creed began to circulate. The Homoians struck a victory over their Homoiousian counterparts, but at the cost of the unity that the emperor had been so insistent upon.

---

5. Nike was named for an ancient Greek goddess of victory. The modern-day athletic shoe company of the same name draws on this same etymology. Perhaps Constantius II would have had better luck getting the bishops onboard if he could have offered them free sneakers in exchange for their support.

The church's constant infighting is especially remarkable in the face of imperial pressure. Some Christians assume that when the church becomes involved in the affairs of government, church leaders will inevitably bow to the whims of authorities. However, that is only partially true. Constantius II was able to wield some influence over the bishops; he could force them to come to a council, and his constant threats of exile did produce some results. Yet his power had limits. The bishops knew full well that Constantius did not particularly care about (and likely did not have the theological education[6] to understand) the intricate, complex differences between their theologies. They had no qualms about modifying the emperor's explicit instructions to pursue their own theological agendas. Moreover, the bishops believed they were discussing something of inexpressible importance: the very nature of the Holy Trinity. Praising God was the heart of the Christian life. If they failed to accurately express God's being, then they had fundamentally failed to be the church. In the face of that pressure, many bishops insisted on defending the doctrine of God as they knew it, even in the face of imperial pressure.

Christianity and the Apostate

Constantius II was about to have much bigger problems than the eternally quarrelsome church. In 360 AD, the Persian Empire launched one of its many invasions of the Eastern Roman Empire. Constantius II mustered his troops and began the long march to stop the invaders. However, his real enemies were not the invading Persians. The Roman emperor was about to be laid low by foes inside his lands and inside his body.

You may remember from chapter 6 that Constantius II purged the family tree to avoid splitting the empire with other male relatives. Only a few of his male relatives survived the purge. The most consequential survivor was a young man named Julian. A scholar by nature, Julian studied in Athens at the same time as Basil and Gregory of Nazianzus. Unlike the two Cappadocian fathers, Julian left his studies to take up politics. Constantius

---

6. The question of the Roman emperors' grasp of Christian theology is somewhat open for interpretation. Constantine seems to have had a rather shallow understanding of theology; the few documents we have that are undoubtedly written by him are fairly unsophisticated in their approach. His sons were tutored in religion, and so probably had a stronger grasp of the subject. However, they also had to be tutored in all the other affairs of state: economics, legislation, military effectiveness, history, etc. I assume that even if they had a reasonable knowledge of the basics of Christian theology, they were nowhere close to the depth of knowledge that church leaders and teachers could acquire.

II named him a Caesar at age twenty-four, much to the young man's dismay. Julian stated throughout his life that he felt like being a Caesar was a death sentence. Julian was thrust into the limelight and forced to make all sorts of important decisions that could get him executed for treason if he incurred the emperor's wrath. Traumatized by the childhood murder of most of his family, Julian lived in fear that Constantius II might decide it was time for another purge if he upset his cousin. But he resigned himself to his fate, and resolved that if he had to be a Caesar, he would put all his effort into it. He turned out to be quite good at being an emperor, administering the empire competently and successfully defeating some of the marauding tribes that threatened its lands.

Julian won the respect and loyalty of his troops. In fact, he had so much respect that when Constantius II summoned his troops to assist in repelling the Persian invasion, many of them refused. Julian's troops were stationed in modern-day France, and were not particularly keen to give up their nice climate to march into a sandy Syrian desert and risk death by exhaustion, thirst, or getting their head lopped by a Persian soldier. The soldiers vastly preferred Julian to the distant Constantius II. They also knew that Julian had almost been killed by his cousin when he was young. As dissatisfaction and rumor mongering grew, the troops took a dangerous, fate-defining step: they hailed Julian as an Augustus, and not just a Caesar. We are not entirely certain if Julian orchestrated this event; there is some evidence to suggest that he did, but it is not conclusive. In either case, there was no turning back. Julian was convinced that Constantius II would never forgive him for what his troops had done. Julian took his army and began to march into his cousin's territory. He had seen what Constantius II had done to usurpers. He was not going to wait for the rebel-crusher to make the first strike.

The feared strike would never come. During his campaign against the Persians, Constantius II fell gravely ill. With a rebellion in the empire and an infection in his body, Constantius II knew he was not long for the world. As he neared the end, he made a choice that would change the fate of the empire forever. He named Julian as his sole heir and the Augustus of the empire.

Emperors typically do not name those who have rebelled against them as their heirs. However, the circumstances were highly unusual. The way he saw it, the empire had no clear successor if he died. His only child was a daughter. Thanks to the purge he had orchestrated, Constantius II had no other male relatives besides Julian. If he did not recognize the rebel as his heir, a bloody power struggle was sure to ensue. So Constantius II did the only thing he felt he could. He acknowledged Julian's claim to be Augustus.

Julian's reign proved shocking in many ways. For the purpose of our story, the most significant change he brought was due to the fact that Julian was not a Christian. As a victim of the purges in the Christian household of Constantine, Julian knew firsthand that the church was no stranger to hypocrisy and violence. Moreover, Julian had been a disciple of some of the most influential pagan philosophers of the day. He sought to renew the Empire's faith in the ancient gods of the Roman pantheon. In order to do so, he would have to destroy Constantine's Christian empire.

Julian knew that he could not accomplish his aims by persecuting the church. He had grown up on the stories of the Great Persecution, and believed that explicit persecution would only give the church more moral authority and sympathy. Furthermore, by the time of Julian's reign Christianity had been the state religion for almost four decades. Every administrator who remembered the old pagan order was either dead or well into retirement. Julian had no established pagan religious bureaucracy to empower, and no cadres of ready-made pagan administrators to run his empire. Instead, he quietly sidelined the church where possible. He moved Christians out of powerful positions. He re-legalized the pagan rites and attended them frequently. And when the quarreling bishops fought with each other and called each other heretics, Julian sat back, laughed, and let them bicker.

Constantius II's imperial policy of forced unity was out the window. Julian didn't want Christianity to prosper, he wanted it to wither. The more the church fought, the more likely that was to happen. Paradoxically, this proved a useful reprieve for the Homoousians. Bishops who dissented from the Homoian victory had freedom to continue ministering and working. With no emperor pressuring the church to unify, they could continue arguing their case to the faithful.

Still Julian's reign did not mean that all was well and good for the plucky, hard-pressed defenders of Nicaea. When Constantius died, Julian had signed a decree allowing all exiled bishops to return home. That meant Athanasius, well into his third exile, could happily return home. And then a letter arrived from Julian stating that when he allowed *all* bishops to return, that did not include Athanasius. The petulant, persecuted promulgator of Nicaea was pushed out of his city yet again to begin his fourth exile. Athanasius retreated to the desert. His monastic friends would not have even had time to repurpose the spare cave he had been sleeping in.

Julian's ambitions were vast. He was not merely content to drive popular bishops into exile and let the church wallow in controversy. He learned from his religious enemies and attempted to build a pagan structure to rival them. One of the largest sources of the church's appeal was its charity program. Christian churches were places where all people, whether believers or not, could receive help and succor. Christian charity attracted more people to the church; it also gave people an avenue of social support that was not directly connected to the imperial hierarchy. Julian began to envisage a parallel system of pagan charity that would ultimately flow down from the emperor—who was ultimately responsible for the welfare of *all* the citizens in the empire, and who could encourage them to worship the traditional Roman gods as he did.

He would never get the chance to see his vision made real. Just two years into his reign, Julian was struck down in battle against the Persian forces that Constantius II had been attempting to repel. With him died the vision of a pagan empire. The church, once again favored in imperial politics, would resume its quest for a unified understanding of the Trinity. As they moved forward, the seemingly indomitable Homoians would lose ground even when the emperors favored them. The Cappadocians began to take the stage, and the first glimmers of light appeared at the far end of the tunnel of controversy.

Chapter 10

Religion After Julian

WITH JULIAN'S DEATH IN 363 AD, the reign of the house of Constantine came to an abrupt end. The dynasty that had dictated Roman life for four decades would never again rule the Roman Empire. However, Constantine's religious legacy would live on despite Julian's best efforts to undo it. After decades of consistent imperial favor, Christianity enjoyed the support of so many officials and military officers that there were simply no pagan contenders for the imperial crown when Julian passed away. Instead, Julian was succeeded by Christian emperors who were more than happy to undo his religious reforms.

The Crisis of Succession

However, it would take some time for a new emperor to lodge a stable claim on the throne. The first successor was a man named Jovian, who had served as Julian's bodyguard—hardly the kind of political pedigree one would expect for the leader of the Roman world. Jovian apparently had the trust of the troops, however, as they quickly recognized him as the empire's new Augustus. He quickly got to work. He ended the conflict with Persia that had just claimed Julian's life by suing for peace and giving the Persians everything they had hoped to gain in the war. Jovian marched back to Constantinople to claim his title and organize the empire. While en route, Jovian revoked most of Julian's religious decrees. He did not outlaw paganism or tear down the temples that Julian had rebuilt. Religious tolerance would be the order of the day. But since Christians were already entrenched in positions of power, removing the barriers to their access effectively gave them the upper hand in political affairs. In fact, there are records of court officials who had converted to paganism under Julian's reign and reconverted to Christianity under Jovian's. Many administrators simply wanted to know which way the wind was blowing and follow it. Jovian also ended Athanasius's exile and apparently met with the stubborn bishop in person, who gave the new emperor a copy of the Nicene Creed and begged him not to let the Arians get away with their heresy.

Jovian had little opportunity to enforce his decrees, however, because he reigned for slightly longer than it will take you to read this chapter. He died en route to the capital in what appears to be a renovating accident. One night Jovian was sleeping in a bedchamber that had just been repainted. The room had a brazier that Jovian kept lit, and its fire created enough paint fumes that Jovian died from inhaling them as he slept. Jovian was one of many emperors to gain the throne through the military; he was the only one to lose it due to his taste in home decor. The imperial throne was vacant once again.

The next emperor of all Rome was Jovian's brother, Valentinian. Valentinian was a military officer who spent a fair bit of time in exile during Julian's reign. Two different accounts are told about his exile. One is that Valentinian had the bad luck to be the commander of a military operation that went awry and wound up taking the fall for it. The other is that a pagan temple attendant accidentally sprinkled Valentinian with some holy water, which offended him. He supposedly muttered, "I am not purified but defiled!" and punched the poor attendant in the face. The pagan emperor Julian had a strict no-punching-pagan-temple-attendants-in-the-face policy, and consequently exiled the pugnacious Valentinian. Whatever the truth of the situation was, his exile was short-lived and he was in the army with Julian again by the time of his fateful campaign against the Persians.

Valentinian enjoyed broad support for his rule largely by virtue of being acceptable to most of the Roman hierarchy. He was competent (which officials and administrators loved), his first loyalty was to the army (which the army loved), he was a pious Christian (which the bishops loved), and he was willing to compromise (which did not make his enemies love him, but did make him more palatable to them). However, his willingness to compromise had limits. While shoring up support for his imperial bid, Valentinian had to agree to name a co-Augustus. Having a co-Augustus as Diocletian had originally intended would prevent the problems of the last decade from recurring. No doubt Constantine, Constantius II, and Julian had enjoyed their supreme authority. However, when the empire's sole Augustus died, it threw everything into complete disarray. So Valentinian was required by his allies to name a co-Augustus. Valentinian promptly named his younger brother Valens. Valens had no real credentials to speak of other than being the emperor's brother, and hence someone whose loyalty to Valentinian was not in doubt.[1] Valentinian may have been willing to compromise, but he would brook no rivals to his authority. Valentinian would reign as Augustus of the West, and Valens would take the East.

With the rapid successions of the past few years mostly settled, the emperors could get down to the business of fending off Rome's military enemies. Valens trotted off to the northern frontier to defeat the Germanic tribes, then off to the eastern frontier to lose against the Persians. (He did manage to avoid getting killed by the Persians while losing to them, much to the relief of his soldiers). Valentinian put down raids and revolts on the Rhine River, then headed off to the northwest to put down raids from the Scots and Picts, and then sent troops to the southwest to put down raids on North African holdings. The empire was never *really* at peace, but its armies were strong enough and its leaders competent enough to keep the frontier tensions manageable.

Religion Under Valentinian and Valens

During their many military activities, both emperors found time to weigh in on questions of religion, albeit in very different ways. Valentinian appears to have been broadly sympathetic to the Nicene Creed and the Homoousians, but mostly took a hands-off approach to religious conflicts. Shortly after he was made emperor, a bunch of bishops asked him to summon a big council to decide controversial matters of faith, including the Nicene Creed. Valentinian replied that he was just a layman and was not going to meddle in the bishop's business. They could have a council if they wanted to organize it, but he would not be the one to call it.

This is a really remarkable change in the relationship between emperor and church. You may remember from chapter 3 that Constantine saw himself as the head of the bishops. He was their commander and superior, and it was his job to marshal them together in order to maintain a unity in worship and doctrine that would safeguard the empire's political unity. Constantius II continued his father's legacy, and had no qualms using his imperial power to enforce his desired outcome. Valentinian was articulating a very different vision. Church controversy was the bishops' business, and they needed to

---

1. Or at least Valentinian assumed his brother's loyalty was never in question. A closer look at the history of Constantine's sons might have given him reason to worry.

handle it without getting the emperor involved. He was not a bishop and did not presume to dictate their doctrines to them.[2]

Valentinian was interested in rooting out corruption, however, and he found some of it had seeped into the church. Bishops of important cities were often plied by wealthy nobles and rich widows, and found that they could become exceedingly wealthy by courting such favors. In fact, the bishop of Rome had so much wealth that his banquets were often more lavish than the emperor's! Where there is wealth, there is often conflict, and such was the case in Rome. In one case when an election for the bishop of Rome was disputed, the conflict grew so fierce that 137 people died in a riot in the middle of church. Valentinian did not approve of such violence, and worried that it was a consequence of men of God gathering so much personal wealth. He prohibited clerics from receiving personal gifts from widows to stem the tide of corruption and violence. Yet even without those gifts, the wealth of bishops increased.

Valentinian's religious legacy was one of moderation. His reign was good for the pro-Nicenes because the majority of bishops in the Western Empire were pro-Nicene, and they could worship and plan without interference. However, he did not actively help their cause because he stayed out of religious conflicts where possible, only intervening when necessary to respond to corruption and vice.

Valens took a more active approach to religious matters. He was also not nearly as fond of the Nicene Creed—or its supporters—as his brother. After Athanasius returned to Alexandria, relieved by the end of his fourth exile, he got a letter from Valens announcing that he was banished yet again. Valens had decided to reinstate all the exiles of Constantius II that had been canceled by Jovian. Athanasius, thoroughly sick of this constant coming and going, packed his bags and went into exile a grand total of two miles away from the city. You see, the order of exile prevented Athanasius from being in Alexandria. It laid out no conditions on how far away he had to be. So Athanasius set up shop in a little cottage just outside of Alexandria's city limits. It is a bold move to obey the letter of an order and not the spirit, especially when the order comes from the Roman emperor who could have you killed just for irritating him. But Athanasius was quite done with all the running

---

2. Although it is tempting to see Valentinian as a precursor of modern liberal democracies in which there is a presumed separation between religious authority and the state, it is unlikely Valentinian had anything like a separation of powers in mind. Valentinian declined to decide matters of doctrine for the bishops, but he was still more than happy to pass laws concerning bishops' behavior, favored and disfavored religions, etc. Valentinian simply chose not to be involved in matters where he saw no pressing need for his intervention.

around. Valens, knowing full well the Alexandrines' habit of rioting when emperors tried to force new bishops on them, eventually issued a special letter ending Athanasius's exile. He would return to his city and finally, after five exiles, have some peace and quiet.

The Cappadocians would not have the same luck as Athanasius when dealing with Valens. Shortly after Basil became the bishop of Caesarea, Valens unilaterally cut the diocese in half, quickly reducing Basil's prominence. In fairness to Valens, his decision was driven by political concerns; he was probably not scheming to reduce the power of one particular bishop. However, Valens definitely favored anti-Nicene theologians. When he had the opportunity to install bishops, he made sure they were in line with his preferences. When the Heteroousian-allied bishop of Constantinople died, the pro-Nicene minority in Constantinople immediately nominated a candidate for the office. Valens promptly exiled him so he would not get in the way of the anti-Nicene bishop the emperor favored. When Athanasius passed away, Valens did the same thing in Alexandria, running the bishop's handpicked successor out of town. He also sent a bunch of the monks and clergy of Alexandria who were presumed loyal to Athanasius to do forced labor in the mines, clearing out some of the old guard that might have resisted their new imperially backed bishop. Valens also had a habit of taking clergy he disliked and naming them to the *curiales*, an elite group of citizens who were considered the leading men of their city. While that sounds like an honor, being in the *curiales* significantly increased one's taxes, which proved to be a particularly effective deterrent for money-conscious clergy.

Several important bishops resisted Valens's anti-Nicene maneuvers, but none did so with more flair than Basil. During one of the emperor's several attempts to force his bishops to sign onto an anti-Nicene creed, Valens sent a high-ranking official to strong-arm Basil into compliance. The official made it very clear to Basil how important it was to remain in the emperor's favor, and mentioned that it would be a shame indeed if Basil were to remain on the wrong side of the dispute. Basil chastised the man for his threats and made it plain that his position would not change. The official, shocked at his boldness, muttered that no one had ever spoken to him in that way before. Basil replied, "Perhaps you have never spoken with a bishop before."

The official scurried back to Valens with his tail between his legs, and the emperor's favored creed did not carry the day. But he remembered Basil's boldness, and would later volunteer the bishop for a dangerous and difficult diplomatic mission to the kingdom of Armenia as payback for his resistance. Basil attempted to perform his diplomatic work well, but Armenia was a political minefield, forever caught between the influence of Rome and Persia. His work with the churches there burdened him for the rest of his life.

However, Basil was not the target of the greatest crisis the Homoousian party would face under Valens. Ironically enough, their greatest crisis may not have been the emperor's fault at all. During his reign, a large delegation of pro-Nicene clergy came to meet Valens and attempted to persuade him that the Nicene Creed was an orthodox statement of the faith. They also asked him to recall many of their exiled clergy, and to perhaps consider exiling fewer of them in the future.

They would never get their chance.

Valens refused to meet with the group and sent a boat to take them home. The boat caught fire mid-journey, and every single member of the delegation died.

We simply do not have enough information to know if this was a deliberate tactic or an awfully timed accident. But for most of those advocating for Nicaea, who had already had enough of Valens's heavy-handed tactics, there was no doubt this was a deliberate escalation of his war against orthodox doctrine. Gregory of Nazianzus, in typically dramatic fashion, wrote an oration savaging Valens for his brutal murder of faithful clerics who were trying to protect the true doctrine. Many Homoousians felt the same way as Gregory, and Valens would go down in church history as a brutal murderer of the faithful.

Searching for a Synod

Fortunately for the pro-Nicenes, Valens was a busy man, and his time was mostly spent dealing with the significant military threats to the empire: the Persians to his east and the Germanic tribes to his north. That gave the Homoousians in his territory time to organize a response, coordinating with their allies across the empire.

No one was more instrumental in this work than Basil of Caesarea. Basil spent most of his career attempting to create alliances with like-minded bishops. His dream was to call new church councils to overrule the disastrous councils that had taken place under the reign of Constantius II.

He faced significant obstacles to his work. While Basil wrote many letters to Athanasius attempting to gain the patriarch's support, Athanasius never wrote back to Basil. It is a truly remarkable fact of history that even as Athanasius was also trying to build a pro-Nicene consensus, he refused to work with another great supporter of his cause. To understand why, we need to return to the city of Antioch.

Antioch has been in a long-simmering feud since just after the council of Nicaea. You may remember that Eustathius of Antioch was kicked out of his bishopric after making some unfortunate comments about the Emperor Constantine's mother shortly after the council. Ever since then, the city's churches had been divided. There was a remnant of Christians who were loyal to Eustathius and refused to recognize his replacement. When Eustathius died, these loyalists elected their own bishop, who was not recognized by imperial officials. Thus there were always dueling bishops vying for the allegiance of Antioch's citizenry, and different parts of the Empire often recognized different candidates.

By the 360s AD, the imperially backed bishop was a man named Meletius of Antioch. Meletius appears to have been originally allied with the moderate wing of the Homoian party, but quickly became allied with no one due to his tremendous talent for annoying everyone. He preached a sermon shortly after his consecration that caused the Homoians to think he had deserted them to become a Homoousian. Meanwhile, Homoousians thought he was simply equivocating and not worth their time. The emperor promptly exiled him for his trouble. Ever the peacemaker and bridge-builder, Basil stood by Meletius. Basil apparently saw him as a kindred spirit, albeit one with a knack for putting his foot in his mouth.[3] Meanwhile Athanasius supported a different figure who had the support of Eustathius's lost flock, a man by the name of Paulinus.

You might think this is a trivial matter to anyone outside of Antioch. On the contrary, few matters were of greater consequence. Antioch was one of the four biggest cities in the empire, rivaled only by Rome, Constantinople, and Alexandria. The bishop of Antioch controlled a huge amount of territory, and was therefore of enormous consequence. Both Athanasius and Basil knew that whoever was bishop of Antioch would have the ability to tip the scales of doctrinal controversy in one direction or another; Athanasius apparently decided that if they could not agree on that question, they had nothing more to say to each other.

Athanasius was thus not an ally in Basil's campaign. He became even less of an option after 373 AD, when Athanasius died. Athanasius's death was perhaps the most surprising thing about his life, because it was the one thing his life had never been—peaceful. The champion of orthodoxy who had spent his life arguing with Ariomaniacs and enduring eternal exile at the hands of emperors died serenely, at home in his bed, surrounded by

---

3. There is probably a parallel between Basil's relationship with Meletius and Athanasius's relationship with Marcellus of Ancyra. Both figures stood by a problematic figure they perceived to be misunderstood. How ironic that Athanasius was not able to recognize the similarity between the two situations.

sympathetic friends and clergy. Athanasius was a fighter, and his personality appears to have been an acquired taste for many of his contemporaries. How remarkable that after fighting for so long and enduring so much, Athanasius was granted a moment of earthly peace before passing into an eternal one.

With Athanasius gone, Basil had to turn to his other potential ally: Damasus, bishop of Rome. Damasus was a vocal and stalwart champion of Nicaea. There was just one problem: Basil could not stand him. He regarded Damasus as an insufferably arrogant know-nothing. Damasus, for his part, simply could not understand why Basil would not recognize his authority as the bishop of Rome, the heir to Peter, and therefore obviously Basil's superior. The Nicene controversy is one occasion among many in which we see this dynamic repeated: the bishop of Rome assumes that he has the last word on matters of church doctrine and law, while other bishops see him as a powerful and influential figure, but one with no more inherent authority than any other bishop of a major city. The disagreement lives on in the division between Roman Catholics and all other Christians.

Basil and Damasus struggled over the question of Antioch as Basil and Athanasius had. Athanasius's handpicked successor bishop was Peter of Alexandria. As you may remember from a few paragraphs above, Peter inherited Athanasius's habit of being persecuted by emperors, and Valens removed him from Alexandria by force. Peter fled to the only place he knew he would be safe: Rome. He became an advisor to Damasus, and Peter held Basil in the same suspicion Athanasius had. Peter slowly but surely turned Damasus against Basil. Damasus decided to test Basil's orthodoxy by sending him a statement of faith and instructing him to sign it without changing a single word.

Basil responded with a letter in which he declined the request. His letter was written with all the niceties and gentle turns of phrase one would expect from a well-educated aristocrat, but his message was clear. Basil had been fighting for Nicaea longer than Damasus. If Damasus thought he could install himself as the singular judge of Basil's (or any other bishop's) orthodoxy, then he was in for a very rude surprise.

Basil's refusal brought things to a standstill. A year later Basil's old Homoiousian mentor Eustathius of Sebaste was exiled,[4] and Basil asked Damasus to intervene on his behalf. Damasus, still smarting over Basil's prior rejection, replied by sending to Basil a statement of faith about the

---

4. Eustathius of Sebaste had a long history of running afoul of councils. Early in his life, he was condemned for excessive ascetical practices. He was believed to have prohibited marriage and taught that no married person would be saved. He also tended to align with anti-Nicene forces. Eustathius also took the radical (for the time) position that slavery was immoral and should be abolished—a view shared by Gregory of Nyssa.

Trinity. He avoided the language of *hypostases* in his statement, which was a deliberate provocation. Basil and the other Cappadocians said there were three *hypostases* in the Trinity. By this they meant that Father, Son, and Spirit were three substantially existing things. They were not mere phantasms or aspects or epiphenomena, like smoke from a fire. In the West, however, there was some suspicion of *hypostasis* language. Damasus left it out of his creed because he wanted to see if Basil would take the bait and adhere to his preferred formula. Simply put, Damasus wanted to be able to call the theological shots in any potential alliance; he wanted to have the last word as to what language was acceptable to use for God. Basil, seeing Damasus's maneuvering, again refused to sign the creed. The matter was dead in the water.

Then Damasus made the mistake of writing a reference letter for a cleric he had met personally but whose theology had not been vetted for orthodoxy. A reference letter from the bishop of Rome was a powerful thing, and the cleric used it to gain a ministry post in Antioch. Unfortunately, the cleric turned out to be widely regarded as a heretic, and his approval letter became a massive embarrassment for Damasus. Damasus then compounded his blunder by sending a letter retracting his approval to Paulinus. By implicitly treating Paulinus as the bishop of Antioch, Damasus had officially taken sides in the controversy—and taken sides against Basil. Basil was furious and sent emissaries to Damasus to express his disapproval. The emissaries became so angry that they began to hurl insults at Damasus and Peter before storming off.

Things continued to go downhill as Basil and Damasus sent a series of statements to each other's churches making demands they knew the other would not comply with. After continuing in this deeply productive fashion for about a year, they finally broke off all contact. The great union between Rome and Caesarea was not to be.

It was a depressing situation for the Homoousians. Even more depressing was the fact that Basil would die just a few years later, his dreams and hope of a great victory for Nicea unfulfilled. With the anti-Nicene emperor Valens on the throne, the cause of the pro-Nicenes seemed as perilous as it ever had. It was quite a tragic end for a man who had spent the majority of his forty-nine years working so hard to advance a victory he would never see. It was even more tragic because the situation was about to change dramatically in ways Basil could not have foreseen.

Despite Damasus's penchant for making enemies with his arrogance, some Homoousian bishops in the East read his statement of faith and realized that there was nothing in it that was heretical—in fact, it agreed with their theologies perfectly. There appear to have been some regional councils in the East in which bishops signed onto the creed of Damasus in hopes of unification. While the bishops were not necessarily sold on Damasus's language, they recognized the intent of his words as pro-Nicene. Even Meletius of Antioch signed onto Damasus's creed, probably trying to get on the bishop of Rome's good side.

Even though Damasus wasn't going to be able to effect that grand universal council, there was a big appetite among the pro-Nicene bishops for just such a move. Basil's words may have fallen on deaf ears at Alexandria and Rome, but other bishops around the empire heard his pleas for unity and were moved by them. While Basil would not live to see it, his attempts at consensus building had prepared the soil in which a genuine affirmation of Nicaea could happen. The next emperor of the East would be able to do just that.

PART 3

Chapter 11

The Council to (Mostly) Settle It All

BY THE 370S AD, the Nicene controversy had been raging for over five decades. Each of the factions had little to show for their trouble. Emperors and dynasties had risen and fallen, bishops had come and gone, and the church was seemingly no closer to a resolution than it had been before the original council. Appearances, however, can be deceiving. The past half-century of arguing had not been as fruitless as it might have appeared, and in a few short years the Nicene controversy would reach a resolution that has held the majority of Christians together ever since. In order for that resolution to be realized, however, a new emperor needed to arise who could coordinate the quarrelsome clerics of the fourth century.

The Rise of Theodosius

Fortunately for world history and unfortunately for Valens, an opening in the imperial college was imminent. Towards the end of the decade, an alliance of Goths and Huns invaded the empire, pushing all the way into modern-day Bulgaria and Greece. Valens quickly mustered his troops to confront the threat, but discovered that he was outmatched. Not only was the Germanic horde more powerful than his legions, they had much better control over their tempers. On one particularly hot day while the two armies were circling each other, a lone Roman unit launched an unprovoked and uncoordinated attack on the enemy. The attack was unfortunate for many reasons. Foremost among them was that Valens had been trying to negotiate a peace with the Goths. With negotiations cut short by Roman aggression, the Goths began their attack and crushed the Roman army. Valens was killed in the battle.

The next Augustus of the East would be a previously unknown military officer named Theodosius. While he was not of particularly high military rank, most of the Eastern Empire's skilled officers had been destroyed along with Valens in the battle with the Goths. Although his pedigree was lacking in the usual prestige, Theodosius possessed deep military experience in a time of military crisis, and therefore quickly garnered support across the empire.

We know shockingly little about Theodosius compared to many of the other emperors. Unlike the scions of the house of Constantine, nobody ever expected Theodosius to be heading up the entire Roman Empire one day. Consequently, very few bothered to write about him before his ascension to the throne. All we know is that Theodosius was born in modern-day Spain to a father also named Theodosius.[1] His family were probably from a minor aristocratic line that had lived on their ancestral land for centuries.

Theodosius was raised as a Christian, almost certainly in a pro-Nicene family. Spain had long been a bastion of pro-Nicene Christianity. Even when the tides of fate turned against the Nicene Creed, Spanish clergy generally tended to hold firm in its defense. Later generations of thinkers remembered Theodosius as a particularly pious emperor, dedicated to the church and to promoting the true religion. During his early life, however, he was not remarkable for his piety—or really for much of anything. He was just a minor lord who would spend his life doing what minor aristocrats did in the empire: managing the family estate and participating in the family business.

The family business was military service. Theodosius and his father served honorably, with sturdy if not extraordinary track records. They lost few battles, but had few brilliant victories. Both Theodosiuses went to Britain to suppress a Celtic and Germanic invasion before the younger man got a commission guarding the Danube river against the Germanic tribes across the river. There he would have stayed had it not been for the disastrous death of Valens and the loss of military personnel. The imperial hierarchy coalesced around the young commander in short order. Just eight days after his thirty-second birthday, Theodosius was named Augustus of the East.

While Theodosius's main objective was the defeat of the invading armies, it was clear from the beginning of his reign that he intended to champion the cause of Nicene orthodoxy. It would take several years for him to put his religious policies in place. There were Goths and Huns to

---

1. Theodosius thus fulfilled one of the most important job requirements for a Roman emperor: having the same name as other people in your family tree and confusing future historians.

be defeated first, which left little time for ecclesiastical politicking. Yet with each territory he brought back into Roman control, Theodosius brought his new vision of church and state to bear.

Theodosius quickly issued a decree that lauded Pope Damasus and Peter of Alexandria as the gold standards of Trinitarian orthodoxy. In so doing, he made his Nicene commitments abundantly clear. He also, perhaps inadvertently, bolstered Pope Damasus's claims to be the final arbiter of Christian doctrine.[2] Theodosius promised that those who contradicted the faith of the Nicene Creed as interpreted by Damasus and Peter would be treated as heretics and punished with the power of the state. Theodosius made good on his threat, albeit in a milder way than his threatening language might have implied. He deprived heretics of the right to public assembly, which essentially meant they could not gather to worship in churches. They could still meet for outdoor worship. Whether the anti-Nicenes took this as an opportunity to create themed "picnic and preaching" services is unknown. In any case, many could continue worshiping even indoors because Theodosius rarely used violence to enforce the decree. Theodosius would use his power to block anti-Nicenes from gaining new converts, but he had no desire to make martyrs of them. The anti-Nicenes went on worshiping in outdoor settings, unmolested by violence—but they probably had a hard time getting new visitors when the weather was rainy.

Theodosius appears to have wanted a state-protected religion, and was willing to disenfranchise groups that could be confused with that state-protected religion. Heretical groups that could be mistaken for orthodox Christianity were thus disenfranchised. Other groups that could not be mistaken for Christians—Jews, pagans, etc.—were mostly free to do as they liked. Pro-Nicene Christianity would thus enjoy a preeminent status among the faiths of the day with its biggest rivals suffering punishments and smaller competitors left alone. This was Theodosius's vision, and it may have been his intent from the very start. It also may have been the result of a frantic deathbed plea.

One year into his reign, Theodosius fell gravely ill. He called for a bishop to baptize him, following the ancient Christian practice of waiting until one's deathbed to get baptized. Theodosius made a full recovery shortly after his baptism. He thus became one of the few Roman emperors to be a baptized Christian for almost his entire reign. His declarations against the anti-Nicenes began shortly after he was baptized. Some historians have interpreted Theodosius's baptism in an almost conspiratorial fashion, as if

2. If Theodosius intended to say that the bishop of Rome was in fact the final arbiter of religious doctrine, then it is unlikely he would have mentioned Peter of Alexandria as an orthodox source as well.

his baptism chained him to the church in such a way that he felt compelled to advocate for the orthodox faith as he saw it. Such a scenario is unlikely. Theodosius had the full power of the Roman army behind him; bishops had no way of forcing him to do anything. Furthermore, emperors like Constantius and Valens had no compunction weighing in on church affairs even when they were not baptized. Emperors did not become involved in church conflict because they feared for their souls; they did so because it had been one of their responsibilities since 325 AD. His miraculous recovery might have given Theodosius a newfound gratitude for God's mercy or reaffirmed his commitment to the faith, but it did not set him on a fundamentally different path. Theodosius had always been a pro-Nicene Christian.

The Road to Resolution

After defeating the Goths and successfully completing several other misadventures and delays, Theodosius arrived in Constantinople and immediately told the sitting bishop of the city, who was an anti-Nicene, that he could either submit to the Nicene Creed or be exiled. The bishop chose exile. Theodosius also began to send out invitations for a grand council to be held in the city, just as Basil and his allies had hoped. Theodosius believed this council would resolve the controversies plaguing Christendom—including the old question of the relationship between Son and Father.

This cleared the way for Gregory of Nazianzus, long waiting in the wings as the voice of the pro-Nicene resistance in the city, to be named bishop of Constantinople. Unfortunately, the brilliant orator faced significant complications. As was often the case in Gregory's life, that complication came in the form of a friend. Gregory had struck up a friendship with a philosopher and fellow cleric named Maximus the Cynic.[3] He did not know that Maximus was in a secret alliance with Peter of Alexandria, who distrusted Gregory because they supported opposing candidates for the bishop of Antioch. While Gregory was sick, Peter sent bishops in the middle of the night to ordain Maximus as the true, rightful, orthodox bishop of Constantinople.

Gregory was shocked and hurt by the betrayal. So were his parishioners, who drove Maximus out of the city. Maximus then fled to Thessalonica to plead his case before Theodosius. Theodosius was still busy with military campaigns and referred the matter to the bishop of Thessalonica, who in turn referred it to Pope Damasus, who wrote a very noncommittal letter

---

3. "Cynic" refers to Maximus's philosophical school. It is not a way of saying that Maximus was a particularly negative or pessimistic person.

saying that someone should figure out who the bishop of Constantinople was. For all the bishop of Rome's claims to be the supreme head of the church, this was one bishop he had no interest in personally selecting.

Gregory of Nazianzus had his work cut out for him as the council began. He was not the uncontested bishop of Constantinople, the pro-Nicenes were deeply divided over the question of the bishop of Antioch, and they had a new emperor who was generally supportive of the cause but inexperienced in ecclesiastical and imperial politics. It would take a master orator and politician to steer this council through the turbulent waters ahead. Gregory would soon have his chance to try as Theodosius's long-awaited council began in the summer of 381 AD.

The Council of Constantinople is usually referred to as an ecumenical council, but unlike Nicaea, not everyone was invited. Only the most important bishops in the West received an invitation; Theodosius was more interested in resolving matters in his half of the empire. Furthermore, most of the prominent bishops in the West were solidly in favor of Nicaea by this point, and hence the need for Western participation was less pressing. Some bishops in the East were not invited because their theologies were beyond the pale. Theodosius was not going to have Eunomius sitting at his council. He did, however, invite over thirty bishops of the Pneumatomachoi. Theodosius hoped to make peace among those factions he considered within the bounds of reasonable religion. He seems to have found the Pneumatomachoi to be reasonable. That description did not apply to the entirety of the Egyptian church, which was also excluded from the council. Meletius of Antioch appears to have gained Theodosius's favor to be bishop of Antioch. The Egyptian clergy, headed by Peter of Alexandria (recently returned from his exile under Valens), were solidly against Meletius and instead favored his rival Paulinus. They had also meddled in Constantinople by sponsoring Maximus over Gregory as bishop. Theodosius decided that matters would proceed much more smoothly if the Egyptians were not invited.

The Council Proceedings

Things would go as smoothly as the emperor hoped for but a few short moments. The emperor Theodosius gave the bishops a grand welcome in the imperial palace and then promptly left the group to attend to his other imperial responsibilities. He kept an eye on the proceedings, but he never attended an actual session. His only intervention was to make Meletius the president of the council, which left no doubt in anybody's mind who the emperor thought was the rightful bishop of Antioch.

As the bishops began their work, they found a city abuzz with gossip and talk about their work. Gregory of Nyssa recounted his experience of Constantinople as follows:

> If you ask for change, the man launches into a theological discussion about begotten and unbegotten; if you enquire about the price of bread, they answer that they Father is greater and the Son subordinate; if you remark that the bath is nice the man pronounces that the Son is from nothing.[4]

Ultimately, the bakers and bath managers had no say in such matters; that was left to the bishops. The bishops settled down and quickly got to work resolving the matters before them. First, they affirmed that Gregory of Nazianzus was the true bishop of Constantinople with remarkably little fuss. The assembled bishops appear to have seen Maximus's consecration as a transparent ploy for power, and they were not about to entertain it further.[5] The council also passed a series of canons regulating the work of bishops. Of particular importance are canons two and three, which attempted to set some boundaries on episcopal interference. They restricted a bishop's authority to minister to his own diocese. A bishop had full power in the territory he served, but would not oversee churches or ordain priests outside of that area unless invited to do so by the appropriate bishop. In other words, the final authority in a diocese was the bishop of that diocese; you could not invite a different bishop to minister to you without your bishop's permission. The council also asserted that Constantinople was to be honored after Rome because it was the New Rome. This was not just a way of thanking the people of Constantinople for their luxurious accommodations. The council was keenly aware that there were many questions about which bishops had seniority, and wanted to establish the bishop of Constantinople's power over nearby clerics. This particular canon has caused discussion and argument ever since. It is frequently quoted in arguments between Orthodox and Roman Catholic writers. You can read it as saying that Constantinople is in second place behind Rome and the bishop of Rome has authority over the bishop of Constantinople. Or you can read the canon as honoring the bishop of Constantinople "along with" the bishop of Rome, suggesting their equality and collegiality as the heads of crucial imperial cities.

The council, blissfully unaware of the centuries of half-informed arguing its canons had inaugurated, continued on with its business. The business

---

4. Gregory of Nyssa, *De Deitate Filii et Spiritus Sancti*, PG 46:557.

5. Those bishops familiar with their history may have remembered that the original council of Nicaea also settled matters related to a bishop's authority—in that case, Alexander's authority over the schismatic Meletius.

would get harder from there. The council's guest list changed dramatically after the opening. After initial negotiations, the Pneumatomachoi decided that the council was not going anywhere they wished to follow. They were asked to affirm their belief in the Nicene Creed in order to be seated. They refused. With the majority of bishops affirming the divinity of the Spirit, the Pneumatomachoi left to ensure their names would not be attached to any creed the council produced. The Council of Constantinople eventually anathematized their doctrines and included them in the list of heretics. Theodosius's dreams of compromise would not be realized.

The Pneumatomachoi were replaced over the summer by a large delegation of bishops from Egypt. At their head was the brand-new bishop of Alexandria, Timothy. Brother of the departed Peter of Alexandria, Timothy was apparently not thrilled that he and his bishops had not been invited. So he and his bishops decided to crash the party. No one even attempted to stop the Egyptian delegation, including the emperor Theodosius. It is unclear if Theodosius wished to avoid using force, or if he was more willing to welcome the Egyptian delegation now that Peter was no longer leading them. Whatever the reason, the Egyptians took their places at the council, argued, and voted. Their right to attend was apparently not in question.

The arrival of such a strong anti-Meletius faction would have been quite troubling for Meletius if he had not conveniently died before their arrival, sending the Antiochene controversy into a whole new direction. The council quickly elected Gregory of Nazianzus as the next president. Gregory would put all his intellectual and rhetorical skills to use in his new role.

The situation confronting Gregory was complicated. Some council members said that Meletius and Paulinus had come to a gentleman's agreement that if one of them died, the other would become the sole bishop of Antioch. Gregory of Nazianzus wanted to honor this agreement and recognize Paulinus as the bishop of Antioch. The majority of the council, however, wanted a fresh start. Some members proposed electing a priest named Flavian to be bishop. Flavian had been ordained by Meletius, which meant he had ties to the Meletian wing of the church. However, by the time of the council Flavian was a card-carrying member of Paulinus's party. Many bishops hoped he could bridge the gap between the two factions.

This must have been a complicated situation for Gregory of Nazianzus. He had hero-worshiped Meletius Gregory thought he was everything that a bishop was supposed to be. Supporting Paulinus would have left a bitter taste in his mouth, but he believed it was what Meletius had wanted. To contravene his hero's wishes must have seemed unthinkable, especially to support an ecclesiastical turncoat like Flavian. But the rest of the council, especially the other Syrian bishops, would have none of it. Most of the council attendees had supported Meletius.[6] As far as they were concerned, Paulinus was a stooge for Western bishops trying to control affairs in the East. They believed they should choose a bishop on their own rather than accepting a candidate propped up by the West.

On top of all this trouble, Gregory was taking significant flak from the Egyptian delegates, who were raising questions about whether Gregory should even be bishop of Constantinople at all. They pointed out that the canons of Nicaea forbade bishops to move from one territory to another. Yet Gregory had started out as bishop of Sasima, then briefly been a bishop under his father in Nazianzus, and was now in Constantinople. His election was invalid, they argued, as was his presidency.

Gregory's situation was perilous. The majority of delegates opposed his choice of bishop for Antioch; even the Egyptians who supported his choice were critical of his own status as a bishop. So Gregory made a gambit. He delivered a grand speech endorsing Paulinus as bishop of Antioch, and explicitly threatened to resign as president of the council and bishop of Constantinople if they did not agree. Whatever else is said about him, Gregory was clearly not afraid of risk. He had just been granted one of the four most important posts in the whole church, and he offered to give it all up if the council did not adopt his distinctly unpopular policy.

The council took the Nazianzen up on his offer to resign and promptly elected a new council president. It chose a rather scandalous figure named Nectarius, who was not at the council at all. He was not even ordained. Nectarius was an aristocrat with no theological education who had a reputation as a bit of a playboy. But he was quickly ordained, made bishop of Constantinople, and named president of the council. From his self-imposed exile, Gregory of Nazianzus fumed at the state of affairs, bemoaning the political machinations of the bishops and the lack of doctrinal conviction in their deliberations. However, in some of his later, more self-reflective poems, Gregory seems to admit that Nectarius had one thing he did not: political acumen.

The New Nicene Creed

Under Nectarius's leadership, the council produced a creed so influential that it has supplanted the original Nicene Creed. When churches today refer to the "Nicene Creed," they are almost always referring to the creed adopted at the Council of Constantinople in 381 AD, not that of Nicaea in

---

6. As one would expect of a council where Meletius was the president.

325 AD. Officially known as the Nicene-Constantinopolitan Creed, it reads as follows:

> We believe in one God, the Father, the Almighty, maker of heaven and earth; of all that is, seen and unseen.
> We believe in one Lord, Jesus Christ, the only Son of God, eternally begotten of the Father, God from God, light from light, true God from true God, begotten not made, of one being (homoousios) with the Father. Through him all things were made. For us and for our salvation he came down from heaven. By the power of the Holy Spirit he became incarnate from the Virgin Mary and was made man. He was crucified under Pontius Pilate; he suffered death and was buried. On the third day he rose again in accordance with the scriptures and ascended into heaven. He is seated at the right hand of the Father. He will come again to judge the living and the dead, and his kingdom will have no end.
> We believe in the Holy Spirit, the Lord, the Giver of Life, who proceeds from the Father. With the Father and Son he is worshiped and glorified. He has spoken through the prophets. We believe in one holy catholic and apostolic church. We acknowledge one baptism for the forgiveness of sins. We look for the resurrection of the dead and the life of the world to come.

This creed clearly follows the structure of the original Nicene Creed, but with a few key differences. The original creed said the Son was generated from the substance of the Father. The creed of 381 simplifies that description with the words "only Son of God." It also adds some meat to the description of the Holy Spirit; the original Nicene Creed abruptly ended at "we believe also in the Holy Spirit." However, the Spirit is not described as *homoousios* with the Father. In fact, the Spirit's substance is never discussed at all. Gregory of Nazianzus had lost the day. His double *homoousios* language did not make it into the council's creed, which does not even describe the Spirit as God. But the creed does affirm that the Spirit is worshiped and glorified with the Father and Son. Since Christians only worship God, the Spirit is God by implication. The framers of the creed apparently preferred to do no more than imply the Spirit's divinity in an attempt to draw in as many Pneumatomachoi as possible. Despite their exit from the council, Nectarius and the other delegates still wanted to come to some kind of agreement with the Pneumatomachoi. Basil may have approved of their discretion; Gregory of Nazianzus was enraged by it.

Nectarius would not be so lucky with the contentious issue of the bishopric of Antioch. Full reconciliation between the feuding parties would wait for over another thirty years, when a single bishop of Antioch was finally recognized by the whole church. Yet he could claim to have brought the council to a conclusion, and take partial credit for a creed he would not have had the theological training to understand.

The Aftermath of the Council

The most shocking result of the Council of Constantinople is that in spite of everything, its creed seemed to actually work. Unlike all the councils before, it unified the empire. After 381 AD, the churches of the empire offered few objections to the new and revised Nicene Creed. The most fervent of Nicaea's detractors would persist in their theologies, but they were marginal voices in the church, and would only become more isolated in the years ahead. Eunomius and his Heteroousian allies established a whole network of dissenting churches that dissolved into internal schism over their disagreements with each other.

While Theodosius's steady and rather firm hand would play a role in the church's newfound stability, his influence was not decisive. Plenty of emperors had tried to settle the matter beforehand—both for and against Nicaea—and failed. Plenty of councils had been called to settle the difficult question of *homoousios*. They had failed. Imperial politics and ecclesiastical infighting plagued every council, Constantinople included.

It seems that somewhere in all those years of fighting and arguing and failed consensus building, the moderate Nicene position represented by Basil and Gregory of Nyssa had won over the majority of the Christian church. The church was not ready to accept Gregory Nazianzus's application of *homoousios* to the Spirit, but it would become commonly accepted in the years after the council. The Council of Constantinople is considered ecumenical not because of who was there (a small handpicked selection of bishops), but because of who accepted it—which was more or less everyone. The vast majority had finally learned to stop worrying and love to call the Son *homoousios* with the Father. From then on, the church praised the Son as being of the same substance as the Father. Nicaea had prevailed. We continue to live and worship in its wake.

Chapter 12

Creeds and Outlaws, Orthodoxy and Heresy

THE COUNCIL OF CONSTANTINOPLE ended the long and occasionally bloody struggle over the Christian conception of the Trinity. After fifty-six years of controversy, the Christians of the Roman Empire were finally (mostly) united in a formula to express the unity of the Son and the Father. While the Holy Spirit's being was not described with the same level of clarity, Christians would eventually acknowledge the Spirit to be *homoousios* with the Father as well. With the history of the Nicene Creed in mind, we can begin to draw some lessons about how churches fight, and about what is at stake when we fight over doctrine.

The first of those lessons comes from two little words that have resounded throughout the Nicene controversy: orthodoxy and heresy. You may recall from chapter 2 that orthodoxy means both "right belief" and "proper praise." Early Christians believed that praising God was central to the church's mission, and they found few things more important than praising God properly. In order to do so, they paid careful attention to the words of the Bible that revealed God to humanity. To be orthodox was to follow the truths of the Bible and thus praise God properly; to be a heretic was to cast aside the wisdom of Scripture by teaching one's own ideas as if they were the church's. All parties to the Nicene controversy were fond of accusing their opponents of heresy. Not only did each side believe the other was wrong, they also believed the other side had departed from Christianity altogether.

In the face of these dueling accusations, the history of Nicaea raises a simple but difficult question: who gets to decide what counts as orthodoxy?

After all, Arius certainly did not see himself as a heretic. On the contrary, he thought he was defending the faith against the newfangled heretical ideas of his bishop. Basil of Caesarea is venerated in the Eastern Orthodox Church as one of the Three Holy Hierarchs—bishops of particular importance as overseers of the church and defenders of the faith. Yet Basil had ties to figures that the Orthodox Church now considers heretical—the Homoiousians and Pneumatomachoi. So who gets to decide what figures and doctrines are orthodox, and which are heretical?

Discerning Orthodoxy

The question has been asked many times. From the Protestant Reformation to modern debates about human sexuality to the scandals caused when megachurch pastors proclaim that God commands their congregations to pay for the pastor's private jet,[1] the church is continually fighting about who gets to decide which teachings are orthodox and which are not.

Several possible answers may come to mind. The first and simplest answer is that God decides what is orthodox and what is heretical. It has the benefit of being the only answer that everyone can agree on; God is the one we are trying to praise, and so of course God should get the final say as to whether what we have said in worship is accurate and appropriate. Unfortunately, God has not recently opened the heavens and spoken in a loud, booming voice to evaluate the Nicene Creed or any other statement of belief. Several figures in the controversy (including Eunomius) claimed to hear God's opinions in private visions, but those have been difficult to confirm. Given the difficulties involved in getting a reply to one's text messages or emails to the kingdom of heaven, a clear answer is probably not forthcoming. Saying that the Bible decides what is orthodox and heretical, as many Protestants do, will run into similar problems. Almost all Christians would agree the Bible is authoritative. However, different people interpret the Bible in different ways, and they can often ground their contradictory interpretations in biblical passages. Since the Bible does not discuss the appropriateness of the word *homoousios*, it could not resolve differences of interpretation in the Nicene controversy. Rules of faith existed for a reason. Simply reading the Bible does not resolve controversies. Fifty-six years of arguing over biblical passages produced no notable conversions on either side of the Nicene debate. Even if the Bible is the arbiter of doctrinal

---

1. Bowen, "Multi-Million-Dollar Jets."

truth, we must still ask who is allowed to decide what constitutes a proper interpretation.

You might instead decide that the emperor of Rome was the ultimate arbiter of what was orthodox. I have often heard folks complain that Christianity was sullied when it became mixed up in politics. The idea is that when Constantine made Christianity the religion of the empire, he introduced earthly power into the church and thereby corrupted it. He made himself the ultimate judge of what counted as orthodox Christianity and what was heresy. He made disagreement with the emperor's theology punishable by exile. However, that idea does not stand up to the actual history. Constantine may have imagined himself to be the leader of the bishops, but there were always bishops willing to stand up to him—and his successors—when they believed him to be out of touch with the true faith. Nor did the assembly of bishops ever take Constantine's word on theological matters as final. Even when Constantine, Constantius II, Valens, or any other emperor proclaimed the Nicene question settled, bishops continued to convene, argue, and draft theological statements on the topic.

Why were the bishops so unwilling to allow the emperor to resolve the matter? There are likely several reasons for the bishops' obdurance. They had long seen themselves as the final authorities on church doctrine and wished to continue in that role. They also had far more theological sophistication than any Roman emperor could have dreamed of. Constantine was a case in point. At the very beginning of the Nicene controversy, he sent a letter to Alexander and Arius scolding them for their fight and ordering them to make peace with each other. In the letter, Constantine informed them that they actually agreed with each other but used different words to make the same point. He also said that the point of their disagreement was so small that it was not worth fighting over anyway. By the end of the letter, it is clear that Constantine had about as much theological sophistication as a college student opining about a book he has not read for his seminar. To say that the mystery of the Son's being is an insignificant matter betrays a staggering ignorance of basic Christian doctrine. Constantine seems to have barely been interested in Christian doctrine, and readmitted the creed's most notorious detractors into the empire upon the flimsiest of pretexts. If he sought theological unity, he lacked the knowledge to actually create or enforce it. Later emperors were more sophisticated in their theologies, but time after time they failed to impose agreement upon the disagreements of the church. For all their military and economic power, they could not force souls to believe as they commanded.

That fact opens up another possible answer to the question. Perhaps councils of bishops, when gathered together, have the power to determine what is orthodox. This answer fits with much of the story of Nicaea. Bishops were not the only source of authority in the early church. However, the rise of Constantine and the Nicene controversy gave them many opportunities to consolidate their power. In the new alliance of church and empire, bishops brought several skills to the table that imperial bureaucrats valued. Compared with charismatic teachers or wonderworking ascetics, bishops were the only class of authorities to offer any reliable administrative acumen or consistency. Monks and other ascetics made a habit of rejecting the trappings of the world, including power. While monks could (and did) participate in riots and protests, they were too scattered and decentralized to be useful conduits of power. Charismatic teachers were as rare in the past as they are today. Roman emperors wanted consistency and reliability in their church. It also did not help that the heresies of the period tended to be promulgated by charismatic teachers: Arius, Aetius, and Eunomius. The most successful teachers of the period were those who were also bishops: Athanasius, the Cappadocians, and Eunomius. They were able to use the security afforded by their hierarchical power to establish a safe base for their teachings to spread. Without the episcopate, teachers had a difficult time holding their own against the power of disapproving authorities.

Thus the weight of the controversy fell on the bishops' shoulders more than any other group. When emperors desired peace in the church, they called councils of bishops together. Bishops were the sole voting members of the council of Nicaea, the Council of Constantinople, and every council in between. Perhaps the task of determining orthodoxy and heresy should fall upon their shoulders. As overseers of the church, they are ultimately responsible for how their churches worship and teach. Has the Holy Spirit empowered them so that they can guide the church to praise God properly? Indeed, the Roman Catholic and Eastern Orthodox churches hold that ecumenical councils are infallible; the bishops who gathered at an ecumenical council were so inspired by the Holy Spirit that they could not have failed to define Christian doctrine correctly.

You may have noticed a caveat in the previous sentence. *Ecumenical* councils are infallible, not all councils. That means that we have another question to answer: who gets to decide which councils of bishops are ecumenical? The Roman Catholic Church believes that there are twenty-one ecumenical councils; the Eastern Orthodox Church acknowledges seven. There were many councils during the fifty-six year controversy over the Nicene Creed, but only the Council of Nicaea and the Council of Constantinople are recognized as ecumenical. Those two councils were not the most well-attended, nor were they particularly representative of the entire church. So if councils decide what counts as orthodox, then we simply push our question back further: which councils get to decide?

Here is another suggestion that may clarify matters. We can simply say that creeds decide what is orthodox and what is not. After all, that is how decisions of orthodoxy and heresy were made in the period. A person would be asked to affirm or deny a particular creed, and (sometimes) to provide an explanation for their decision. If they affirmed the creed, then they could be considered orthodox. If not, they were heretics. The quest for the revised Nicene Creed of Constantinople was nothing more than a quest to find a document that could reliably serve this function.

If you like, it might be helpful to think of a creed as an additional layer of clarification on top of a rule of faith. Rules of faith were general statements of what one expected to find in the Bible and what a Christian was expected to believe. They were useful in defining broad features of the faith, but were not specific enough to resolve the Nicene controversy. In response to this dilemma, the church began to construct creeds. Creeds enforced stricter boundaries than a rule of faith, but also more clarity on questions of the day. The Nicene controversy was an attempt to find a creed that the Christians of the empire could agree to use as a measure of orthodoxy.

You may still be unsatisfied with this answer. Many creeds were offered as possible solutions to the controversy. Who got to decide which creed became the official creed of the church?

Historically speaking, the answer is everyone. Emperors, bishops, monks and ascetics, teachers of the church, the masses of ordinary faithful Christians whose voices we can only faintly detect in the documents that have survived—each of these groups had their say in the formulation of the creed. If emperors were opposed to a creed, they could use their considerable resources to pressure the church to change it. When dissatisfied, bishops regularly called dueling councils to draft rival creeds. Monks, ascetics, and teachers lent their authority to whichever creed they found most appropriate. Even ordinary Christians of the period would riot in defense of a beloved figure like Athanasius if he was persecuted for his adherence to a creed. Only when a critical mass of these groups united behind a creed would it become accepted as a criterion of orthodoxy. To attain such a critical mass is a rare feat indeed. The church has been frequently split because of doctrinal differences in which no side attained such a critical mass. Among some groups today it is common to say that each Christian gets to decide for themselves what counts as the gospel, which abandons any hope that Christians might be able to come to a consensus at all. A creedal consensus is different. It requires everyone to have a say in a document that is to be authoritative for *all* Christians, whether they personally agree with every word of it or not. The Nicene Creed was the first to accomplish the feat; few have done so since.[2]

The Fate of the Heretics

Ironically, Nicaea's dissenters may have done as much to confirm its authority as anyone else. Eunomius and his Heteroousian allies had set up a whole network of churches sympathetic to their views throughout the empire. This network could have been a powerful bastion of resistance to the pro-Nicenes. Instead, the network descended into internal strife as those within it accused other non-Nicenes of heresy. Their reaction is a common one among groups that lose political power. Rather than try to get it back, they attempt to marginalize others within their group as a way of feeling powerful in the face of loss. Many of the other non-Nicene churches were more moderate than Eunomius, and wanted to affirm that the Son and Father were similar to each other, just dissimilar in substance. They had similar wills, similar natures, similar creative powers, and more.

Eunomius was not interested in giving the Nicenes an inch of ground. He was interested in telling everybody else how they were wrong. In particular, Eunomius thought that if you affirmed any similarity between Father and Son, you were eventually going to wind up affirming the *homoousios* and becoming a pro-Nicene. Eunomius and his followers spent much of their time and energy arguing with their theological allies. They even began to fight over God's other attributes. For example, Eunomians began to argue over when the Father could be called a Father, given that he preexisted his Son and hence was not a Father for all time. One cleric wrote a whole treatise to resolve this troublesome problem. The Eunomian church read it, decided they did not like his answer, and excommunicated him for his trouble.

Eunomius made out fairly well even as his church declined. He continued to meet his followers in private and was virtually hero-worshiped by them. He did not use his influence to build up his churches, however. After almost two decades of internal squabbles and increasing marginalization, in 396 AD Eunomian teachers and clerics were expelled from the cities. An energized church that had invested in evangelization and public debate

---

2. You may hear some writers claim that the Apostles' Creed is the earliest creed in Christianity. The history gets complicated on this point. The Apostles' Creed was not accepted as a standard until the fifth century, well after the council of Nicaea. Many historians think that the Apostles' Creed is based on earlier rules of faith than the Nicene Creed, and therefore treat it as the earlier of the two. Since I am focusing on when creeds are accepted by the church and formally written down as liturgical documents, I treat the Nicene Creed as the earlier of the two.

with the Nicenes could have used this incident as a rallying cry, showing the broader empire how they suffered persecution for their convictions. They could have won public sympathy for their cause—and perhaps greater influence. Previous anti-Nicene bishops and churches had done exactly that. Instead, the church that Eunomius had spent his life building up would slowly dissolve in the face of internal dissent and external pressure. The Eunomian church had tacitly agreed not to contest the wider church's judgment. They were content to fight amongst themselves until the realities of their decline caught up to them. Many churches in the modern West, faced with declining attendance and internal divisions, make the same choice.

The ideas of Nicaea's dissenters have not been as willing to fade as Eunomius was. There have been periodic revivals of interest in the theologies of Arius and Eunomius throughout history. One of the most famous sympathizers of Arius was Sir Isaac Newton. The English genius and inventor of classical physics also had a passion for theology and church history. He spent a lot of time obsessing over end times prophecies and appears to have predicted the end of the world. At one point, he calculated the end of days to occur in 2060 AD.[3] If this book has the good fortune of staying in circulation until then, those readers will know whether he was right or not. Newton considered the church's Nicene doctrine to be the great apostasy prophesied in Revelation that set the end of the world in motion. He kept his views private during his life because he knew that contravening long-established orthodoxy was not going to help him win friends and influence people in early modern England. But he did write down in private journals a series of theses on the Trinity that Arius and Eunomius would have likely applauded. They were kept a secret until the 1930's when the famous economist John Maynard Keynes was allowed to view his private papers. Keynes then presented Newton's views and theses to the world. Here they are, in all their heretical infamy:

> 1. The word God is nowhere in the scriptures used to signify more than one of the three persons at once.
>
> 2. The word God put absolutely without restriction to the Son or Holy Ghost doth always signify the Father from one end of the scriptures to the other.

---

3. Petre, "2060 for End of World." It is important to note that Newton also frequently complained about those who predicted a specific date for the end of the world, and some of his other writings do not contain any reference to 2060. For a more reserved perspective on the 2060 date, see Snobelen, "'Time and Times and the Dividing of Time,'" 2003.

3. Whenever it is said in the scriptures that there is but one God, it is meant the Father.

4. When, after some heretics had taken Christ for a mere man and others for the supreme God, St John in his Gospel endeavoured to state his nature so that men might have from thence a right apprehension of him and avoid those heresies and to that end calls him the word or logos: we must suppose that he intended that term in the sense that it was taken in the world before he used it when in like manner applied to an intelligent being. For if the Apostles had not used words as they found them how could they expect to have been rightly understood. Now the term logos before St John wrote, was generally used in the sense of the Platonists, when applied to an intelligent being and the Arians understood it in the same sense, and therefore theirs is the true sense of St John.

5. The Son in several places confesseth his dependence on the will of the Father.

6. The Son confesseth the Father greater, then calls him his God etc.

7. The Son acknowledgeth the original prescience of all future things to be in the Father only.

8. There is nowhere mention of a human soul in our Saviour besides the word, by the meditation of which the word should be incarnate. But the word itself was made flesh and took upon him the form of a servant.

9. It was the son of God which He sent into the world and not a human soul that suffered for us. If there had been such a human soul in our Saviour, it would have been a thing of too great consequence to have been wholly omitted by the Apostles.

10. It is a proper epithet of the Father to be called almighty. For by God almighty we always understand the Father. Yet this is not to limit the power of the Son. For he doth whatsoever he seeth the Father do; but to acknowledge that all power is originally in the Father and that the Son hath power in him but what he derives fro the Father, for he professes that of himself he can do nothing.

11. The Son in all things submits his will to the will of the Father, which could be unreasonable if he were equal to the Father.

12. The union between him and the Father he interprets to be like that of the saints with one another. That is in agreement of will and counsel.[4]

Newton's arguments would have been right at home in the controversies of the fourth century. The anti-Nicenes pointed to the Son's dependence on the Father and description of the Father as greater just like Newton did. They also interpreted the Son's union with the Father to be one of will (both of them desired to save the world and defeat evil) rather than substance.

Newton was not the only self-identified Christian to side with Arius. The Jehovah's Witnesses manage to reproduce the arch-heretic's doctrines with startling accuracy. They believe that God is one person or *hypostasis*, whose name is Jehovah. Jehovah created exactly one thing: Jesus. Then the whole world was made through Jesus, who came down from heaven to redeem the world as the Bible teaches. We do not know if Arius taught anything about the Holy Spirit, but the Jehovah's Witnesses deny that the Spirit is a personal being at all; it is a name for God's active force. Some of the Pneumatomachoi would likely have approved.

Nor do we have to look to official church teachings to find anti-Nicene theology alive and well. In a 2022 survey of American Christian evangelicals, 73 percent agreed with the following statement: "Jesus is the first and greatest being created by God."[5] You should be careful reading too much into a single poll, as such numbers are prone to error. The wording of the question might also be misleading. Some respondents may have thought that the question was referring to Christ's human nature, not the Second Person of the Trinity. Still, it is a startling statistic, and implies that most churches have committed Arians in their pews, faithfully praying, perhaps not even realizing the ancient controversies that condemned their beliefs.

What do we make of the recurring power of anti-Nicene ideas?

One reason these ideas keep popping up is because there are biblical passages to support them. Jesus said that "The Father is greater than I" in John 14:28; small wonder that many Christians have thought as much. Of course there are plenty of passages that support a Nicene interpretation as well. But people, being the incomplete and imperfect readers that they are, will naturally tend to favor one passage over another, or to make a single passage the interpretive lens for all of Scripture, or simply to not read verses that contradict their theologies. The fact that a group of people draw the same conclusions from the same set of texts need not be surprising. While the Nicene Creed has maintained a critical mass of support, that does not

---

4. Christianson, *In the Presence of the Creator*, 253.
5. Carter, "State of Theology."

mean it has entirely overcome its critics. Even the most definitive resolutions of conflict rarely satisfy everyone—and it is very difficult indeed to force people to believe something they are not convinced is true.

There is a deeper story behind these dueling interpretations, however. The Bible contains resources to tell the salvation story in all kinds of different ways. Take, for example, the Eunomian story of salvation. Eunomius so heavily emphasized the mutual relationship between Christ and the world that he further distanced us from the Father by making Christ the God of this world and the Father Christ's God. Our Christian relationship is not really with the Father at all; we are saved by Christ, and it is Christ that we come to know. While Eunomius occasionally says that we can learn a bit about the Father by thinking about the ways he is different from the Son, in the end our relationship with the Trinity stops at the Son. The Father remains beyond us. There are biblical passages and Christian writers who allow us to tell the story exactly as Eunomius tells it. There are others that instead cast Jesus Christ as the perfect image of the Father, *homoousios* with him, whose life and death inject us into the very life of the Trinity, into unspeakable union with the eternal Father himself.

Nor are these dueling visions the only two stories we can tell. Some tell Christianity as a story of endurance: complete this life in the faith and fear of God, and no matter what you suffer you will be taken away to glory and happiness in the sweet by and by. Others treat Christianity as a force for liberation. Stand in solidarity with Jesus and you will be empowered to liberate the oppressed, free the captives, and turn the unjust order of the world upside down. Still others think of Christianity as a mindset, a mystical freedom that one can carry into even the deepest traumas of life and maintain inner peace.

It is these stories that animate the emotional life of our religious practices. They give religion its power to bind together and make sense of our whole life story. They bring us joy in moments of ease and comfort in times of trial. It is only natural that an attack on our salvation story would feel like an attack on our very lives. No one would give one's life to the defense of the mere word *homoousios,* but many people did just that for what they thought that word represented—the reality that in Jesus Christ, they had encountered the Eternal Life and Being that *was* blessedness and salvation itself.

Sometimes, these various stories are compatible with one another. One can see Jesus Christ as *homoousios* with the Father and as the ultimate expression of the Father's solidarity with the oppressed, for example. In other cases, a story might be appropriate for one time and place and not another. Other stories are flatly contradictory to each other, as in the case of the Nicene controversy. It falls to each church, in each time and place, to tell the gospel story in the ways appropriate to its present context and ancient creeds. It is what makes religion so mystifying, but also so rich. Understanding our history can help in this process. By seeing how our forebears told the story, we may gain some wisdom for our own tellings.

There is an old statement that orthodoxy is more true than clear, while heresy is more clear than true. That applies well to the problem of the Trinity. Arius and his allies offered a solution to the problem that was clear. They ultimately lost the day to a Homoousian solution that offered a radical, exciting, and confusing vision of God's being. The church ultimately judged the more mysterious vision to be the truer one. The judgment was not without cost, but it has also endured the ages. Perhaps the modern church, in the midst of its many controversies, could learn the importance of seeking a truer vision of God instead of an immediately clearer one.

Chapter 13

Religious Violence After Nicaea

THE COUNCIL OF NICAEA was a watershed moment for the use of power in the church. Emperors, bishops, charismatic teachers, monks and ascetics, and everyday churchgoers all saw their powers expand or contract over the course of the ensuing controversy. We traced those changes over the course of chapter 12. Now it is time to examine how the Nicene controversy shaped religious violence. For where power is used, violence (or the threat of violence) is usually close at hand.

Defining Violence

One of the most worrying aspects of any faith is the frightening regularity with which religious conviction leads to violence. Violent conflict exploded at several points during the history of the Nicene controversy. If we are to understand why this is, however, we must first be very clear as to what we mean by violence.

In the twenty-first century, it has become increasingly popular to define violence as any attempt to influence another person to do something they would not like. The French philosopher Paul Ricoeur incisively defined violence as that which diminishes or destroys another's power.[1] In Ricoeur's view and those like it, violence can take all kinds of forms that are not necessarily physical. A system of government that disproportionately favors the rich at the expense of the poor would be considered violent, even if the poor are never harassed or attacked. Similarly, a society that depicts white people

---

1. Ricoeur, *Oneself as Another*.

of European descent as good and valuable while denigrating black people of African descent would be not just racist, but violent. A groundbreaking study of African American children found that children as young as three years old had been conditioned to prefer white dolls to black ones—limiting their power to develop self-esteem and see themselves as equal members of society.[2]

Seen in this light, the entire Roman imperial system was shot through with violence from top to bottom. Those not fortunate enough to be born into an aristocratic family had no official voice in the decisions made by their government. Those condemned as heretics were not just shunned from the church. They faced exile from their home city, and that exile was often enforced at swordpoint. Moreover, Romans tended to hold strong racial prejudices against those who lived outside their lands. Goths and other Germanic tribes who immigrated into Roman territory faced especially harsh prejudices.[3] Structural violence often makes physical violence more likely—and even necessary in some cases.

The Riot: The Voice of the People

The most common form of physical violence in the Nicene controversy was the riot. The people of Alexandria rioted several times when soldiers arrived to exile Athanasius. Constantinople was thrown into a riot over the successor to Bishop Eusebius. The original Heteroousian Aetius preached sermons so controversial that his congregations exploded in protest. And people rioted over more than matters of religion. Riots happened regularly in the Roman Empire, caused by everything from food shortages to protests over military policy.

Several factors made riots relatively common. The first and most important factor is that the average Roman citizen had absolutely no say in matters of state. The vast majority of public affairs were decided by the emperor or the governors of regional territories, who were appointed by the emperor. The legislative body of the Roman Empire was the Senate. However, only aristocrats were allowed to become senators, and senators had very little power anyway. An average Roman citizen who was disturbed by

2. "Legacy of Dr. Kenneth B. Clark."
3. Interestingly, Roman prejudices appear to have had very little to do with the color of one's skin. The racial categories we use today—white, black, Asian, etc.—did not exist in the ancient world. For the ancients, one's race had to do with the place of one's birth. Those born in the empire were assumed to be civilized, whether they were from Egypt, Syria, Spain, or anywhere in between. Those outside the empire were assumed to be savages and barbarians who could not be trusted.

a political decision had only one outlet to make sure their voice was heard: the riot. Roman leaders may not have listened to peaceful protests, but they did listen to riots. You have surely heard of Pontius Pilate, the governor of Judea who ordered that Jesus Christ be crucified. What you may not know is that Pilate was unceremoniously removed from his position several years after the crucifixion. The people rioted frequently under his leadership, and Roman officials got tired of having to expend time and resources putting down the revolts. That is mostly likely why Pilate was afraid of a riot at Jesus' trial. He was not afraid he would get killed; his soldiers could put down a revolt easily. Pilate knew that there had already been too many riots and if there were many more, Rome was going to start asking uncomfortable questions. So he agreed to the crucifixion of Jesus because he thought that was what would keep the people calm. His calculation was incorrect in the long term, but he proved that the populace could use the threat of riots to influence policy.

The second factor is that it is surprisingly easy for large gatherings to turn violent. A sociologist I knew once put it this way: out of ten thousand people, how many will try to flip a car on their own? How many will throw bricks through store windows, or climb up flagpoles? Probably very few. Now, imagine you put those same ten thousand people in a stadium, watching a sporting event in which their favorite team is playing. Imagine that the game goes very well or very poorly. Riots often happen in precisely those circumstances. Cars are flipped, windows are broken, goalposts are removed from the stadium and thrown into a nearby river.

Crowds have a way of magnifying our emotions and loosening our inhibitions. In a group we can do things we would never dream of doing as individuals. It is one of the main reasons people come to church. Of course you can worship at home, but it is not the same as joining with a group of people to sing and pray and share a sacrament. And as many pastors can tell you from firsthand experience, there is nothing quite like a church meeting where things have started to go off the rails. Groups amplify our negative feelings as much as positive ones. Churches are no exception.

Systemic oppression and group dynamics can explain much about ancient riots. When Roman soldiers came to town to remove Athanasius, the people of Alexandria were doubly outraged: the bishop they loved was being ousted, and they had absolutely no say in the matter. They gave themselves a say in the matter by rioting. After Athanasius had left town, tensions simmered and eventually boiled over again when the people murdered the poor fellow sent to be Athanasius's replacement. Riots often start out as a response to some great wrong, either real or perceived. When Aetius preached a sermon that offended his listeners' deeply held beliefs, they were incensed.

Their emotions magnified by the crowd, the listeners knew that they could not remove Aetius due to his position of power. Instead they rioted, forcing the man to flee the city and reconsider his future preaching plans. Interestingly, Eunomius also caused offense (though not a riot) by preaching that he did not believe Mary had remained a virgin after Jesus' birth. Apparently his congregants found the perpetual virginity of Mary to be a matter of dire importance and made a formal complaint to the emperor. Fearing the emperor's retribution, Eunomius left the city for a time.

Still, a nagging question looms over the Nicene riots. Of course people want a voice in their government. Of course groups can magnify anger and reduce inhibitions. That still does not explain why religion should provoke riots. Riots over food shortages are easy to explain. After all, if people run out of grain, they die. If people get a bad governor, they could die due to his poor choices. But if people think someone else is a heretic, they could go on living as they liked and worshiping as they liked perfectly well in most circumstances. In fact, in the majority of cases that is precisely what happened. Why did riots break out over theological matters? And if riots are the language of the powerless, then why did the powerful riot against the marginalized, as when the anti-Nicene majority attacked Gregory of Nazianzus's tiny church in Constantinople? We are often tempted to explain rioting and violence purely in terms of the social and political contexts of the day. But those explanations will only take us so far. There is more to religious violence than money, power, and structural violence.

Theology Is a Riot

Why did people riot over religion in the fourth century? There are many answers we could give, but the simplest answer is the most important. They rioted because they believed in their faith and became angry when they perceived it was attacked.

The Christians of the fourth century cared passionately about how best to praise God. They believed it was the purpose of the church. Many of them devoted their lives to God's service as clergy, monastics, or dedicated laypeople who strove to live faithfully. They worried deeply about what it would mean if false doctrine was proclaimed from their pulpits. The church on which they set their eternal hopes would be unable to fulfill its mission; it might even cease to be the church altogether. When an emperor attempted to install a heretical bishop, or clergy preached a sermon offensive to the congregation, it was not simply an inappropriate use of power. It was a threat to their faith and salvation. They responded accordingly, using the means available to them. Gregory of Nazianzus presented no physical threat to the anti-Nicene majority in Constantinople during the reign of Valens; his church was attacked because the majority found his ideas heretical and threatening.

If you are a Christian, then I suspect that reading this might make you feel uncomfortable. Christians purport to follow Jesus, the Prince of Peace. The staggering amount of violence that Christians have committed in his name is a challenge to our religion. Skeptics often ask why Christianity's followers engage in so much violence. One common response is to say that those who commit violence are not real Christians—or at most, bad Christians. We might brush off critique by saying, "Ah, but you see, anyone who commits violence in Christ's name has simply not understood his message. Jesus rejected violent force. He even ordered his disciples not to fight back when he was arrested! He told them that 'all who take up the sword will die by the sword.'[4] So if anyone thinks violence is the means of spreading God's word, they have simply not understood God's word."

To which the skeptic might reply, "I don't care what you think God's word says. You may be right; Jesus may not have endorsed the use of violence. But who cares? All around the world, actual Christians are using violence to get their way. Maybe they don't have the 'proper theology' you think they should. Maybe they are uneducated. But they are out there, right now, doing harm to real people. You can call them bad Christians all you want —they are still Christians, and they are still doing harm." In other words, whether we approve of violent Christians' theology is a secondary matter. The bigger scandal is that they have read the same Bible as everyone else, attended the same churches as everyone else, and have come to feel that violence is an appropriate way of expressing power and resolving conflict. Violent Christians truly believe in the articles of faith; in fact, they believe in their faith so much they think it is worth taking up the sword to defend it.

There are no easy answers to the problem of religious violence. We cannot simply say that violent religion is bad religion and be done with it. We also cannot say that religious violence is *really* caused by social problems and that theological conflicts are just the spark that lit the flame. Group dynamics may exacerbate anger, but that anger comes from peoples' fury that their cherished beliefs are denigrated. People may be angry not to have a say in the appointment of a bishop, but that is because they believe their bishop was a key leader in the church, responsible for safeguarding their immortal souls and bodies. Belief can spark conflict; conflict can lead to violence. However we respond to religious violence, we must begin by looking at the

---

4. Matthew 26:52.

matter with clear eyes. Passionate belief raises the possibility of conflict, even when those beliefs are about Jesus. We cannot stop religious violence until we acknowledge that fact.

Violence, Power, and Politics

You may have noticed that the violence in the Nicene controversy was mostly unplanned. Riots are usually not scheduled in advance, after all. While emperors would occasionally send troops to enforce their decrees, the troops did not resort to violence unless people resisted. If Valens truly did order the sinking of a ship full of pro-Nicene bishops, it would be the only instance of bona fide premeditated violence in the Nicene controversy.[5]

As the allegiance between church and empire further solidified after the Council of Constantinople, premeditated violence would become increasingly common as a means of preserving and increasing power. After a fresh round of controversies over Jesus Christ began, the emperor would call the bishops of the empire to a council at Chalcedon (451 AD) to resolve it. Bishops were forced to attend this council at spearpoint. Later emperors would become increasingly comfortable using violence to compel bishops' assent. Violence rarely produced the unity they sought. Rather than unifying the church, the Council of Chalcedon split it apart. While the churches that followed Rome and Constantinople endorsed the council, the Egyptian, Ethiopian, and Syrian churches rejected it. The split continues to the present day.

Nor were bishops above using violence to solidify their power. One instructive case of such violence occurred in Alexandria about a hundred years after the Nicene controversy.

Here, in brief, is what happened.[6] In the fall of 485 AD, a promising young pagan student named Paralius came to Alexandria to complete his studies. He was following the same course of study that Basil and Gregory of Nazianzus had completed a century earlier, albeit in Alexandria instead of Athens. Paralius quickly integrated into the school and was assigned a personal tutor, who happened to be a pagan teacher of rhetoric and philosophy. Paralius had two older brothers in the city who welcomed him. They gave him just one simple order: do not talk to your other brother.

---

5. Athanasius has been accused of plotting violence against his enemies, but I find the evidence of such charges unpersuasive. See Arnold, *Early Episcopal Career of Athanasius of Alexandria*, for a full treatment.

6. See Watts, *Riot in Alexandria*, for a detailed treatment of this event.

Paralius's other brother had converted to Christianity and lived in a monastery close to Alexandria. Paralius's family was not on speaking terms with this brother due to his conversion. In the inimitable style of young men everywhere who have just been told not to do something, Paralius walked right up to the monastery and had a chat with his long-lost third brother. During that conversation his brother made some arguments in favor of Christianity and against paganism that must have affected Paralius rather deeply, which is probably exactly what his other brothers were afraid would happen. Paralius, hoping to find answers to these questions, repeated them to his teacher at school, but his doubts only deepened.

Hoping to ease his doubts, Paralius visited a shrine of the Egyptian goddess Isis in Menouthis, a suburb about forty miles away from Alexandria. At the shrine, Isis appeared to Paralius in a vision and told him a secret: one of his classmates was a magician. It is unclear what (if anything) Paralius was supposed to do with this information, but he was quite excited that Isis had spoken to him and departed with his faith restored. Paralius went back to school and quite naturally started telling all his friends about his amazing visit and how one of their classmates was a sorcerer. He was shocked to discover that his magician classmate had been telling everyone almost the exact same story. The classmate had recently gone to the shrine of Isis as well and had a vision in which Isis told him that Paralius was the magician. I suspect that Paralius's classmates were engaging in the time-honored tradition of teasing the new student. But Paralius took it very seriously. He went back to the shrine and demanded Isis reappear and explain the situation. But Isis did not show up this time.

Paralius's faith was broken. He began to tell his classmates how foolish the pagan faith was, and even compared the high priestess of Isis to a prostitute. Worst of all by the school's standards, he insulted his tutor and called him a fool.

Paralius had crossed a line.

Traditionally, when a student did something like this, he was beaten up. Teachers turned a blind eye when the senior students administered some corporal punishment. And so it was that, on a day when the teacher conveniently happened to be working from home, a group of the senior pagan students cornered Paralius to teach him what happened to people who insulted the teacher.

It just so happened that there was a class of Christian students meeting next door. Paralius ran to them to get protection, and the Christian students took him in. The pagan students, realizing they were about to provoke a much bigger conflict, backed down, trusting that Paralius had received the message.

Over the course of the next two days, a very curious thing happened. Christian leaders began to talk about Paralius as a confessor—someone who had suffered for his faith in Christ. Anger began to rise among the Christians of Alexandria. Paralius's pagan tutor fled the city, fearing for his life. As riots broke out among the Christian citizenry, the bishop of Alexandria Peter Mongus organized a mob to assault the shrine of Isis at Menouthis. The centuries-old temple was destroyed. The next Sunday, Peter walked into church as the congregation chanted insults about Paralius's teacher. Peter spent his sermon telling the congregation how many idols they had captured and invited them to come and see the idols right after church in the courtyard. They would be seeing them for the last time. Leaders of the community would be destroying the idols that very day.

Of course, the story upon which the riots began was a lie. Paralius was not even a Christian; how could he have suffered for a faith that he did not hold? Moreover, he was not persecuted for his religious beliefs, but for insulting his teacher. The pagan students might have been bullies, but they were not zealots. Still, the lie traveled around the city in the blink of an eye. There are several reasons why this lie took hold. Tensions between pagans and Christians were especially fraught at the time, Christians had been trained to expect persecution for following the faith, and the Egyptian church was deeply angered by the Council of Chalcedon, which had occurred only a few decades earlier. Most importantly for our story, however, the bishop found the lie to be quite useful for shoring up his precarious position.

If there is one constant truth in ancient history, it is that it is really, really hard to be the bishop of Alexandria. No matter what Peter Mongus did, everyone was angry with him. Peter's predecessors had fiercely resisted the Council of Chalcedon's proclamations, and had even suffered persecution because of their resistance. Peter had a gentler approach. He called a small council with the emperor's blessing and drafted a statement of faith that affirmed traditional Egyptian beliefs without explicitly denouncing Chalcedon's conclusions. The emperor agreed to accept the agreement and declared Peter (and the whole Egyptian church) to be back in communion with the rest of the church. The rest of the church was irate, and Constantinople even sent some theological investigators to make sure Peter was truly orthodox. Peter passed their test, and his pseudo-compromise over Chalcedon appeared to be on the way to becoming reality.

The citizens of Egypt, and especially its monks, were furious. They had endured imperial persecution for three decades for their anti-Chalcedonian beliefs. They had friends and spiritual leaders who had suffered greatly. They would be satisfied with nothing less than a full-blown rejection of

Chalcedon and everyone who had signed it. In their eyes, Chalcedon was an attack on the Egyptian church and everything it stood for. It was not enough to ignore the council; they would not rest until the empire declared it null and void.

Their anger put Peter in quite a bind. As the bishop of Alexandria, he had a lot of power. He could get people jobs; he could distribute the church's fund for the poor to whomever he chose in whatever amounts he deemed appropriate; and, of course, he could excommunicate people if they violated church discipline. But bishops can only wield their power effectively when people believe they are worthy of their office. If people think that a bishop is acting like a tyrant, they will just ignore him or riot against him. And by making peace with Egypt's theological opponents, Peter had undermined his congregants' trust in him, which was never particularly firm to begin with. Peter had not been a strong candidate for bishop, and had fended off a credible challenge from a rival cleric for the role. Many Egyptian Christians wondered if his rival would have made a better bishop.

The case of Paralius gave Peter Mongus an opportunity to solidify his credibility and score some points with his most passionate enemies. He could rally the Christians of Alexandria around the common enemy of pagan religion. Peter had a story on his hands that he could use to cast himself in the mold of legendary bishops who had gone before him. Earlier bishops of Alexandria had become legends for their destruction of pagan temples and idols. Not all Christians accepted such violence as appropriate. But these predecessor bishops had run very effective PR campaigns, and the majority of Alexandrine Christians were conditioned to see a faithful, effective bishop as one who would reduce the worship of pagan gods by whatever means were available. Peter admonished the crowd to stand up for poor Paralius who had been persecuted for the faith, and to not give the old pagan gods any quarter.

Peter had calculated correctly. By the end of the riot, the crowd was shouting his praises in the streets.

If there are any lessons we can learn from this sad sequence of events, it is this: riots happen frequently, but they do not come from nowhere. Anger can flare up at any time, but if that anger results in the organized destruction of a pagan temple forty miles out of town, it is because those in power have shaped and harnessed that narrative for their own ends. We cannot understand violence without understanding the political and ecclesiastical fault lines that existed beforehand. If Peter had been more secure, he probably would not have tried to whip up the crowd into a destructive frenzy to cement his power. If the Christians of Egypt had not already felt so marginalized by the politics of Chalcedon, they might not have been so ready to see persecution in what was little more than prep school violence.

However, Peter's political calculations only got him so far. Peter enjoyed a short-term boost in his reputation. He attempted to parlay that boost into a long-term advantage by summoning an imperial official to conduct a thorough investigation of Parlalius's school. Peter probably hoped the investigation would uncover more outrages at the pagan school that he could exploit for political gain. But it did not, and the goodwill Peter enjoyed evaporated. Within a year everybody was just as upset with Peter as before. Violence rarely accomplishes long-term political aims.

The Cross Against the Sword

While bishops could use violence to enhance their own power, they could also use their power to oppose violence. The greatest example comes from a figure named Ambrose of Milan. Ambrose was not the sort of person who was ever supposed to become a bishop. He was an unbaptized layman who served in various political roles over the course of his long and distinguished career. He happened to be the regional governor of Milan when the previous bishop died. There was a huge storm brewing between pro- and anti-Nicene factions as to who the next bishop should be. When it became clear that violence would result if no one intervened, Ambrose arrived with a contingent of troops to enforce a peaceful election of the next bishop.

All the folks in the room quickly decided that Ambrose should be the next bishop.

This was not the way that Ambrose was expecting things to go. Perhaps no one was expecting things to go this way. The events of the day conspired against their expectations. The election had been contentious, the church was divided, and Ambrose happened to be one of the few Christians in the city who was almost universally respected. The assembled bishops knew a solution when they saw one. They took Ambrose and ordained him on the spot three times over: first as a deacon, then a priest, and finally as a bishop.

Ambrose was thoroughly pro-Nicene in his theological sentiments. He did not write any of the long treatises on the subject like the Cappadocians, but he read their works and was responsible for promoting them in the Latin-speaking West. Anywhere that christological controversies could be found, Ambrose was there supporting the cause of Homoousian theology. Ambrose was an excellent ally to have because in addition to being widely respected, he was also stone-cold brilliant. He was one of the very few men in his time period who did not read aloud. He read silently, which was really hard to do in antiquity because most books did not have spaces between the words.[7] The average reader needed to speak the text aloud in order to figure out where the word breaks were. Ambrose was intelligent enough to decipher the text with his mind alone.

All of his brilliance would be needed, because Ambrose would have the most important congregant of all: the emperor Theodosius, who moved the imperial capital to Milan later in his reign. Ambrose was Theodosius's personal bishop during one of the worst sins of the pious emperor's reign.

To make a long story short, there was a massive riot in the Greek city of Thessalonica in which tens of thousands of citizens were murdered by Roman soldiers. We are not entirely certain of the details. It appears that a very popular Roman charioteer was credibly accused of sexually assaulting an important government official's aide. The closest modern example would be if someone like David Beckham was accused of attacking the prime minister's personal secretary. The charioteer was duly arrested and charged, but the populace was so angry their hero had been imprisoned that they rioted and killed the arresting officer. In response, the Roman military brutally put down the riot, killing everyone who got in their way—and more besides. They did so on orders from Theodosius himself.

In response, Ambrose imposed the harshest penalty a bishop had available to him: excommunication.

The bishop went about the matter gently.[8] Ambrose quietly counseled Theodosius that he needed to go through a period of penitence before he could receive communion again. Until Christmas of that year, Theodosius attended church quietly, without pomp or circumstance, and without wearing his imperial regalia. After his penance was over, Ambrose publicly welcomed Theodosius back into the communion of the church.

Ambrose's boldness is striking. He knew that such massive violence needed to be met with consequences, and he was not afraid to impose those consequences on the most powerful man in the entire empire. Ambrose benefited from his time as the governor of the city; many troops remembered him fondly and still felt loyal to him. Ambrose was also well-connected to important families in the area. Even if he had wanted to, Theodosius

---

7. Making a book was extremely expensive and difficult before the invention of the printing press, and so it was crucial to fit as many words as possible onto a single page. Spaces between words would have made books even more expensive.

8. There is a popular story that Ambrose dramatically met the emperor and his full imperial retinue at the gates of the church and barred his entry. The story is exciting and inspiring; it is also an urban legend. There is no good evidence that Ambrose went about his discipline so publicly. History, unfortunately, is often a killjoy.

could not have retaliated against the bishop without significant political consequences.

The case of Ambrose is probably the high-water mark for a single bishop's influence over an emperor. He proved that bishops could use their spiritual authority to guide emperors down a path of peace and repentance. Even with the security his position and class afforded him, it is remarkable that Ambrose was able to impose a penance on an emperor and the emperor accepted it without question.

The changes wrought by Constantine and the councils after Nicaea created two parallel streams of authority. The emperor held immense political authority by virtue of his imperial grandeur, public persona, and command of myriad Roman legions outfitted with extremely pointy swords. A Christian emperor was believed to rule by divine permission, and therefore to have spiritual authority as well. But his spiritual authority was not absolute. Christianity also taught that all people were equal before God, that all were sinners who stood in need of the graces of the church. Those graces were ultimately overseen by the bishops. A resourceful and well-connected bishop could claim spiritual authority over even the emperor. Bishops had the power to check the emperor's worst tendencies and be voices for peace.

The post-Nicene church had new opportunities to weigh in on matters of public importance. It could use its power to foment violence or to oppose it. Over the course of the next seventeen centuries, the church would do both. Its ambivalent relationship to power and force is part of its enduring legacy—one which the Council of Nicaea did not invent, but certainly complicated.

Chapter 14

Nicaea and the Suffering, Relational God

THE LAST FEW CHAPTERS of this book have focused on understanding Nicaea's impacts on world history. In this chapter and the next, we will focus on what the players in the controversy were focused on: how the Nicene Creed changed the Christian understanding of God and the church. There was no doubt that calling the Son *homoousios* with the Father would impact the way Christians worshiped. Nicaea's defenders claimed that it was a necessary evolution in the church's understanding of God and perfectly continuous with the faith of earlier Christians. Moreover, they said that it guarded against the heretical innovations of Arius and his ilk. Anti-Nicenes, on the other hand, believed the phrase to be a radical innovation that departed from the faith Christ revealed to the apostles.

As they pondered the implications of this word, each side attempted to answer a burning question: if the Son is truly of the same substance as the Father, what does it mean to say the Son suffered?

Accounting for a Scandal

The question was not a new one. Christians had been forced to give an account of Christ's suffering ever since Peter rejected the idea.[1] In the ancient world, the notion that God would suffer and die was scandalous. Most other religions gloried in their deities' strength, not in their capacity to suffer and

1. Matthew 16:22.

die. When nations went to war, they often viewed their gods as guarantors of victory in battle. A god who could be crucified by mere mortals would be of no help in such matters. Ancient Romans found the Christians' worship of a crucified human man not just strange, but ludicrous. One piece of Roman graffiti[2] depicted a man worshiping a crucified figure with the head of a donkey—an ass's head, in other words.[3] Beneath the image was carved the simple phrase, "Alexamenos worships his god." The author of this graffiti wanted to make fun of his neighbor Alexamenos, and chose to do so by mocking his suffering God. Nor was he alone in his criticism. Early Christian thinkers were constantly trying to explain to their pagan neighbors why they worshiped a man who had suffered and died. They repeatedly insisted that Christ's suffering was not a result of his weakness or failure to plan, but part of God's loving plan to bring salvation to the whole world. Their arguments met with varying levels of success depending on their rhetorical skills and the goodwill of their audience. Some pagans were convinced and converted to the worship of the Crucified One, but most remained deeply skeptical of Christianity until the time of Constantine.

The Nicene controversy shed new light on this old dilemma. Since this conflict was between Christians, not between Christians and pagans, all parties agreed that Christ had suffered as part of God's divine plan. However, they were very careful in how they described that suffering, because they also believed that God was immune from outside change, compulsion, or suffering.[4] They summed up all of these nasty things that God was not subject to with a single nifty Greek word: *pathos* (PAH-thos). It refers to being overcome by something else: another's violence or force, one's own emotions, the pain of disease or infirmity, etc. To say that God was immune to *pathos* simply meant that God could not be overcome by anything else. God was supreme, and nothing could change that—not even divine emotions.

Different thinkers had different understandings of what exactly this meant. One school of thought suggested that God could experience pleasant emotions but not destructive ones. For example, God could feel joy and peace, but never became envious or despairing. Other thinkers argued that God could experience strong emotions like anger, sorrow, or pain if they were morally justified. A good God must feel outrage at the state of the world, for example. They simply believed that God remained in control when angry—something very difficult for humans to manage. Others suggested that since God's being is incomprehensible to us, we cannot say for

---

2. Yes, the Romans had graffiti just like we do.
3. Yes, Roman graffiti was about as crude as modern graffiti.
4. The ten-dollar word for this doctrine is "divine impassibility."

certain that God has emotions. When we say that God is emotional, we are saying that God behaves in a way analogous to a human being experiencing emotions. For example, when God punishes someone for doing evil, we might say that God is angry because humans are often angry when they punish someone. When God provides nurture and comfort, we say that God is compassionate, since people often feel compassion when caring for others. We attribute emotions to God as a way of comprehending God on our own terms.[5]

Nicaea and the Suffering God

Central to each of these theories was the notion that God could not be controlled or influenced by any other force. Christians differed on the specifics of what level and kinds of emotion God might experience. They were united, however, in their conviction that God was the ultimate power in the universe and hence was above any kind of harmful *pathos*. For many of the anti-Nicenes, the Nicene Creed was dangerous because it implied the opposite.

Jesus Christ suffered the most excruciating torture the Roman Empire could devise. Moreover, the Gospels portray Jesus as being not entirely in control of his mind and body during the crucifixion. Luke 22:44 reports that Jesus was so nervous before his crucifixion that he began to sweat blood. Matthew 27:46 depicts Jesus crying out, "My God, my God, why have you forsaken me?" Ancient Christians interpreted this cry as an expression of fear or even despair—precisely the sort of thing God was supposed to be immune from. Moreover, Jesus' death was humiliating. Those being crucified had one last way to assert their dignity in the face of death: they could hold out as long as possible. A strong man might easily last a day or more before succumbing to death, and in so doing earn some measure of respect from the watchful crowds. Jesus died so quickly that the soldiers did not even need to break his legs to speed up the process,[6] hardly the glorious ending that one might have expected of the Son of God.

If Jesus Christ was *homoousios* with the Father, then that meant the Father was vulnerable to precisely those emotions of fear, despair, and pain. Yet if the Father was vulnerable to those things, then he was clearly not the omnipotent, highest God they proclaimed him to be. The anti-Nicenes were horrified by this implication. In fact, Eunomius specifically referred to the

---

5. See Gavrilyuk, *Suffering of the Impassible God*, for a detailed treatment of each of these schools of thought.

6. John 19:33.

crucifixion as evidence that the Son and Father could not be *homoousios*: "If ... God Who is over all, Who is the unapproachable Light, was incarnate, or could be incarnate, came under authority, obeyed commands, came under the laws of men, bore the Cross, then let him say that the [Son's] Light is equal to the [Father's] Light."[7] For Eunomius, Christ's suffering was proof he was a second, lower deity. A lower deity could suffer and die as God's plan required without implying that the Unbegotten experienced *pathos*—a logical impossibility in Eunomius's mind.

The pro-Nicenes responded to the charge of incoherence in several ways. First, they made a distinction between Christ's humanity and divinity. Because Christ was fully human, he suffered with respect to his humanity, but not with respect to his divinity. Athanasius frequently described the Son as having "put on flesh," almost like one might put on a garment. The flesh can suffer even when the Son's divinity does not, almost like how a coat can be torn without harming the body underneath it. The Cappadocians made similar arguments to Athanasius. Gregory of Nazianzus's rule of applying "higher" descriptions to Christ's divinity and "lower" descriptions to his humanity was a case in point—Christ's suffering was to be attributed to his humanity. The pro-Nicene strategy was to point out that Jesus Christ was a composite of different natures and realities. Eunomius and his allies were playing fast and loose with logic by applying what was said of one nature to another. Someone can wear a garment that might become frayed at the ends, faded in color, or suffer from fabric degradation. However, we would not then say that the person had faded in color or become frayed at the ends.[8]

If you are finding yourself confused by this line of argument, you are not alone. For while Athanasius and the Cappadocians drew a clear line between divinity and humanity in Christ, they were rather ambiguous about what exactly that meant for Jesus Christ. Did he, for example, have a human soul, or just a human body? Was he fully human and fully divine, or did his humanity and divinity combine into one unified nature? These questions would occupy the church in the next major controversy after Nicaea (which led to the Council of Chalcedon, which we touched on in chapter 13). The story of that controversy is fascinating, important, and the topic for a different book entirely. For now, simply know that you are not confused because you are failing to understand. You are confused because there are ambiguities in the arguments themselves.

---

7. Quoted in Gregory of Nyssa, *Against Eunomius* 5.3, in *NPNF* 5.

8. Except metaphorically, as when said person is attempting to meet the next deadline in the book writing process.

The pro-Nicenes had another reply to Eunomius that was equally important, but less frequently noticed. Far from being a mark against his divinity, the Homoousians saw Christ's suffering as proof of his greatness. Gregory of Nyssa was appalled at Eunomius's blasphemous mockery of Christ on the cross. For Gregory, there was no clearer proof of the man's divinity than his ability to endure humiliation, torture, and death for our sake. Unlike Eunomius, Gregory did not claim that Jesus Christ's full divinity required him to be immune from fear, despair, and pain. On the contrary, he saw Jesus' ability to maintain his faithfulness in spite of those feelings as proof of his divinity. Who else but God could have endured such suffering in the flesh and still remained sinless? Gregory has quietly repurposed the notion of divine self-control. Other thinkers had said that God might experience anger, sadness, despair, etc. but was never overcome by them. Gregory added that a human nature united to God's divine nature can stay faithful in the face of truly overwhelming emotions.[9]

What did God's suffering mean for the average Christian? There were several implications one could draw. If Jesus Christ is fully divine, then his suffering is the most profound expression of empathy and solidarity possible. Even if the divine nature does not die, God knows what it is like to die because God took on human flesh. Even if divinity cannot suffer, divinity has united to a human life that does suffer. God is with us in our pain as intimately as possible. Moreover, if Jesus Christ is fully divine and felt fear and despair as a human, then Christians do not have to worry that they are doing something wrong when they feel fear and despair. Fear of suffering and death are natural parts of being human; it is natural to wonder if God is with you when all seems turned against you. It is not a lack of faith to feel these emotions.[10] If Christ genuinely felt them without sin, then so can we.

Homoousians did not just have to defend how Jesus Christ could suffer as a man. They also had to describe how the Son could be fully divine and a son. There are fewer external influences greater than another being causing you to be born. If being God means being free from external influence, then it is difficult to imagine that a being begotten by another could be fully divine. The infamous blasphemy of Sirmium said as much explicitly:

> There is no uncertainty about the Father being greater [than the Son]: it cannot be doubted by anyone that the Father is greater

---

9. Gregory of Nyssa, *Against Eunomius* 5.3

10. This is not to say that *all* negative emotions are always natural. It is possible to wallow in one's fear, sorrow, etc. A negative emotion can also lead to sinful thoughts, such as when a fear that God has abandoned you turns into a firm belief that God has abandoned you. These sins are not the result of feelings, however. They are the result of choices we make about our feelings.

in honor, in dignity, in glory, in majesty in the very name of "Father," for he himself witnesses.[11]

In the ancient world, it was assumed without question that fathers were greater than sons because fathers caused sons to be born and not vice versa. The idea that the Son might be equal to the Father was a cause of scandal. Yet the pro-Nicenes were driven by their convictions to square this seeming circle: the Son was the Father's equal in a way that did not diminish the Father's glory in the slightest.

In so doing, the pro-Nicenes quietly expanded the vision of divinity.

The presumption of most ancient (and many modern) authorities is that God is so utterly powerful and impervious to influence as to be unable to receive anything from creatures. The ancient Jewish thinker Philo of Alexandria famously claimed that "God never ceases to act. As it is the property of fire to burn and that of snow to chill, so it belongs to God to act."[12] God acts on other beings, but other beings do not act on God. Christian philosophers tended to take a similar view. Because God is omnipotent, no being can influence God without God being willing to be influenced—and if God is willing to be influenced already, then one's efforts are superfluous anyway. Perhaps the most famous formulation of this attitude comes from the medieval theologian Thomas Aquinas,[13] who stated that God was not in a real relationship with creatures. Aquinas did not mean that God had failed to compliment creation enough or to take creation out on enough dates. For Aquinas, a real relationship is one in which both parties are changed by the other, and God did not change. The relationship of a person to God was in that way rather like one's relationship to the sun. When we move out of the shade and into the sunlight, we are warmed and comforted. The sun, however, does not change. It remains as brilliant as it was before we ever stepped into its light.

While each of these theologies has their unique aspects, all share a common conception of God. God acts, but is not acted upon; God changes us, but is unchanged; God cannot be surprised or taken back, but is always in perfect control.

If we take the Nicene Creed seriously, this picture of God must change.

If the Son is truly *homoousios* with the Father, then that means that God can experience a certain kind of receptivity. God does not just act;

---

11. "The Second Creed of Sirmium," in Hahn, *Bibliothek*, 199–201.

12. Philo of Alexandria, *Allegorical Interpretations* 1.5.

13. Thomas Aquinas lived approximately eight hundred years after the Nicene controversy. However, his formulation of divine impassibility captures a pattern of thinking that existed in both the fourth century and in our modern times.

God can be acted upon. The Son is begotten of the Father. The Son (and Spirit, for that matter) submit to the Father's will and carry out the Father's commands. The Son suffered and died according to the flesh. Per the Homoousians, the Son did all of this without his divinity being degraded or compromised in any way. The beloved preacher David Bartlett once said that "God is most God just when God is most vulnerable, most human."[14] His sentiment would make no sense without the theological insights of the Homoousians. There are limits to the kind of receptivity or passivity the pro-Nicenes could imagine in the Son. They insisted that he did not suffer with respect to his divine nature, and that he was begotten in a way that is incomprehensible to human minds. His submission to the Father's will was a natural consequence of the fact that he was the Father's Word. The Father did not force him to submit. This limited version of divine receptivity had profound implications for how Christians worship. It suggested that when Christians glorify God, they do not merely glorify God's activity, freedom from external control, or unchanging truth. They also glorify God's humility, openness to created experience, and capacity to be begotten.

A New Vision of God

The Cappadocians knew that they were not merely trying to refute a particular group of heretics; they were attempting to faithfully explain the doctrine of the Trinity in a way appropriate for the fourth century. In so doing, they left the church with a new vocabulary for understanding God's being as a fundamentally relational phenomenon.

In emphasizing the similarities between the persons of the Trinity, the Cappadocians pointed out that they are alike in almost every way. All three members of the Trinity always work together because they are inseparable. They have a unity that is closer than we can imagine as human beings. Divine persons are not the same thing as human persons, and their relationships to each other are correspondingly different (and closer) than ours. As Basil said, the goodness, glory, compassion, and wisdom of the three persons are *exactly the same*. Everything that really makes God God is the same in them. What we know of one, we automatically know of the other two. The only differences between them are differences of relationship. The Father begets, and the Son is begotten. Whereas the Son is begotten, the Spirit processes. We do not know the details of the Son's begetting or the Spirit's procession. We simply know that the three persons of the Trinity stand in different relationships to each other. One member gives and another receives. One

14. Bartlett, *Collected Sermons*, 218.

member begins a work, another mediates the work to creation, and a third perfects it.

In modern times, some theologians have been so inspired by the Cappadocians' insight that they have come to see this social dimension of the Trinity as their most important insight. This movement is referred to as social trinitarianism, and its proponents generally think that the relationships between the Father, Son, and Spirit provide a blueprint for how relationships between human beings should work. Since we are made in the divine image, if God is a society of divine persons, then perhaps human societies are meant to be patterned on the Trinity. For example, a social Trinitarian might suggest that since the three persons of the Trinity are equal, then democratic societies that respect human rights should be preferred to authoritarian societies or societies with strong caste systems. They might also argue that the Son and Father's self-giving, self-sacrificing love should be the model for human marriages.

Social trinitarianism has inspired much controversy. It is unclear to me that the Cappadocians would endorse the movement. Basil, Gregory of Nyssa, and Gregory of Nazianzus were all quite clear that the mysteries of God's being are unknowable, and that includes God's relationships. We do not and cannot know what it is for the Son to be begotten, or for the Spirit to process. We revere God and hence revere those relationships, but it is difficult to see how we could build a just society by imitating a set of relationships that are beyond our understanding. Moreover, humans are not God. The Father and Son are infinite, and can give of themselves infinitely without harming themselves. It might not be helpful to tell a person suffering abuse from their partner that they ought to sacrifice themselves infinitely. Many twelve-step groups have found that when partners try to be self-sacrificial, they only enable their partner's addiction.[15]

Regardless of your opinion about social trinitarianism, the Cappadocians left behind a rich legacy for thinking about the Three Persons that endures even to this day. God is not a monolithic, solitary aloneness. God is not an isolated and impersonal ruler dispensing commands from on high. God is relational all the way down; community and communion are fundamental realities of God's being. One person of that triune God has become incarnate. Through his ministry, we are not just united with the Son. We are united with the Father and Spirit because the Son is forever bound to them. We experience the whole life of the Trinity, not just the Son.

---

15. See Tanner, "Social Trinitarianism," for a detailed description of criticisms of social trinitarianism.

The Filioque Clause

The Cappadocians insisted that we cannot know the nature of the divine relationships. There is one particular relationship that the church has been particularly keen to fight over in Nicaea's wake.

If you are a keen-eyed reader and attend a non-Orthodox church, you may have noticed one difference between the creed listed in chapter 11 and the Nicene Creed you have come to know. In the creed of the Council of Constantinople, it says that the Spirit proceeds from the Father, but makes no mention of the Son. In most Western churches, the Spirit is said to proceed from the Father and the Son. This is referred to as the *filioque* clause, after the Latin phrase *filioque* (FEE-lee-oh-quay), meaning "and the Son." The *filioque* clause is an important statement about the way the Holy Spirit comes to be. To say that the Spirit "proceeds" from the Father is to imagine the Spirit coming forth from the Father's mouth, just as breath proceeds from my lips whenever I speak. Just as the Bible uses the metaphor of childbirth to explain how the Son comes to be from the Father, the creed uses the metaphor of procession to describe the Spirit coming to be from the Father. To say the Spirit proceeds from the Son is to say the Spirit depends on the Son for being as well as the Father.

We are not quite certain when Western churches began to include the *filioque* clause in their version of the creed. All we really know is that by about the year 600 AD, some of the Western churches had started incorporating the filioque into their creed. The roots of the *filioque* probably go back earlier—we know of Latin theologians in the fourth and fifth centuries who seem to believe it. As the *filioque* clause gained steam in the West, churches in the East began to oppose it with increasing vehemence.[16]

To understand why this single Latin word became so controversial, we have to take a look at the reasons for and against its usage.

The *filioque* appears to have been added to the creed as an anti-Arian measure. Arian and Eunomian theologies survived in northern Europe for centuries after the Council of Constantinople. Before his exile as a heretic, Eunomius had sent missionaries to evangelize the Goths, and they had been quite successful in their work. Pro-Nicene Europeans needed to counter the prevalent Eunomian theology of their Germanic neighbors. The idea appears to be that if the Son could help generate a whole new divine person like the Spirit, then he absolutely had to be equal to the Father. There are also some biblical passages that could be read to support the idea. Jesus says that he will send the Spirit into the world in John 16:7. While the passage

---

16. See Siecienski, *Filioque*, for a full history of the controversy.

only refers to the Son sending the Spirit into the world at Pentecost, Jesus might also be indicating something about their eternal relationship. Perhaps he had also "sent forth" the Spirit from the Father before the beginning of time.

Those opposed to the *filioque* clause pointed to the lack of explicit biblical support for the notion. Nowhere does the Bible say the Spirit proceeds from the Son; the Bible does say that the Son was begotten of the Father, most famously in John 3:16. It is the Father's role to generate the other divine persons. To ascribe that role to the Son is to dilute the Father's uniqueness and praise the Trinity improperly. Eastern opponents also pointed out that the whole point of creeds is that you are not allowed to go around changing one without telling anybody. In fact, a council held in Ephesus had prohibited anyone, even a future council, from changing the text of the Nicene-Constantinopolitan Creed. The Western churches were not allowed to change a creed's text, even if they had the best of intentions.

In other words, what was at stake in the *filioque* clause was exactly what had been at stake in the whole Nicene controversy: the proper roles of the three persons and the right way to interpret the Bible.

You might be wondering how the church settled this disagreement. If you figure it out, please let the church know. East and West have argued about the *filioque* clause for seventeen centuries with no resolution in sight. Because the *filioque* was adopted in a piecemeal way, there was no one decisive moment that caused a break between the two sides. In the early centuries of the conflict, theologians criticized each other across the increasing linguistic and cultural divides between the Eastern and Western Roman Empires. A few brave souls attempted to come up with a compromise, but none of their solutions caught on.

Resentments and misunderstandings related to the *filioque* contributed to the Great Schism of 1054 in which the Pope of Rome and the Ecumenical Patriarch of Constantinople excommunicated each other. The Roman Catholic and Eastern Orthodox Churches have been out of union ever since.

Yet there are glimmers of hope for reconciliation. Numerous solutions to the *filioque* controversy have been proposed in the past few decades. Perhaps Western churches could continue to use the *filioque* clause without insisting that Eastern churches use it. As long as both groups recognize the orthodox intentions of the other side, perhaps that difference in doctrine need not divide them. Or perhaps the Western churches could drop the *filioque* from the creed but continue to teach it as doctrine. They could believe it to be true without claiming it to be a part of the Nicene Creed. Or perhaps both sides could come up with some new formulation that would fully satisfy everyone.

No one knows what solution will prevail, if any. For the moment, the impetus seems to be behind the second option. Since 1995 AD, popes have generally omitted the *filioque* clause from joint worship services held with Orthodox patriarchs. And in the Anglican Communion, some of the newest liturgical resources offer the text of the Nicene Creed without the *filioque* clause. Such concessions are meant to cool the temperature of ecumenical relations while the work of theological compromise continues. It is a strategy that I suspect Basil would have approved of. Perhaps the Spirit of unity would, too. If a deeper understanding of God's mysteries proceeds from these solutions, then one of the lasting wounds of Nicaea would finally be healed.

Chapter 15

One Body, Many Councils

THE CHURCH HAS NEVER been the same since its bishops gathered in a nondescript town seventeen centuries ago. The Council of Nicaea was the end of a great many things, and the start of even more.

Ecumenical Councils

You have read throughout this book that the Council of Nicaea came to be accepted as the first in a series of ecumenical councils. An ecumenical (also sometimes spelled oecumenical) council is one that has secured the assent of the large majority of Christians throughout the world. Not since the twelve apostles gathered in Jerusalem in Acts 15 had a council's findings enjoyed such broad support as those of Nicaea. The Nicene Creed was something really new in church history—for the first time, the vast majority of bishops in the world settled on a formal statement of faith that excluded those who disagreed from communion with the church. While smaller councils had drafted such creeds, they had never done it on such a vast scale. For most of previous history, Christians settled arguments by voting with their feet. The churches that survived and grew defined what was orthodox; the churches that shrank and closed defined what heresy had been. Now a new method of doctrinal definition was available. Creeds were not without cost; as we have seen, the Nicene Creed's acceptance would not have occurred without fifty-six years of tireless advocacy, argumentation, and enduring persecutions. Still, by the time of the Council of Constantinople, there was no denying that the Nicene Creed had achieved a genuine majority of support—not just from the assembled bishops, but from Christians of every rank and ethnicity throughout the empire. In a world filled with people of contrary opinions and contrary personalities, that agreement alone must have seemed miraculous. Later controversies would look back to the Nicene controversy as a blueprint for how to resolve their own questions of faith.

Nicaea's shadow was evident at the next major ecumenical council: the Council of Chalcedon in 451 AD. Chalcedon has reared its head in our story several times already; if you have read this book straight through, then you already know that the Egyptian church despised the council, and that its theological controversies had something to do with Christ's humanity. You need to know a little bit more about the council in order to make sense of how Nicaea influenced it. The Nicene controversy had definitively settled the question of Christ's divinity. He was just as divine as the Father, and *homoousios* with him. He was not a lesser god, as Arius or Eunomius had claimed, and he was not merely an aspect of the Father as the modalists taught. He was a distinct divine person, an *hypostasis*, fully equal to the Father, receiving his own will and thoughts from the Father in a way analogous to how we produce our own internal monologues.

As with most good answers, the Nicene Creed produced new questions to ponder. Now that Jesus' divinity was more defined, theologians began to wonder about his humanity. Did Jesus have a human mind? What about a human soul? If Jesus received his will from the Father, then how is it possible that he prayed that the Father's will and not his own be done?[1]

Each of these questions was an attempt to clarify how Christ's divine nature interacted with his humanity. Just as with the Nicene controversy, one proposed solution was so horrendous that everyone avoided it like the plague. For the Nicene generation it was modalism; for the Chalcedonian generation, it was the theology of Apollinaris of Laodicea. Apollinaris proposed that Jesus had a human body, but no human soul or mind. The Word took the place of the soul and mind in Jesus, controlling his body in the way one might control a puppet or a character in a video game.[2] Interestingly enough, Basil had attempted to court Apollinaris as an ally in the Nicene controversy before he understood his theology. After learning more about Apollinaris, Basil cut off all contact with him. Basil's enemies were less willing to forget about his scandalous associations, which dogged him for the rest of his career.

---

1. Luke 22:42.

2. Obviously Apollinaris of Laodicea, living in the fourth century, was tragically ignorant of video games. Nevertheless, I believe the analogy captures the point he was trying to make.

Having thus become the theological bogeyman of two generations of theologians, Apollinaris enjoyed the dubious honor of having three different theologies crafted to counter his beliefs. One school of thought, which was formulated by a bishop named Nestorius and became popular in Syria, proposed that Jesus Christ was a composite entity, formed of a full-fledged human man and the divine Word who joined together by God's good pleasure. In modern terms, this theology asserts that Jesus Christ is a bit like table salt. Salt is a composite of two chemicals, sodium and chlorine. When you put them together, you get something that looks quite different from either, although if you were to examine salt closely you would realize that it is nothing other than sodium and chlorine existing side by side. This school of thought, designed to reject the horrifying implications of Apollinaris, managed to horrify most of the bishops in Ethiopia and Egypt. These bishops thought the Nestorian proposal implied there were really two Christs existing side by side, not one. Led by Cyril, the bishop of Alexandria, they proposed that the Son took upon a human nature that was united with and dissolved into his divine nature like a drop of vinegar in an ocean. They were thus clear that there was only one Christ and not two; however, their solution in turn provoked horror from bishops throughout the empire who worried at the implication that Christ suffered as a divine being. Since there was no human nature "unmixed" with divinity in Cyril's proposal, bishops were afraid that they could no longer say with the pro-Nicenes that Christ suffered in his humanity but not in his divinity. Horror at the prospect of divine suffering led some bishops to propose a third solution: that Christ had two distinct natures, divine and human (which Nestorius affirmed) but was only one *hypostasis* (as Cyril and his bishops affirmed).

The Roman emperor at the time, a fellow named Marcian, continued the grand tradition of Roman emperors calling a council out of their frustration with bishops' constant arguing. Like Constantine, Constantius II, and Theodosius before him, Marcian had high hopes of solving all theological problems once and for all. To do so he modeled his council on the Council of Nicaea. Like Constantine, he would attend the council in person. When he arrived, he planted enthusiastic supporters in the crowd who hailed him as the new Constantine. In the literature, Marcian's council was depicted as having 636 attendees—precisely double the number of those supposed to have convened at Nicaea. He even planned to host the council at Nicaea, just in case anyone missed the parallels he was so earnestly drawing. Unfortunately, Marcian was not able to call a second council of Nicaea[3]—and it was all because of Attila the Hun.

3. There would be a second ecumenical council in Nicaea, but it would not be called

At the time, Attila was looming menacingly over the Danube River, poised to strike at the Roman Empire when the moment was right. Marcian decided to reconvene the council at Chalcedon, which was a bit closer to Constantinople and allowed the emperor to return to the military in case the situation deteriorated.

Marcian was not the only one to run the Nicene playbook at Chalcedon. Each of the bishops in attendance was aware of the weight of what they discussed. Christ's humanity was no less central to the faith than his divinity, after all. Gregory of Nazianzus had famously said that what Christ did not assume he did not redeem. If the church failed to accurately describe Christ's humanity, it would not be able to tell the story of salvation at all. With so much at stake, it was only natural that the bishops looked back to Nicaea to shape the council's progress—or obstruct it.

The Egyptian delegation had a terrible time at Chalcedon. The reigning bishop of Alexandria[4] had been deposed because his theology was out of favor. The rest of the Egyptian delegation was in the theological minority. At one point the emperor had to use soldiers to force the Egyptian bishops to remain at the council. To defend their orthodoxy, they pointed to Nicaea's canon law, which stated that the bishop of Alexandria had authority over the other bishops in Egypt. In a brilliant act of malicious compliance, the bishops stated that they could not sign Chalcedon's statement of faith without the permission of the bishop of Alexandria. Since there was no bishop of Alexandria at the moment, they had no choice but to refuse to sign the document.

The majority at Chalcedon were irritated at the Egyptians' obdurance, but they were also concerned to show their continuity with Nicaea. In fact, most of the creed they produced was not about the problem of Christ's humanity and divinity at all. Their document was mostly devoted to explaining how they were completely and totally in line with the Nicene Creed. Chalcedon's positive contribution to church doctrine was limited to a few lines in which the council upheld the third school of thought against the Egyptian and Syrian delegations. The emperor Marcian then proceeded to impose the council's result by force, with tragic consequences.

Perhaps Marcian imagined that his firm hand would steer the course of church history along the channels he desired. After all, Theodosius had enforced the Council of Constantinople's results with much success. There was one crucial difference, however. Theodosius promulgated a pro-Nicene

---

until 787 AD—more than four hundred years after the original Nicene controversy was settled, and long after Marcian lost his chance to convene it on account of being dead.

4. This bishop was not Cyril, but a successor whose name I will not trouble you with. Cyril had passed away before the Council of Chalcedon was called.

position that had already won the acceptance of the majority of the church. The Council of Chalcedon had not had time to win the same level of support. Instead of uniting the faithful, Marcian's council split the church into three distinct groups: the Egyptian and Ethiopian churches that emphasized Christ's united nature, the Syrian churches that emphasized his two natures; and the other churches that accepted the results of the Council of Chalcedon. That split continues today in Christianity's major denominations. The Egyptian and Ethiopian position is held by the Coptic and Ethiopian Churches, the Syrian position by the Assyrian Church of the East, and the Chalcedonian position by Roman Catholicism, Eastern Orthodoxy, and most branches of Protestantism.

Redeeming Church Politics

Marcian's foolhardy move might seem to you like yet another entry in the depressingly long list of church scandals. Nowadays, it is fashionable to bemoan the role that politics plays in church decisions. Politics does not just mean one's opinions on the national government or what candidates one supports (although churches are increasingly split along those lines, too). Rather, politics is the messy business of making controversial decisions, often by relying on church policies or behind-the-scenes negotiations to achieve desired ends. Many people react to politics with disgust, especially in church. In the house of God, can we not just come to an agreement? Can we not all just get along?

If those thoughts have ever crossed your mind, then it is important to remember that there is one group of people in the Nicene saga that has consistently agreed with your complaint. That group is the Roman emperors.

Roman emperors were consistently frustrated by and dismissive of the church's theological controversies. Constantine thought that Arius and Alexander disagreed over a trivial matter. He thought the status of Christ's divinity to be a small matter compared to the larger work of uniting the Roman Empire so it could continue to conquer the world with God's blessing. Even though he called the Council of Nicaea, he seems to have cared very little what the Nicene Creed actually said. He only cared that bishops said they agreed with it. Constantius II and Valens had stronger theological opinions than Constantine, but they were united in their belief that they could only reach unity by force. Rather than allow the church to engage in further politicking and argument, they wielded their military power to exile bishops they found disagreeable. Even Marcian's imposition of Chalcedon is more of a rejection of politics than anything else. He was unwilling to allow passionate disagreement to continue in the church. He simply called one council and then forced its dissenters to agree.

When we prize the apparent unity of the church and scoff at passionate disagreement, we risk falling into an imperialistic ideology of power. People will inevitably disagree. Those disagreements usually take longer to resolve than we would like, both because it takes a long time to understand what the disagreements are really about and because disagreements are uncomfortable, so *any* length of time spent in disagreement is more than we would desire. Yet the only way to avoid disagreement is to silence people. Disagreement is human. To suppress conflict is to suppress our humanity.

As long as the church is full of people, the church will have conflict. Conflicts are how groups of people clarify what is important to them and why. If the church has conflict, then the church will have politics, for politics are nothing other than the means by which groups of people resolve their conflicts. We cannot remove politics from the church without removing people from the church. We can, however, draw some lessons from the Nicene controversy that might help our politics stay constructive.

The first lesson is that politics are not the same thing as violence. In fact, church politics are often a defense against violence. When the church is engaged in political debate, it is ultimately attempting to persuade rather than force. Most bishops probably did not enjoy the many councils they attended, or the heated arguments they had. Yet those councils ultimately resulted in a creed that has united the church for seventeen centuries. Athanasius and the Cappadocians did not write their works out of a complacent desire to think about God. They wrote them out of anger at anti-Nicene theologies and a genuine fear of heresy. Yet many of those same works are now regarded as timeless classics of the faith. No one, pro- or anti-Nicene, was thrilled to spend fifty-six years of controversy without much to show for it. Yet that time was necessary for the Nicene Creed to slowly but surely win acceptance throughout the world. The work of church politics was incredibly slow. It happened on the timescale of generations. Little has changed today; the implications of Vatican II, for instance, are still hotly debated among Roman Catholics. Roman emperors had little patience for politics. Church unity was but one item on their very long to-do lists. They were often tempted to use violence to speed up the process of attaining unity. Alas, unity cannot be rushed. Exiling a troublesome bishop or threatening a council with military force may produce compliance; it cannot create genuine unity. As frustrating as it is, faithfully navigating church politics alongside deep theological reflection remains the best (and perhaps only) way of generating unity in the midst of conflict.

The second lesson is that most conflicts are complex and multifaceted. The Nicene controversy ostensibly began as a simple question: was the theology of Arius heretical? That question proved to be the tip of a massive iceberg. Within it were packed all sorts of other questions that the story's protagonists spent decades unraveling. Arius had learned his theology in his home of Libya, but ministered in Egypt. How were two disparate provinces of the empire, whose churches had different traditions of prayer and worship, going to unite in a single confession? How much authority did Arius's bishop have to decide what theologies would be taught in his city? In what circumstances could a group of bishops claim to speak for the whole church? What role did authorities like the emperor play in the conflict? Was God unbegotten and ungenerated by definition, or was there room in the Godhead for a limited kind of begottenness, dependency, and receptivity? How could so many people who had suffered for the name of Christ just a few decades earlier disagree so passionately about who Christ was? By the time churches realize they are in conflict, they are usually involved in several conflicts. One of the reasons church fights can seem so impossible to resolve is because underneath each fight, there are more controversies than meet the eye.

Seen in that light, it is surprising that the Nicene controversy took only fifty-six years to resolve. Such questions could easily have stumped thinkers for centuries!

The third lesson is that external authorities like the emperor cannot create unity, but they can reveal it. One problem with attempting to force a consensus is that you cannot force someone to change their mind; at best, you can force them to act like they have changed their mind. In the heyday of Constantinian Christianity, many believed that imperial force could change minds. That power turned out to be a mirage. This was difficult for the players in the controversy to see; it is much clearer for us today. Constantius II and Valens tried very hard to codify an anti-Nicene theology as the law of the land. To the Homoousians, it seemed as though they might succeed and the whole church might turn away from the Nicene Creed. The emperors were unable to overcome the consciences of the pro-Nicene party, however. By contrast, Theodosius's edicts were broadly accepted, and anti-Nicene theology faded away. In retrospect, the anti-Nicene emperors had been propping up a theological minority whose time was over. Theodosius spoke for the majority. As fourth-century Romans were blissfully ignorant of the concept of public opinion polls, there was probably no way for anyone to know where the majority stood until the emperors put their thumb on the scale for one side or another. It turned out that by the end, the majority stood with Nicaea. This suggests that there is a time and place for leaders to "call the question" on controversies within the church. However, they should not imagine that they will dramatically persuade all the holdouts to agree with their position. They will simply learn where the mind of the church is at that moment.

The fourth lesson of the Nicene controversy will likely not shock you: people are strange, and if the Holy Spirit is at work in the church, then the Spirit works through people's oddities. The story of Nicaea is a profoundly human story. It would have been wildly different if Athanasius had the diplomatic skills to avoid being exiled five times. If Eustathius of Antioch had been able to keep his foot out of his mouth and avoid insulting the emperor's mother, then perhaps the purge of pro-Nicene bishops would have been stemmed. Certainly Gregory of Nazianzus would not have had to stake his whole bishopric on a doomed attempt to reunify Antioch. Eunomius might have been able to carry the day if he had focused more on his reputation as a wonder-worker instead of insisting on preaching controversial sermons about Mary that got him in trouble with the emperor. Gregory of Nazianzus would never have found his way to Constantinople had he not insisted on dramatically running away from every church job he had been forced into. If a whole slew of Roman emperors had the good fortune not to die in battle against their enemies, who knows how the political landscape would have been different?

Much of our frustration at church conflict comes from the oddities of the people involved. Our opponents do not always make sense. They contradict themselves. They become angry over matters that seem trivial to us. They continue to disagree with us no matter how often we explain our positions. To which the players of the Nicene controversy would likely say: welcome to the club. History is full of unexpected twists and turns because history is made by humans. I have known many people who believe that the best conflict is one in which each side arrives perfectly well-adjusted and in full command of their faculties, proceeding to hold a calm, rational discussion that leads to a tidy resolution within an hour. Alas, people are not so simple. Each of us brings our God-given strangeness to a conflict, and when the conflict is important, emotions tend to run high. The reason that church politics are so often awkward and uncomfortable is because strong feelings and human oddities make for an awkward and uncomfortable combination. Yet this is how we are. We would do far better to accept this as a natural part of conflict than to fight against it. Christians believe the Holy Spirit is at work in the church. Most of them also believe the Holy Spirit to be divine. Surely God can work through our idiosyncrasies and not just our most buttoned-up, put-together selves!

Embracing the Mess

If the church is to fight constructively, it can only do so by becoming comfortable with discomfort. The messiness of conflict and the strong feelings associated with controversy often drive Christians to seek tidier methods of conflict management. Christians have even tried to make the Nicene controversy a tidier story than it actually is.

Those who claim the mantle of Nicaea often portray the council as a unanimous endorsement of obviously orthodox theology against its obviously heretical opponents. On this account, Christians had been searching for centuries to find the language to express that Christ was perfectly God and perfectly human, but scratched their heads in bafflement until the Nicene Creed came along to solve their problems. When the council was called, all the assembled bishops condemned Arius and happily walked forward into the new Nicene era without any backsliding or further debate.[5] The fact that some dissenters were exiled is ignored, as are the fifty-six years of backlash and debate that followed it. Far from being serenely accepted by an empire eager to find a single solution, the Nicene Creed was often opposed by those in power, especially in the eastern half of the empire. Nor were the creed's opponents cynical villains consciously attempting to undermine the faith of the empire. Arius, Aetius, and Eunomius were not perfect people, but all evidence suggests they were sincere in their convictions. Those with significant political power, like Eusebius of Caesarea and Eusebius of Nicomedia, often used it to manipulate the imperial hierarchy in their favor. However, the anti-Nicenes were hardly alone in their use of such methods. Nor does that mean they were insincere in their beliefs; far more likely that they thought their theology so important that it was worth fighting for.

On the other side of the aisle, many people tell an equally simple story in which Nicaea is the villain. Prominent religious writers have described the Council of Nicaea as "bought and paid for" by the emperor Constantine, who ensured that no free religious discussion could take place.[6] If Constantine bought the council, then it is clear that the *homoousios* was the emperor's personal theology imposed by force. On this telling, Nicaea is not a high point of Christian truth, but the beginning of the church's long and disturbing history of collaboration with world power at the cost of its own soul. Of course, these stories tend to leave out the fact that bishops continued to argue no matter what the Nicene Creed said—and in many cases, no

---

5. See, for example, the summary of *Catholic Digest*: "Short History."
6. Tooley, "Diana Butler Bass vs the Council of Nicaea."

matter what the emperor said. Ignored as well are the travails of Nicaea's defenders, who spent at least as much time resisting the dominant theological trends of their day as riding them. No one can deny that emperors and powerful bishops wished to resolve the Nicene controversy; to assume that they had the power to do so is to give them far more credit (or blame) than they deserve.

The Council of Nicaea was a church fight, and like most church fights, it was neither a single glorious triumph of truth nor a single heinous victory of cynical power over marginalized minorities. If we make Nicaea either of these, then we will walk into church conflicts with unrealistic expectations. Truth rarely triumphs without significant effort or significant opposition, and those in power are rarely able to simply dictate the outcome of theological arguments. If our expectations are realistic when we fight in the church, then we may enter our conflicts with more patience—and more good humor.

The Monastic Virtue of Being Annoyed

At least one Nicene figure was aware of how important these realistic expectations were. When he was not busy refuting Eunomius or managing the affairs of the church in Caesarea, Basil maintained relationships with many monastic communities. The monks would occasionally write to Basil with questions about how they ought to live. While writing with them, Basil had an opportunity to opine on what kind of monasticism was best. Some monks lived solitary lives, praying in silence and making contact with other monks only a few times per month. These monks are often referred to as eremitical monks. Others lived in communities in the desert, praying, eating, and working together. These monks are called cenobitic monks. Basil found the cenobitic approach to life superior. The cenobitic life was a better way for the monk to grow in love because it provided more opportunities to grow in moral character by tolerating annoyance. Monks were to become humble. How could they be humble if they lived alone, where no one could wound their pride? How could monks love their enemies if they had no one nearby to even frustrate them? Patience was most difficult of all in the solitary life. How can you be patient if no one is around to deny your desire for some peace and quiet?[7]

Whatever else the Nicene controversy did, it gave everyone involved ample opportunities to exercise themselves in patience. The various attempts by emperors and bishops to force a conclusion to the controversy were failures of patience. So many people in power could not tolerate the

7. Basil, *Rule*, 7.4.

tension, discomfort, confusion, and headaches that the church's disagreement caused. Yet by some miracle of fate, the church had enough time and space to come to a real conclusion that has held the majority of the church together for the last seventeen centuries. Not all conflicts have had the same good fortune. The Council of Chalcedon was hailed as ecumenical by the churches of Rome and Constantinople; when Alexandria and Antioch rejected it, they were simply cast out of the church. And the wounds of the Protestant Reformation are still healing five hundred years after they first opened.

Yet when conflicts are given the time and space they need to heal, real growth is possible. The church did not emerge from the Nicene controversy with the same faith it had before. It gained a deeper and richer understanding of the God it worshiped. The church embraced a notion of God that was more capacious than the anti-Nicenes', able to incorporate limited forms of receptivity and dependence. Preachers now heralded the doctrine of salvation more clearly, drawing the links between God's incarnation, our predicament, and our ultimate deification that Athanasius had first articulated. Thanks to the work of the Cappadocians, the church was able to better grapple with the central paradox of its task: to praise a God whom it could not hope to comprehend. You can argue (and many have) that the *real* church already knew all of this. Perhaps Origen, Tertullian, and the other great thinkers of prior centuries assumed all of these Nicene developments and simply never bothered to express them in the same way as Nicaea. The fact nevertheless remains that the church was not able to explicitly express these ideas until they were refined in the fire of controversy. Only because of conflict did the church sharpen its praises of the One who is worthy of the highest worship mortal tongues can sing.

Conclusion

Churches are made up of humans. Churches fight because humans fight. Churches are perhaps never more human than when they are fighting over divine things.

The Council of Nicaea met seventeen centuries ago, but much of its story could have been written today. The egos of the parties involved, the abortive attempts at preemptive compromise, the frustration of each party as it failed to convince the other side of its theology, the indefatigable weirdness of the humans involved are as true of the average board of elders or parish council meeting as they are of the fourth-century church. The fourth-century church brought its full self to bear on a question that involved its whole self: how was it to praise the Christ who had redeemed it from sin and death? The answer to that question would only reveal itself after decades of conflict, pain, and frustrated searching. Yet the church deemed it a fight worth having.

Not all modern church fights are over matters of such substance, thankfully. Yet a fight does not have to be Nicaea-sized for it to be worth having. Every day, churches fight over what ministries they will prioritize, what music and words they will use in their worship services, who will lead them, and what they will teach about God. Each of these touches on the church's core mission. And, of course, churches fight over all kinds of things that probably do not matter quite so much: whether to file documents alphabetically or chronologically, how much of the service text to print in the bulletin, and where the mysterious spill in the kitchen came from. Peer underneath the hood, however, and you will find that these conflicts are proxies for larger questions that people value enough to fight about: whether their expertise and skills are valued, the place for beloved traditions, and who is responsible for what in a community. The fights are messy and often frustrating, but truth can still be found in the mess for those with the patience and persistence to look.

That patience and persistence have never been more important than they are today. The church is divided into thousands of denominations. Each of those denominations has its own list of councils (or general assemblies, or synods, or conferences, or meetings) through which it makes decisions. Each one of those councils may deal with multiple kinds of disagreements. Churches are divided between each other, but also among themselves. Questions of gender and sexuality, of authority, and proper doctrine continue to bedevil Christians seeking to be faithful in a rapidly changing world. If the church is to be the one body of Christ, then it might do well to look to the past as it navigates its present conflicts. It might do well to look back on the lessons of Nicaea.

Appendix A

A (Mostly) Jargon-Free Glossary of Key Terms

Cappadocian fathers: Also known as "the Cappadocians," this term refers to three important figures in the later years of the Nicene controversy: Basil of Caesarea, Gregory of Nyssa, and Gregory of Nazianzus. All three figures were born in the Roman province of Cappadocia and had personal relationships with each other. While their theologies share many similarities, the Cappadocians were not in perfect harmony and occasionally disagreed with each other. Basil and Gregory of Nazianzus famously disagreed on whether to describe the Holy Spirit as *homoousios* with the Father.

Council of Nicaea: A church council convened in 325 AD by the emperor Constantine in the town of Nicaea. Bishops from across the Roman Empire issued pronouncements on matters of church governance and theology. Most importantly, the council created a document known as the Nicene Creed, which asserted that the Son was *homoousios* with the Father. The council also condemned the theology of Arius of Alexandria as heretical.

Creed: A document, usually (but not necessarily) formulated by a church council, that expresses the council's beliefs on matters of faith. Creeds often (but not necessarily) also contain a list of beliefs that the council rejects. Creeds began to be written in the fourth century, though the Apostles' Creed may have roots in the second or third century.

Heteroousios: A Greek adjective meaning "of different (or dissimilar) substances." Those who described the Son as being of a different substance than the Father are referred to as Heteroousians.

Homoi: A Greek adjective meaning "similar." Homoians were those willing to describe the Son as similar to the Father but who refused to describe the Son's *ousia*.

Homoiousios: A Greek adjective meaning "of similar substance." Those who described the Son as being of similar (but not the same) substance as the Father are referred to as Homoiousians.

Homoousios: A Greek adjective meaning "of the same substance." Those who described the Son and Father as being of the same substance are sometimes referred to as Homoousians.

Hypostasis: A Greek noun meaning a real existing thing, rather than a thing that is merely an effect of something else. Human beings, rocks, and angels are *hypostases*. A reflection in a mirror is not.

Modalism: A theology which teaches that Father, Son, and Holy Spirit are modes or aspects of the one God, not distinct persons. Modalism might claim that God was Father in the Old Testament, became Son in the New Testament, and is currently the Holy Spirit. Modalism was repeatedly condemned as a heresy by multiple church councils.

Nicene controversy: The period during which churches in the Roman Empire debated questions related to the Son's divinity and its relation to the Father's divinity. While the precise dates of the controversy change from historian to historian, it begins no later than 325 AD and ends no earlier than 381 AD.

Ousia: A Greek noun meaning a thing's substance or being. The *ousia* of a human being is humanity; the *ousia* of God is divinity.

Rule of faith: A statement of the basic elements of Christian faith, as expressed by a particular writer or community. Ancient Christian writers referred to a "rule of faith" as a standard against which theologies could be evaluated. Rules of faith typically did not provide much doctrinal specificity, and occasionally did no more than list topics that Christian faith was supposed to cover without describing what Christianity said about them. There is no universal rule of faith that all early Christians recognized as authoritative. However, several principles are common to extant rules of faith: belief in God the Father, Jesus Christ, and the Holy Spirit. It is arguable that creeds evolved out of a need to provide more doctrinal specificity than rules of faith offered.

Tetrarchy: A system of governance in which rulership of the Roman Empire was shared between four emperors. The empire was divided into eastern and western halves, and two emperors ruled over each half. Each half had a senior emperor, called an Augustus, and a junior emperor, called a Caesar. The tetrarchy was implemented by the emperor Diocletian in an effort to stabilize the Roman political system. After Diocletian's retirement, the tetrarchy collapsed due to infighting among the four emperors and was eventually replaced by Constantine's dynasty.

Appendix B

A (Mostly) Jargon-Free Glossary of Key Players and Their Relationships

Alexander of Alexandria: The reigning bishop of Alexandria at the beginning of the Nicene controversy. Alexander taught that the Father and Son were *homoousios* and disciplined Arius for teaching otherwise. He was Arius's bishop and the adoptive father of Athanasius.

Arius of Alexandria: The Libyan-born priest whose theology was condemned by the Council of Nicaea. Arius taught that the Son was not *homoousios* with the Father, but was rather a created being who originated at a particular point in time. His bishop was Alexander of Alexandria, who disagreed with his theology. He sought support from Eusebius of Caesarea and Eusebius of Nicomedia in his conflict with Alexander. While most of his works have been lost, sections of his poetic creed, known as the *Thalia*, survive today.

Athanasius of Alexandria: An Egyptian-born priest who later became bishop of Alexandria. Athanasius was a secretary at the Council of Nicaea and spent most of his life writing and preaching in defense of the Nicene Creed. Athanasius endured five different exiles during his ministry. He was the adoptive son of Alexander of Alexandria. He was the author of *On the Incarnation* and *Orations Against the Arians*.

Basil of Caesarea: One of the Cappadocian fathers and bishop of the imperial province of Caesarea in modern-day Turkey[1] during the later years

---

1. Not the same Caesarea that Eusebius was bishop of. The Roman Empire had multiple provinces named Caesarea.

of the Nicene controversy. Basil is most remembered for his attempts to build pro-Nicene alliances of bishops across the empire, as well as his philanthropic work in his diocese. Basil also wrote important theological works defending the Nicene cause, most notably *Against Eunomius* and *On the Holy Spirit*. He was the brother of Gregory of Nyssa, on-again-off-again friend of Gregory of Nazianzus, and a political foe of the emperor Valens.

Constantine: The first Roman emperor to adopt Christianity as a state religion and the convener of the Council of Nicaea. Constantine was the son of emperor Constantius I and eventually conquered all other emperors to become the undisputed head of the Roman Empire, ending the tetrarchy. Constantine was responsible for Arius's brief exile and promoted Eusebius of Nicomedia to key positions of power. His three sons became emperors in their own right: Constantine II, Constantius II, and Constans.

Constantius II: The third son of the emperor Constantine (and the only one of Constantine's sons important enough to get an entry in this glossary). Constantius II initially ruled over the eastern third of the Roman Empire, but eventually came to rule the entire empire after the deaths of his brothers. He applied significant imperial pressure to bishops to adopt his preferred anti-Nicene theology, often threatening bishops with exile if they opposed him. Constantius II was also responsible for several of Athanasius's many exiles.

Eunomius of Cyzicus: The bishop of Cyzicus in modern-day western Turkey during the later years of the Nicene controversy. Eunomius was the leading spokesperson for the Heteroousian school of thought, and is remembered for his emphatic denial of the Son's equality with the Father. Due to his reputation as a theological radical, he became a favorite target of pro-Nicene writers, who criticized his position to illustrate the absurdity (as they saw it) of anti-Nicene theologies. Eunomius had a reputation as a wonder-worker and established an alternate network of anti-Nicene churches that continued to worship after the Council of Constantinople. He was also responsible for the evangelization of most of the Gothic tribes who lived in modern-day Germany.

Eusebius of Caesarea: The bishop of the imperial province of Caesarea (in modern-day Palestine) at the beginning of the Nicene controversy. Eusebius is noteworthy for his many scholarly writings, his quiet support of anti-Nicene theologians, and his enthusiastic support of Constantine. Athanasius accused Eusebius of Caesarea of fabricating charges against pro-Nicene bishops to have them removed from their posts. Eusebius presided over a council at which Athanasius was tried for crimes of murder and extortion.

Eusebius of Nicomedia: The bishop of the imperial province of Nicomedia at the beginning of the Nicene controversy. Eusebius of Nicomedia was one of Arius's most ardent supporters and was exiled by Constantine after the council of Nicaea. After a short exile, Eusebius returned and gained favor in the imperial court. He baptized Constantine on his deathbed and became the bishop of Constantinople. From this position of power, Eusebius spread anti-Nicene theology across the eastern Roman Empire.

Gregory of Nazianzus: One of the Cappadocian Fathers, reluctantly consecrated to be a bishop due to pressure from Basil of Caesarea. Gregory was briefly bishop of a small town called Sasima, then briefly bishop of his hometown of Nazianzus, before accepting an invitation to serve as the pro-Nicene bishop of Constantinople. Gregory was not recognized by the majority of Constantinople's Christians until the Council of Constantinople affirmed his title in 381 AD. Gregory was a skilled orator and writer, and is most known for his *Five Theological Orations* expounding his doctrine of the Trinity. Gregory was briefly president of the Council of Constantinople before resigning his post in disgust when the Council refused to back his preferred candidate to be bishop of Antioch. Gregory of Nazianzus met Basil of Caesarea as a student and was a close friend of his before they fell out as adults.

Gregory of Nyssa: One of the Cappadocian fathers and bishop of the imperial province of Nyssa in modern-day Turkey during the later years of the Nicene controversy. Gregory was an important writer for the pro-Nicene cause, and his most important works were *Against Eunomius* and his *Letter to Ablabius*, also known as *On Not Three Gods*. Gregory was present at the Council of Constantinople in 381 AD that reaffirmed and edited the Nicene Creed. He was the brother of Basil the Great, and was on friendly terms with Gregory of Nazianzus.

Marcellus of Ancyra: The bishop of the imperial province of Ancyra at the beginning of the Nicene controversy. Marcellus was a fervent supporter of the Nicene Creed, but his theology was widely perceived as modalistic. Homoousians struggled to distance themselves from Marcellus's theology, while anti-Nicene theologians feared that all pro-Nicenes sympathized with Marcellus.

Theodosius: Emperor of the eastern half of the Roman Empire after the death of Valens. Theodosius was born in modern-day Spain and was raised in a pro-Nicene family. Upon ascension to the throne, Theodosius began to implement pro-Nicene religious policies and called the Council of Constantinople (381 AD) to reaffirm the theology of the Nicene Creed. Theodosius worked closely with Gregory of Nazianzus before Gregory resigned his post as bishop of Constantinople.

Valens: Emperor of the eastern half of the Roman Empire after the death of Julian. Unlike his predecessor Julian, Valens was a Christian and restored many privileges to the Christians under his rule. Valens favored anti-Nicene Christianity and exiled prominent pro-Nicene bishops under his rule. Valens came into conflict with Basil of Caesarea, whose power he undercut by dividing Basil's diocese in two. While Valens did not exile Basil, he exerted significant pressure on Basil to force him to assent to pro-Nicene theology. His efforts were unsuccessful. Valens's death at the hands of a Gothic army led to the ascent of Theodosius, the first pro-Nicene emperor of the eastern empire in decades.

Bibliography

Anatolios, Khaled. *Athanasius*. New York: Routledge, 2003.
———. *Retrieving Nicaea: The Development and Meaning of Trinitarian Doctrine*. Grand Rapids: Baker, 2018.
Arnold, Duane W. H. *The Early Episcopal Career of Athanasius of Alexandria*. Notre Dame: University of Notre Dame Press, 1991.
Athanasius of Alexandria. *The Life of Antony and the Letter to Marcellinus*. Translated by Robert C. Gregg. Mahwah, NJ: Paulist, 1980.
———. *On the Incarnation*. Translated by John Behr. Yonkers, NY: St. Vladimir's Seminary Press, 2011.
———. *The Orations of St Athanasius Against the Arians*. Translated by William Bright. Cambridge: Cambridge University Press, 2014.
Ayres, Lewis. *Nicaea and its Legacy: An Approach to Fourth-Century Trinitarian Theology*. Oxford: Oxford University Press, 2010.
Ballan, Joseph. "Basil of Caesarea on the Ascetic Craft: The Invention of Ascetic Community and the Spiritualization of Work in the Asketikon." *Heythrop Journal* 52, no. 4 (2011) 559–68.
Balthasar, Hans Urs von. *Presence and Thought: An Essay on the Religious Philosophy of Gregory of Nyssa*. San Francisco: Ignatius, 1995.
Barnes, Michel Rene. *The Power of God: Dynamis in Gregory of Nyssa's Trinitarian Theology*. Washington, DC: Catholic University of America Press, 2016.
Barnes, Timothy David. *Athanasius and Constantius: Theology and Politics in the Constantinian Empire*. Cambridge: Harvard University Press, 1993.
———. *Constantine: Dynasty, Religion and Power in the Later Roman Empire*. Chichester, West Sussex, UK: Wiley Blackwell, 2014.
Bartlett, David L. *The Collected Sermons of David Bartlett*. Louisville: Westminster John Knox, 2020.
Basil of Caesarea. *Against Eunomius*. Translated by Mark Delcogliano and Andrew Radde-Gallwitz. Washington, DC: Catholic University of America Press, 2011.
———. *On Social Justice*. Edited by C. Paul Schroeder. Yonkers, NY: St. Vladimir's Seminary Press, 2009.
———. *The Rule of St Basil in Latin and English: A Revised Critical Edition*. Translated by Anna M. Silvas. Collegeville, MN: Liturgical, 2013.
Beeley, Christopher A. *Gregory of Nazianzus on the Trinity and the Knowledge of God: In Your Light We Shall See Light*. New York: Oxford University Press, 2013.

———. *The Unity of Christ: Continuity and Conflict in Patristic Tradition*. New Haven: Yale University Press, 2012.
Behr, John. *The Nicene Faith: Formation of Christian Theology*. Vol. 2. Yonkers, NY: St. Vladimir's Seminary Press, 2004.
———. *The Way to Nicaea*. Vol. 1. Yonkers, NY: St. Vladimir's Seminary Press, 2001.
Blaising, Craig A. "Creedal Formation as Hermeneutical Development: A Reexamination of Nicaea." *Pro Ecclesia* 19, no. 4 (2010) 371–88.
Bowen, Barry. "Televangelists Keith Moore And Creflo Dollar Acquire Multi-Million-Dollar Jets." *The Roys Report*, August 24, 2024. https://julieroys.com/televangelist-keith-moore-creflo-dollar-acquire-multi-million-dollar-jets.
Brown, Peter. *The World of Late Antiquity: AD 150–750*. London: Thames & Hudson, 2024.
Burton-Christie, Douglas. *The Word in the Desert: Scripture and the Quest for Holiness in Early Christian Monasticism*. New York: Oxford University Press, 2023.
Cameron, Averil. *The Later Roman Empire*. New York: HarperCollins Publishers, 2013.
Carter, Joe. "The State of Theology: What Evangelicals Believe in 2022." *The Gospel Coalition*, September 22, 2022. https://www.thegospelcoalition.org/article/state-theology-2022/.
Catholic Digest. "A Short History of the Nicene Creed." April 1, 2020. https://www.catholicdigest.com/amp/faith/rayer/a-short-history-of-the-nicene-creed/.
Christianson, Gale E. *In the Presence of the Creator: Isaac Newton and His Times*. New York: Free Press, 1994.
Coakley, Sarah. *Re-Thinking Gregory of Nyssa*. Malden, MA: Blackwell, 2004.
Crawford, Peter. *Constantius II: Usurpers, Eunuchs and the Antichrist*. Barnsley, South Yorkshire: Pen & Sword Military, 2016.
Daley, Brian E. *God Visible: Patristic Christology Reconsidered*. Oxford: Oxford University Press, 2019.
Daniélou, Jean. *Platonism and Mystical Theology: The Spiritual Doctrine of St Gregory of Nyssa*. Edited by Ignatius Green. Translated by Anthony P. Gythiel and Michael Donley. Yonkers, NY: St. Vladimir's Seminary Press, 2022.
DelCogliano, Mark. "Basil of Caesarea on Proverbs 8: 22 and the Sources of Pro-Nicene Theology." *Journal of Theological Studies* 59, no. 1 (2008) 183–90.
Edwards, Mark. "The Concept of God at Nicaea." *Apulia Theologica* 10, no. 2 (2024) 265–88.
Elm, Susanna. *Sons of Hellenism, Fathers of the Church: Emperor Julian, Gregory of Nazianzus, and the Vision of Rome*. Berkeley: University of California Press, 2015.
Fedwick, Paul J. *The Church and the Charisma of Leadership in Basil of Caesarea*. Eugene, OR: Wipf & Stock, 2001.
Frazee, Charles A. "Anatolian Asceticism in the Fourth Century: Eustathios of Sebastea and Basil of Caesarea." *The Catholic Historical Review* 66, no. 1 (1980) 16–33.
Gamble, Harry Y. *Books and Readers in the Early Church*. New Haven: Yale University Press, 2015.
Gavrilyuk, Paul L. *The Suffering of the Impassible God: The Dialectics of Patristic Thought*. Oxford: Oxford University Press, 2004.
Greer, Rowan A., and Margaret M. Mitchell. *The "Belly-Myther" of Endor: Interpretations of 1 Kingdoms 28 in the Early Church*. Atlanta: Society of Biblical Literature, 2007.
Gregory of Nazianzus. *Gregory of Nazianzus: Autobiographical Poems*. Translated by Carolinne White. Cambridge: Cambridge University Press, 2005.

———. *Gregory of Nazianzus's Letter Collection: The Complete Translation*. Edited by Bradley K. Storin. Berkeley: University of California Press, 2020.

———. *On God and Christ: The Five Theological Orations and Two Letters to Cledonius*. Translated by Frederick Williams and Lionel R. Wickham. Yonkers, NY: St. Vladimir's Seminary Press, 2002.

———. *Poems on Scripture: Greek Original and English Translation*. Edited by Brian Dunkle. Yonkers, NY: St. Vladimir's Seminary Press, 2012.

Gwynn, David M. *The Eusebians: The Polemic of Athanasius of Alexandria and the Construction of the Arian Controversy*. Oxford: Oxford University Press, 2006.

Hahn, August. *Bibliothek der Symbole und Glaubensregeln der Alten Kirche*. Breslau: E. Morgenstern, 1897.

Hanson, Richard Patrick Crosland. *The Search for the Christian Doctrine of God: The Arian Controversy 318–381 AD*. London: A&C Black, 2005.

Heffernan, Thomas J., ed. *The Passion of Perpetua and Felicity*. New York: Oxford University Press, 2012.

Heine, Ronald E. *Origen: Scholarship in the Service of the Church*. Oxford: Oxford University Press, 2011.

Henderson, David E. *Constantine and the Council of Nicaea: Defining Orthodoxy and Heresy in Christianity, 325 CE*. Chapel Hill: University of North Carolina Press, 2024.

Hopkins, Keith. "Christian Number and Its implications." *Journal of Early Christian Studies* 6, no. 2 (1998) 185–226.

Jasper, David. *The Sacred Body: Asceticism in Religion, Literature, Art, and Culture*. Waco, TX: Baylor University Press, 2009.

Johnson, Aaron P., and Jeremy M. Schott. *Eusebius of Caesarea: Tradition and Innovations*. Washington, D. C.: Center for Hellenic Studies, 2013.

Jones, Arnold H. M. *The Later Roman Empire*. Oxford: Blackwell, 1964.

Kim, Young Richard. *The Cambridge Companion to the Council of Nicaea*. Cambridge: Cambridge University Press, 2021.

"The Legacy of Dr. Kenneth B. Clark." CUNY Academic Commons. https://kennethclark.commons.gc.cuny.edu/the-doll-study/. Accessed December 1, 2024.

Lienhard, Joseph T. "Ousia and Hypostasis: The Cappadocian Settlement and the Theology of 'One Hypostasis.'" *The Trinity* (1999) 99–121.

Marcellus of Ancyra. *Fragments*. In "Marcellus of Ancyra: Problems of Christology and the Doctrine of the Trinity," by Maurice James Dowling, 288–357, PhD thesis, Queens University Belfast, 1987.

McGuckin, John Anthony. *St. Gregory of Nazianzus: An Intellectual Biography*. Yonkers, NY: St. Vladimir's Seminary Press, 2001.

Meredith, Anthony. *The Cappadocians* London: Bloomsbury, 1995.

Migne, J. P., and C. Blum. *Patrologia Graeca sous la direction de Claude Blum*. Paris: Classiques Garnier Numérique, 2006.

Murdoch, Adrian. *The last Pagan: Julian the Apostate and the Death of the Ancient World*. Rochester, VT: Inner Traditions, 2008.

Opitz, Hans-Georg. *Untersuchungen zur Überlieferung der Schriften des Athanasius*. Vol. 23. Berlin: Walter de Gruyter, 1935.

Origen of Alexandria. *Origen: Commentary on the Gospel According to John, Books 1–10*. Translated by R. E. Heine. Washington, DC: Catholic University of America Press, 1989.

———. *Origen: Commentary on the Gospel According to John, Books 13–32*. Translated by R. E. Heine. Washington, DC: Catholic University of America Press, 1993.

———. *Homilies on Jeremiah and 1 Kings 28*. Translated by John Clark Smith. Vol. 97. Washington, DC: Catholic University of America Press, 2010.

———. *On First Principles*. Translated by John Behr. Oxford: Oxford University Press, 2019.

———. *Treatise on the Passover; and, Dialogue of Origen with Heraclides and His Fellow Bishops on the Father, the Son, and the Soul*. Translated by Robert J. Daly. Mahwah, NJ: Paulist, 1992.

Petre, Jonathan. "Newton Set 2060 for End of World." *The Daily Telegraph*, February 22, 2003. https://www.telegraph.co.uk/news/uknews/1422794/Newton-set-2060-for-end-of-world.html.

Philo of Alexandria. *Allegorical Interpretations*, 1.5. In *The Works of Philo*, translated by C. D. Yonge. Peabody, MA: Hendrickson, 1993.

Prestige, G. L. *God in Patristic Thought*. Eugene, OR: Wipf & Stock, 2008.

Pseudo-Aurelius Victor. *Epitome de Caesaribus*. Translated by Thomas M. Banchich. Buffalo, NY: Canisius College Translated Texts, 2018.

Ricoeur, Paul. *Oneself as Another*. Chicago: The University of Chicago Press, 1992.

Roberts, Alexander, ed. *The Ante-Nicene Fathers: Vol. 3. Latin Christianity: Its Founder, Tertullian. I. Apologetic; II. Anti-Marcion; III. Ethical*. Revised and chronologically arranged with brief prefaces and occasional notes by A. Cleveland Coxe. Boston: Cosimo, Inc., 2007.

Rousseau, Philip. *Basil of Caesarea*. Berkeley: University of California Press, 1994.

Rukuni, Rugare, and Erna Oliver. "Nicaea as Political Orthodoxy: Imperial Christianity versus Episcopal Polities." *HTS Teologiese Studies/Theological Studies* 75, no. 4 (2019). https://www.ajol.info/index.php/hts/article/view/213618.

Schaff, Philip, and Henry Wace, eds. *A Select Library of Nicene and post-Nicene Fathers of the Christian Church: Second Series*. Vol. 1. Grand Rapids: Christian Literature Company, 1904.

Schlumberger, Jörg A. *Die Epitome de Caesaribus. Untersuchungen zur heidnischen Geschichtsschreibung des 4. Jahrhunderts n. Chr*. Munich: C. H. Beck, 1974.

Seznec, Jean. *The Survival of the Ancient Gods*. New York: Harper, 1961.

Siecienski, A. E. *The Filioque: History of a Doctrinal Controversy*. Oxford: Oxford University Press, 2013.

Smith, Mark S. *The Idea of Nicaea in the Early Church Councils*. Oxford: Oxford University Press, 2018.

Snobelen, Stephen D. "'A Time and Times and the Dividing of Time': Isaac Newton, the Apocalypse, and 2060 AD." *Canadian Journal of History* 38, no. 3 (2003) 537–52.

Stead, G. Christopher. "'Eusebius' and the Council of Nicaea." *The Journal of Theological Studies* (1973) 85–100.

Stephenson, Paul. *Constantine: Unconquered Emperor, Christian Victor*. London: Quercus, 2011.

Tanner, Kathryn. "Social Trinitarianism and its Critics." *Rethinking Trinitarian Theology* (2012) 368–86.

Tooley, Mark. "Diana Butler Bass vs the Council of Nicaea." *Juicy Ecumenism: The Institute on Religion & Democracy's Blog*. November 21, 2019. https://juicyecumenism.com/2019/11/21/diana-butler-bass-vs-council-of-nicaea/.

Trigg, Joseph W. *Origen: The Early Church Fathers*. New York: Routledge, 1998.

Vaggione, Richard Paul. *Eunomius of Cyzicus and the Nicene Revolution*. Oxford: Oxford University Press, 2023.
Ward, Benedicta. *The Sayings of the Desert Fathers: The Alphabetical Collection*. Kalamazoo, MI: Cistercian, 1984.
Watts, E. J. *Riot in Alexandria: Tradition and Group Dynamics in Late Antique Pagan and Christian Communities*. Berkeley: University of California Press, 2010.
Williams, Stephen, and Gerard Friell. *Theodosius: The Empire at Bay*. London: Routledge, 1998.
Williams, Rowan. *Arius: Heresy and Tradition*. Grand Rapids: Eerdmans, 2001.

Scripture Index

Old Testament

Genesis
1:2	109

Exodus
4:24–26	12n12

Leviticus
19:19	11n8

1 Samuel
28:3–25	11n9

Psalms
104	101

Proverbs
8	25, 101
8:22	90, 93
26:11	102n4

Isaiah
53:8	126
58:11	101

Jeremiah
2:13	101

Ezekiel
29	23, 24

Amos
4:13	93–94

New Testament

Matthew
11:19	51n9
16:22	180n1
26:52	172, 172n4
27:46	182

Luke
22:42	192
22:44	182

John
1	25
1:1–3	20
1:1	50–51, 51n6
1:3	95, 95n5
1:14	94
1:18	94
3:16	94, 189
3:18	94
8:58	118, 118n16
10:30	50, 50n5
14:6	101
14:28	95, 95n3

John (continued)

16:7	188–189
17:3	26
17:21	xi
19:33	182, 182n6
20:17	20n2, 95, 95n4

Acts

15	191

Romans

9	24

1 Corinthians

1:24	51n9
2:11	109n10
8	12n11
10:14–22	12n11
11:17–34	8n7
15:22	85, 85n1
15:24	103

Galatians

4	24

Philippians

2:6	50, 50n4

Colossians

2:3	51n9

Titus

1:12	11n10

Hebrews

6:1–6	6

1 John

4:9	94

Apocrypha

Wisdom

7	51
7:25–27	51, 51n8

Baruch

3:12	101

Authors Index

Alexander of Alexandria, 55n12
Arnold, Duane W. H., 173n5
Arius of Alexandria, 45n1
Athanasius of Alexandria, 99n2, 102, 102n4
Ayres, Lewis, 90n2

Bartlett, David L., 186, 186n14
Basil of Caesarea, 107, 107n9, 200n7
Bowen, Barry, 158n1
Brown, Peter, 5n3, 59, 59n3

Carter, Joe, 165n5
Christianson, Gale E., 165n4

Gavrilyuk, Paul L., 182n5
Gregory of Nazianzus, 118, 118n15, 119, 119n17
Gregory of Nyssa, 113, 113n14, 152, 152n4, 183n7, 184n9

Hahn, August, 185n11
Hanson, Richard Patrick Crosland, xv, 77
Heffernan, Thomas J., 4n1
Hopkins, Keith, 5n2

Lienhard, Joseph T., 105n7

Marcellus of Ancyra, 104, 104n5

Origen of Alexandria, 25n5, 26n7

Petre, Jonathan, 163n3
Philo of Alexandria, 185, 185n12
Pseudo-Aurelius Victor, 36n4

Ricoeur, Paul, 168, 168n1

Seznec, Jean, 23n4
Siecienski, A. E., 188n16
Snobelen, Stephen D., 163n3
Socrates, 69n1

Tanner, Kathryn, 187n15
Tertullian of Carthage, 27n9
Theognostus of Alexandria, 52n10
Theophilus of Antioch, 28n12
Tooley, Mark, 199n6

Watts, E. J., 173n6
Williams, Rowan, 45n1

Topic Index

Acacius of Caesarea, 92
Aetius of Antioch, 84–86, 128, 160, 169–71, 199
agenetos, 77
agennetos, 77, 80, 123
Alexamenos graffiti, 181
Alexander of Alexandria, 49–57, 61–63, 65, 70, 72, 97, 152n5, 159, 195
Alexandria, city of, 13, 4n14, 23, 41, 43–44, 53–55, 54n11, 65, 70–73, 75, 78, 80, 86, 114, 125, 137–38, 140–41, 143, 169–70, 173–76, 194, 201
Ambrose of Milan, 177–78, 178n4, 179
anathema, 47, 64, 122, 153
Anthony the Great, 17
Antioch, city of, 14n14, 44, 60, 72, 79–80, 84, 110, 122, 139–42, 150–51, 153–55, 198, 201
Apocrypha, 51n7
Apollinaris of Laodicea, 192, 192n2
Apostle's Creed, 10–11, 162n2
Aquinas, Thomas, 185
arche, 118
Arius of Alexandria, xiv, 43–49, 52–57, 61–64, 66, 69–71, 79, 83–84, 100–101, 108, 157, 159–60, 163, 165, 167, 180, 192, 195, 197, 199
 Thalia, 44–45, 101
Asterius, 104
Athanasius of Alexandria, xv, 61, 70, 72–75, 77, 80, 82–83, 90, 92–94, 97–104, 107, 111, 113, 118, 123, 125–26, 128, 132, 135, 137–41, 160–61, 169–70, 183, 196, 198, 201
 On the Incarnation, 98–100
 Orations Against the Arians , 100–101, 111
Athens, 106, 110, 114–15, 130, 173
Attila the Hun, 193–94
Aurelius, 64

Bartlett, David, 186
Basil of Ancyra, 89–91, 95
Basil of Caesarea, 105–10, 113, 115–16, 118, 138–42, 150, 155–58, 187, 190, 192, 200
 Against Eunomius, 106–8, 110
 On the Holy Spirit, 106, 108–9
Bell, Rob, xi
biblical inspiration, 23
bishop, role and power of, 14n14, 64, 70, 83, 127, 152, 160, 176

canon, 64–65
Cappadocians, the, 104–6, 113, 133, 138, 142, 160, 177, 183, 186–88, 196, 201
catechumens, 6–7
Constans, 74–75, 78–79, 81, 121
Constantine, 36–64, 66, 69–72, 74–75, 124, 130n6, 134–36, 148, 159, 179, 181, 193, 195, 199
 military career, 36–38
 vision, 38–39
Constantine II, 74, 78

Constantinople, xv, 57, 71, 75, 86, 93, 116, 138, 150–52, 154, 156, 169, 171–72, 194, 198, 201
Constantius, 36–37
Constantius II, 74–75, 78–79, 81, 91–92, 121–33, 135–37, 139, 150, 159, 193, 195, 197
Council of Antioch, 60, 79, 122
Council of Ariminum, 128–29
Council of Chalcedon, 173, 175, 183, 192, 194n4, 195, 201
Council of Constantinople, 151, 153, 156–57, 160, 173, 191, 194
creed, definition of, 79, 161
curiales, 138
Cyril of Alexandria, 193, 194n4

Damasus, 141–42, 149–50
Dated Creed, 128–29
Decius, 15
Dedication Creed, 80
Demetrius, 14–15
diakonoi, 8
diocese, , definition of, 32–33
Diocletian, 32–36, 40, 135
  administration, 32–33
  Great Persecution, 34–35
  cabbage farming, 35–36
doxa, 19

ecumenical, 60
  councils, 191
episkopos, 8
Era of Too Many Creeds, 79–81
Eucharist, 6–8
Eunomius of Cyzicus, 84, 86–88, 95–96, 104, 106–7, 110–11, 117, 128, 151, 156, 158, 160, 162–63, 166, 171, 183–84, 188, 192, 198–200
  philosophy of language, 87–88
Eusebius of Caesarea, 55, 59–63, 66, 71–74, 78–80, 82, 84, 92, 109, 199
Eusebius of Nicomedia, 55–57, 61, 64, 71, 74–75, 75n3, 78–80, 82, 84, 109, 116, 169, 199
Eustathius of Antioch, 72–73, 140, 198

Eustathius of Sebaste, 106, 108, 141, 141n4

filioque clause, 188–90
first cause, 48
Flavian, 153

Galerius, 37, 40
George of Capppadocia, 75
Great Persecution, 34–35, 40–41, 44, 53–54, 65, 105–6, 132
Great Schism of 1054, 189
Gregory of Nazianzus, 106, 108–9, 113–20, 139, 150–56, 171–72, 183, 187, 194, 198
  Five Theological Orations, 117–19
Gregory of Nyssa, 105, 109–11, 118, 141n4, 152, 156, 184, 187
  Against Eunomius, 111–13
  On Not Three Gods, 111, 113

Helena, 38
Heracleides, 14
heresy, 9–10, 157, 167
Heteroousian party, 84–86, 88, 90–92, 106, 108, 124, 128, 138, 156, 162, 169
heteroousios, 84, 86
homoi, 89, 91
Homoian party, 91–93, 121, 123, 127–29, 132–33, 140
Homoiousian party, 89, 91, 93, 95, 106, 108, 128–29, 139–41, 158
homoiousios, 50, 89–90
Homoousian party, 90, 93, 97–98, 111, 117–18, 121–23, 126–28, 132, 136, 139, 142, 184, 186, 197
homoousios, 62–64, 72, 76, 82–84, 93–94, 99–102, 108–9, 116, 121, 125–27, 155–58, 162, 166–67, 181–83, 192, 199
hypostasis, 26, 47, 76, 79–80, 103, 112, 112n13, 142, 192

idios, 102
Ignatius of Antioch, 9
Isis, goddess, 174

Jehovah's Witnesses, 165

Jerusalem, 70, 191
Jovian, 134–35
Julian, 114–15, 130–35
Julius, bishop of Rome, 77–79

Keynes, John Maynard, 163

Libya, 44, 47, 64–65, 70, 197
Licinius, 40–41
logos, 25
Lucian of Antioch, 44, 47
Lucifer of Cagliari, 124n1

Macedonius, 93
Macrina, 105
Macrostitch Creed, 80
Marcellus of Ancyra, 71, 77–80, 83, 103–4, 110, 122, 140n3
Marcian, 193–94, 194n3, 195
Marcion of Sinope, 10, 27
Maxientius, 37–38, 40
Maximus the Cynic, 150–52
Meletius of Lycopolis, 53, 65, 74, 152n4
Meletius of Antioch, 140, 143, 151, 153–54
modalism, 21–22, 47, 52, 71–72, 76, 80, 89, 103–4, 192
monarchia, 117–18
monasticism, 15–17, 200
Montanists, 29

Nectarius, 154
Nestorius, 193
Newton, Isaac, 163–65
Nicene Creed, xii-xii, 63, 80, 82, 94, 123–25, 127, 135–37, 139, 149–50, 153–57, 160–61, 165, 182, 185, 189, 191, 194–96, 199
Nicene-Constantinopolitan Creed, 155, 161, 189
Nicholas of Myra, 62–63

Origen, of Alexandria, 12–15, 22–27, 47, 51, 53, 66, 79, 105, 114, 201
biblical interpretation, 23–25
Hexapla, 13, 59
On First Principles, 13
orthodoxy, 19–20, 157, 167

ousia, 50, 52, 63, 76, 80, 91–92, 100, 108, 112, 112n13, 122, 126–28

Paralius, 173–74, 176–77
pathos, 181–83
patripassianism, 22
Paul of Constantinople, 93
Paul of Samosata, 64
Paulinus, 140, 142, 151, 153–54
Perpetua, 4n1
Peter Mongus, 175–77
Peter of Alexandria, 53, 141–42, 149, 149n2, 150, 153
Philo of Alexandria, 185
Photius, 122
physis, 112
Piper, John, xi
Pneumatomachoi, 93–94, 106, 108–9, 116, 151, 153, 155, 157, 163
Pontius Pilate, 170
presbyteros, 8
prosopon, 77

Ricouer, Paul, 168
riot, 75, 169–71, 178
Roman religious practice, 4–6, 2, 33–34, 38, 132
Rome, 5, 13, 14n14, 30–31, 33–35, 40–41, 45, 61, 65, 71, 74, 75, 77–78, 104, 123, 135, 137, 140–43, 149n2, 151–52, 159, 170, 173, 189, 201
rule of faith, 10–12, 158, 161

schism, definition of, 9
Sirmium, 122, 126–28
social trinitarianism , 187
substantia, 29, 50

Tertullian of Carthage, 27–29, 52, 102–3, 118, 201
tetrarchy, 33
Theodosius, 87, 148–49, 149n2, 150–51, 153, 156, 178, 193–94, 197
Theognostus of Alexandria, 51–52
Theophilus of Antioch, 28
Timothy of Alexandria, 153
traditores, 35, 53, 65

Trinity, xiii, 14, 17, 20–22, 25–29, 44–45, 48, 71, 79–80, 86, 92, 103–5, 108, 112–13, 117–19, 121, 130, 133, 142, 157, 163, 165–66, 186–87, 189

Valens, 115, 120, 136–39, 141–42, 147–48, 150, 159, 172–73, 195, 197
Valentinian, 135–37
Vatican II, 196

www.ingramcontent.com/pod-product-compliance
Lightning Source LLC
Chambersburg PA
CBHW020407230426
43664CB00009B/1217